AMERICA
IS NOT FINISHED,
PERHAPS
NEVER WILL BE;

NOW AMERICA
IS A DIVINE
TRUE SKETCH....

ALWAYS AMERICA
WILL BE
AGITATED
AND TURBULENT.

FROM JACKSON TO LINCOLN

FROM JACKSON TO LINCOLN: DEMOCRACY AND DISSENT

Robert Parks, Christine Nelson,
Stephanie Wiles, and Lori E. Gilbert

With an introduction by
David Brion Davis

The Pierpont Morgan Library
New York 1995

The Pierpont Morgan Library
14 September 1995 to 7 January 1996

Library of Congress Cataloging-in-Publication Data

From Jackson to Lincoln: democracy and dissent /
catalogue by Robert Parks . . . [et al.].
p.   cm.
Catalog of an exhibition held at the Pierpont Morgan Library,
New York, N.Y.
Includes bibliographical references (p.).

ISBN 0-87598-113-5 (alk. paper)
1. United States—Civilization—1783–1865—Exhibitions.
2. United States—History—1815–1861—Exhibitions.
3. Americana—Exhibitions.
4. Pierpont Morgan Library—Exhibitions.
5. Gilder Lehrman Collection
(Pierpont Morgan Library)—Catalogs. I. Parks, Robert
(Robert E.) II. Pierpont Morgan Library.
E165.F85 1995
973.5—dc20

95-589
CIP

ISBN 0-87598-113-5
(The Pierpont Morgan Library)
ISBN 0-8122-1577-X
(University of Pennsylvania Press)

Photography by David A. Loggie

Published in 1995 by
The Pierpont Morgan Library
29 East 36th Street
New York, NY 10016–3490

Distributed by
University of Pennsylvania Press
1300 Blockley Hall
423 Guardian Drive
Philadelphia, PA 19104–6097

CONTENTS

PREFACE

CHARLES E. PIERCE, JR.
Director, The Pierpont Morgan Library

From Jackson to Lincoln: Democracy and Dissent is the largest exhibition on an American theme organized by the Morgan Library since 1976, when *America from Amerigo Vespucci to the Louisiana Purchase* was mounted to celebrate the nation's bicentennial. The impetus for this exhibition is one of the world's greatest private collections of Americana, the Gilder Lehrman Collection, which is on deposit at the Library. Richard Gilder is a Trustee and a Fellow in Perpetuity of the Library, and Lewis E. Lehrman is a Fellow. With remarkable energy and acuity, they have put together an extraordinary collection of historical documents. They share a passion for preserving our nation's heritage as well as a keen interest in American history. Their intention in placing their collection at the Morgan Library is twofold: to make it available for scholarly study and accessible to the public through exhibitions.

Since the Gilder Lehrman Collection was placed on deposit at the Library in 1992, we have integrated it with our own holdings to produce several exhibitions. They include *Stormy Politics and Tranquil Pursuits*, which honored the bicentenary of Thomas Jefferson's birth; *Seeds of Discord*, which surveyed the politics of slavery from the nation's founding through the Civil War; and an ongoing series of smaller displays.

For all of these exhibitions, we have organized documents around a particular theme, rather than presenting them as a series of individual icons, in order to interpret and elucidate their meaning. *From Jackson to Lincoln* explores the decades from 1820 to 1860—a particularly exciting period in American history. The dynamic spirit and contradictions of the period are conveyed through a rich combination of historical documents, literary manuscripts, printed books, maps, and drawings.

While most of the historical documents are from the Gilder Lehrman Collection, the literary manuscripts and drawings are from the Library's own American holdings. Our objective is to emphasize some of the strengths of our American collections, which, though considerable, are much less known than our European holdings. With a strong interest in American history, Pierpont Morgan acquired letters and manuscripts of George Washington, Thomas Jefferson, Abraham Lincoln, and other influential personalities from the founding of the republic through the Civil War. His 1900 purchase of a collection of books from the library of Theodore Irwin of Oswego, New York, played an important role in augmenting what would eventually become the Library's American holdings. Irwin, who began collecting books in 1853, was described by a contemporary as having "illuminated manuscripts, incunabula, specimens from the famous presses, Americana, monuments of literature, the Greek and Roman classics, and books that refused to be classified" as well as manuscripts and marvelous collections of prints and etchings, including some 270 by Rembrandt that are in the Library today. The six spectacular Audubon drawings of quadrupeds entered the collection, along with splendid copies of *The Birds of America* and *The Viviparous Quadrupeds of North America*, as part of the Irwin collection.

Except for a few isolated examples, notably the acquisition of the manuscript of James Fenimore Cooper's *Deerslayer* in 1895, Morgan's collecting did not encompass American literary manuscripts. Nevertheless, in 1909, he boldly rectified this by purchasing the Stephen H. Wakeman collection of American literary works, which included major manuscripts of Henry David Thoreau, Nathaniel Hawthorne, Edgar Allan Poe, and many others. That same year he acquired the manuscripts of *Life on the Mississippi* and *Pudd'nhead Wilson* directly from Mark Twain.

Important additions to the American collections were made by J. P. Morgan, Jr., as well, but, in general, the focus has been on European holdings. As *From Jackson to Lincoln* reveals, the Morgan Library has the foundation of a great American collection. In the future, we plan to share other aspects of it through exhibitions, and we hope to strengthen it through acquisitions.

I am deeply grateful to Mr. Gilder and Mr. Lehrman for placing the magnificent Gilder Lehrman Collection on deposit at the Morgan Library and for their encouragement and support of this exhibition and its accompanying publication through the Gilder Foundation. Paul Romaine, Mr. Gilder and Mr. Lehrman's liaison, generously shared his detailed knowledge of their collection. The New-York Historical Society graciously lent to the exhibition.

Support for the publication has also been provided from an endowed fund at the Library for research and publications, established by a grant from The Andrew W. Mellon Foundation. A generous gift from an anonymous donor, through the New York Community Trust, has been received in support of the project's educational programs.

I should like to add a very special note of thanks to Professor David Brion Davis for his fine introduction, which so eloquently surveys the period from 1820 to 1860.

A DOCUMENTARY MOSAIC OF AMERICA

RICHARD GILDER AND LEWIS E. LEHRMAN

America is, we think, the greatest country the world has ever known. We are not alone in this conviction; nor is it merely a patriotic observation. From its earliest origins America has been morally judged a city upon a hill, a new Jerusalem, a testimony to the world of how a free people, "dedicated to the proposition that all men are created equal," can and will govern itself. From time immemorial these judgments have been held by astute foreign observers of the American experiment. The most famous, Alexis de Tocqueville, 150 years ago, went so far as to insist that "America is great because she is good; and if America ever ceases to be good, America will cease to be great." The distinguished British historian Paul Johnson has recently made the case for America as the hope of the world. But opinions of distinguished intellectuals are not sufficient. It is more compelling to observe, after the recent moral and economic collapse of the worldwide socialist and communist experiments, that every emerging country struggling to be free and prosperous now emulates the American system or evokes the rhetoric of American constitutional democracy.

Given this overwhelming evidence of the centrality of American history, need there be further justification to collect, preserve, and study the historical record of our country? And so, over the years, with the help of friends, scholars, and manuscript authorities, we have struggled to piece together the intricate and brilliant mosaic of American history from the fifteenth through the twentieth centuries. Our task has been daunting, for much of the record is already housed in library depositories the world over. Indeed, the project could not have been undertaken without the excellent team of dedicated scholars and archival experts who have helped us. We are, therefore, grateful to Paul Romaine, our curator; to Seth Kaller, our liaison to manuscript owners; and to Charles E. Pierce, Jr., Robert Parks, Christine Nelson, and Lori E. Gilbert of the Morgan Library, one of the most distinguished libraries of the world.

Because of the scale and density of American history, we deliberately specialized in the founding era of our country—the revolutionary and federal periods—and in the era of Abraham Lincoln and the Civil War, that extraordinary epoch we have come to call "the refounding of America." Thus, scholars and students of our collection have already discovered the immense riches of the Henry Knox archive, drawn from the revolutionary and federal periods, preserved almost intact in our collection. General Knox was General Washington's closest military partner in war; subsequently he was President Washington's first secretary of war. Secretary Knox left us an incomparable archive of state papers, letters, and manuscripts. This archive, when joined to the letters in the collection of Washington, Adams, Jefferson, Franklin, Hamilton, Madison, and other founders, puts us in immediate and intimate touch with a young nation whose leaders were struggling to give birth to the first great democratic republic.

The generation of the founders is linked to the generation of the Civil War through the letters and manuscripts in our collection of Webster, Clay, Jackson, Marshall, Monroe, John Quincy Adams, and many of their contemporaries. This link is indispensable, for most important to us has been the effort to recapture the historical origins of the struggle against slavery that led to the Civil War. The world-girdling consequences of this bloody war and the remarkable achievements of President Lincoln's sublime statecraft made possible the ultimate fulfillment of the promise of the Declaration of Independence—that all human beings should be free and equal before the law. Thus, in the documents of our collection, many scholars and students have been able to rediscover the peerless genius of Abraham Lincoln, as revealed in his original letters, in the Emancipation Proclamation, the Thirteenth Amendment to the Constitution, his state papers, and some original manuscripts of his speeches and policy decisions. In our collection one will also find—in their own words, in letters, and in official documents—the taciturn and relentless General Ulysses S. Grant; the literate and indomitable warrior, General William T. Sherman; and their bold and genteel antagonist, General Robert E. Lee. Above all, a vast archive of thousands of mournful battlefield letters by brave and simple soldiers, of the North and of the South, reminds us why they gave their lives in war that a great nation might live in peace.

We believe that nothing surpasses American history, for it is the *Iliad* and *Odyssey* of the pilgrimage of the modern world. If one would know our country, nothing can surpass the letters, the documents, and the manuscripts of the men and women who made our history. This fact, alone, has been our inspiration.

At the Morgan Library, we have put on deposit this treasure of the American spirit, convinced as we are of the noble purpose of the founders of the Library, its Trustees, and its curators.

Richard Gilder and Lewis E. Lehrman are New York businessmen and collectors of American historical documents. Together they have built the Gilder Lehrman Collection, which is on deposit at The Pierpont Morgan Library and is represented in the exhibition by over eighty documents.

FROM JACKSON TO LINCOLN: DEMOCRACY AND DISSENT

DAVID BRION DAVIS

By the 1820s (beginning the so-called Age of Jackson), it was becoming clear that the American people would quickly leap across restraints and limits of every kind. They were expansive, self-assertive, and extravagantly optimistic, and they believed that they had a God-given right to pursue happiness. In a nation of supposedly infinite promise, there could be no permanent barriers to the people's aspirations toward wealth and self-improvement.

This absence of barriers, of distinctions of rank, and of prescribed identities was what the famous French social critic Alexis de Tocqueville meant by "the general equality of condition among the people." When Tocqueville visited the United States in 1831, nothing struck him more forcibly than this leveling of ancient and inherited distinctions of rank. He took it to be "the fundamental fact" about American society; all other facts seemed "to be derived" from it. Tocqueville was acutely aware of the economic and racial inequalities of American society. Indeed, he suggested that the lack of traditional restraints, such as those associated with a landed aristocracy, precisely opened the way for racial oppression and for a new kind of aristocracy created by business and manufacturing. A racial minority, such as African Americans, seemed more vulnerable in a society in which all white males were eager to assert their own equality.

The United States, as Tocqueville repeatedly emphasized, had thus far managed to avoid anarchy while greatly expanding most people's possibilities of life. From the time of the first colonial settlements, Americans had evolved institutions that ensured a degree of order and stability in social life, protecting the public good from the worst excesses of acquisitive self-interest. This protection of the public good had been the preeminent goal of republican political culture. By the early 1800s, however, there was a growing faith that the public good would best be served by allowing maximum freedom to the individual pursuit of self-interest.

In the period from 1820 to 1860, this drive for individual self-betterment led to the beginnings of industrialization, unprecedented economic and territorial expansion, the migration of millions of Europeans to America, and the settlement of millions of Americans in the new states and territories of the West. Much of the nation's foreign policy was devoted to extending territorial boundaries and to preventing European attempts to impose barriers to American influence and expansion in the Western Hemisphere. Federal land policy encouraged rapid settlement of the West. Both national and state governments committed a large share of public resources to the construction of roads, canals, and railroads to overcome the barriers of mountains and increasing distance. Government at all levels actively sought to stimulate growth and economic opportunity, and as states extended suffrage to virtually all white males, an intensely competitive two-party system (Democrats versus Whigs) stimulated exceptionally high voter turnout. Much of the political ideology of the period was directed against forces and institutions, such as the Freemasonic Order and the Second Bank of the United States, that could be portrayed as restricting individual opportunity.

But for many thoughtful Americans, reformers as well as conservatives, Southerners as well as Northerners, there was a danger that these expansive energies would erode all respect for order, balance, and community purpose. The fear arose that the competitive spirit would lead to a fragmented society ruled by the principle "every man for himself and the devil take the hindmost." Some worried that the American people would become enslaved to money, success, and material gratification, and that the centrifugal forces of expansion would cause the nation to fly apart. A spirit of dissent generated a multitude of movements, especially in the North, that called for public schools, women's rights, more equal and cooperative communities, and the abolition of slavery, war, capital punishment, and the sale and use of alcoholic beverages.

Most of the proposed remedies to social problems, such as urban poverty, centered on the need to shape and reform individual character. Rather than looking to constitutional reforms or governmental programs, most Americans sought social change through the moral reformation of individuals. They believed that if self-interest could be enlightened by a sense of social responsibility, the nation could be saved from the dehumanizing effects of commercialism and competitive strife. This improvement of the individual was the great goal of the public schools, the religious revivals, and most of the new reform movements. It was a mission that gave a new importance and an educational role to mothers and the middle-class home. In one sense these efforts at shaping character embodied a nostalgic desire to restore a lost sense of community and united purpose. But the crusades for moral improvement also served to modernize society, for they encouraged predictable and responsible behavior and moreover aimed at giving moral legitimacy to a market-oriented society—that is, to a society governed by the standards of economic exchange, of supply and demand.

In the half century preceding the Civil War, a modern market economy emerged in conjunction with the rapid settlement of "virgin land" and the unprecedented expansion of the western frontier. By 1860, the settled area of the United States was five times what it had been in 1790, and nearly half the people lived beyond the 1790 boundaries of settlement. No other nation had populated so much new territory or absorbed as many immigrants in so short a time. No other had combined rapid urbanization with the dramatic expansion of an agricultural frontier and a transportation network. Yet, despite a generally rising standard of living, the pre-Civil War decades witnessed growing economic inequalities. Moreover, the nation's triumphs in economic and territorial expansion depended on two forms of outright racial exploitation: the forcible removal of the Indian people from rich lands east of the Great Plains; and the forced labor of black slaves, who produced the most valuable exports, mainly cotton and sugar, that helped finance America's economic growth.

White Americans, determined to go where they pleased and to seize any chance for quick profit, regarded the millions of acres of western land as a well-deserved inheritance to be exploited as quickly as possible. But in 1820, approximately 125,000 Native Americans still inhabited the prairies and forests east of the Mississippi River. Although millions of acres had been cleared of Indian occupancy rights in accordance with Anglo-American law, the physical presence of the Indians blocked the way to government sale of much public land that could lead to increased revenues, profits from land speculation, and the creation of private farms and plantations.

Indians, hopelessly outnumbered by an invader with superior technology, had little room to maneuver. Although they had long sought trade and alliances with whites, Native Americans had learned that advancing white settlements undermined tribal culture and destroyed the fish and game on which their economy depended. They had little understanding of whites' conceptions of private property and competitive individualism. But whites were just as blind to the diversity and complexity of Native American cultures, their traditions of mutual obligation and communal ownership of land, and to other factors, such as the crucial role Iroquois women played in political and economic decisions. These cultural barriers made it easier for whites to think of Indians in terms of negative stereotypes as deceitful and bloodthirsty savages or as a weak and "childlike" race doomed to extinction.

Native Americans had proved to be the major losers in the War of 1812. By ending the long conflict between Western settlers and European empires, this war had removed their last hope of finding white allies who could slow the advance of white Americans. Andrew Jackson, whose decisive military victory over the Creeks opened the Old Southwest to white settlers and hundreds of thousands of black slaves, thought that all Indians should be required as individuals to submit to the laws of the states, like everyone else, or to migrate beyond the Mississippi River, where they could progress toward civilization at their own pace.

As president, Jackson had no doubt that the vast majority of Indians, when liberated from "tribal tyranny," would willingly emigrate to the West. The civilized few would be free to cultivate modest tracts of land and would become responsible citizens of state and nation. To deal with tribes as privileged corporate groups, Jackson thought, was simply to reinforce the power of corrupt chiefs and cunning half-breeds who prevented tribesmen from following their own best interest.

In 1830, Congress supported President Jackson's policy by voting funds that enabled the president to negotiate treaties for the removal of all the Indian tribes then living east of the Mississippi River. Because most Indians had no concept of land as a measurable and salable commodity, white speculators cornered between 80 and 90 percent of the rich cotton lands that were supposed to be allotted to individual tribal leaders. Victims of wholesale fraud, trickery, and intimidation, the great mass of Indians had no choice but to follow the so-called Trail of Tears to the vacant territory of what is today Oklahoma. Subjected to disease, starvation, and winter cold, thousands died along the way. By 1844, except for a few remaining pockets mainly in the backcountry of New York, Michigan, and Florida, removal had been accomplished. In his farewell address of 4 March 1837, Jackson applauded this brutal policy of Indian removal as a great humanitarian achievement that had also happily removed the main block to America's economic growth: "While the safety and comfort of our own citizens have been greatly promoted by their removal, the philanthropist will rejoice that the remnant of that ill-fated race has been at length placed beyond the reach of injury or oppression and that paternal care of the general government will hereafter watch over them and protect them."

It was the removal of Indians from Georgia, Alabama, and Mississippi that led to the South's "cotton kingdom." It was the issue of black slavery—what James Madison called "the dreadful fruitfulness of the original sin of the African trade" or in Lincoln's phrase, "the sum of all villainies"—that finally dramatized the conflict between self-interest and the ideal of a righteous society, a society that could think of itself as "under God." And it was the westward expansion of black slavery that ultimately became the testing ground for defining and challenging limits—the territorial limits of slavery, the limits of federal power, and the limits of popular sovereignty and self-determination.

For most of the period, all these matters remained ambiguous. This ambiguity allowed the North and South to expand together and to resolve periodic conflicts by compromise. By the 1850s, however, Southern leaders were insisting that the equal rights of slaveholders would be subverted unless the federal government guaranteed the protection of slave property in the common territories. Northern leaders, eventually including many moderates who had always favored compromise, drew a firm line against imposing slavery on a territory, such as Kansas, against the wishes of the majority of settlers. In one form or another, Americans had to face the question of whether in a supposedly free society limits could be imposed on the total domination of one person over another, the hallmark of chattel slavery.

As slavery gradually disappeared in the North during the first decades of the nineteenth century, antiblack racism became more intense. Free blacks were barred from schools, colleges, churches, and public accommodations. Excluded from all but the most menial jobs, they were also deprived of the most elemental civil rights, including in most states the right to vote. But racism did not necessarily mean an approval of human slavery. As the North moved rapidly toward an urban and industrial economy, Northerners celebrated the virtues and benefits of free labor, which they hailed as the keystone of free institutions. Having earlier assumed that slavery was a "relic of barbarism" that would be gradually destroyed by the forces of social and economic progress, they looked on the South with dismay as black slavery became the basis for a vigorous, expanding economy and as Southerners took the lead in the rush for western land.

For the South, black slaves provided a highly mobile and flexible supply of labor. Large planters and speculators could quickly transport an army of involuntary workers to clear rich western land or could sell slaves to meet the labor demands of expanding areas. Even prospering family farmers could buy or rent a few slaves to increase their output of cotton or other cash crops. The flexibility of the system also enabled planters to allocate needed labor to raising livestock and growing foodstuffs for domestic consumption. And when market conditions improved, slaveholders could increase the proportion of work time devoted to cotton or other cash crops.

These various advantages also meant that slaves became the major form of Southern wealth, and slaveholding became the means to prosperity. Except for the bustling port of New Orleans, great urban centers failed to appear, and internal markets declined. Investment flowed mainly into the purchase of slaves, whose soaring price reflected an apparently limitless demand. The large planters, who profited from the efficiency of mobilizing small armies of slaves in specialized working groups or "gangs," soon ranked among America's richest men. In 1860, indeed, two-thirds of the richest Americans—men with estates of $100,000 or more (equivalent to several million today)—lived in the South.

There can be no doubt that investment in slaves brought a considerable return or that the slave economy grew rapidly throughout the pre-Civil War decades. Yet, essentially the system depended on the world's demand for cotton as it entered the age of industrialization, led by the British textile industry. For brief periods, the South's production of cotton exceeded international demand, and cotton prices fell sharply. But until the Civil War, the world market for cotton textiles grew at such a phenomenal rate that both Southern planters and British manufacturers thought only of infinite expansion.

By 1840, the South grew more than 60 percent of the world's cotton; during the pre-Civil War boom more than three-fourths of the South's cotton was exported abroad. Throughout the antebellum period, cotton accounted for over half the value of all American exports, and thus it paid for the major share of the nation's imports. A stimulant to Northern industry, cotton also contributed to the growth of New York City as a distributing and exporting center that drew income from commissions, freight charges, interest, insurance, and other services connected with the marketing of America's number-one commodity. In Louisiana, wealthy sugar growers expanded production by using new technology for the processing of cane. Plantation owners effectively applied slave labor to cultivating hemp, corn, and grain; to mining and lumbering; to building canals and railroads; and even to manufacturing textiles, iron, and other industrial products. Yet the South's economic growth and prosperity depended ultimately on foreign markets.

In theory the Southern slaveholder possessed all the power of any owner of chattel property. This power was limited only by state laws (which were generally unenforceable) that protected slaves from murder and mutilation; that set minimal standards for food, clothing, and shelter; and that prohibited masters from teaching slaves to read or allowing them to carry firearms or roam about the countryside. These slave codes acknowledged that bondsmen were human beings who were capable of plotting, stealing, fleeing, or rebelling and were likely to be a less "troublesome property" if well cared for under a program of strict discipline. Yet the laws also insisted that the slave was a piece of property that could be sold, traded, rented, mortgaged, and inherited. They did not recognize the interests and institutions of the slave community or the slave's right to marry, hold property, or testify in court.

In practice it proved impossible to treat human beings as no more than possessions. Most masters were primarily motivated by the desire for profit. They wanted to maximize their slaves' productivity while protecting the value of their capital investment, a value that kept rising with the generally escalating trend in slave prices. Accordingly, it made sense to provide a material standard of living that would promote good health and a natural increase in the size of slave families, thus increasing capital gains. It also made sense to keep slaves' morale as high as possible and to encourage them to be willing and even cheerful to do the work that would be forced upon them in the last resort. Convinced of the moral legitimacy of the system, most slave owners sincerely believed that their own best interests were identical with those of their slaves. They therefore sought to convince them of the essential justice of slavery and expected gratitude for their acts of kindness, indulgence, and generosity, and even for their restraint in inflicting physical punishment.

But slaves were not passive, agreeable puppets who could be manipulated at will, as Nat Turner, Gabriel, Denmark Vesey, and other rebels demonstrated. As human beings they had one overriding objective: self-preservation at a minimal cost of degradation and self-respect. To avoid punishment and win rewards, they carried out their owners' demands with varying degrees of thoroughness. But black slaves became cunningly expert at testing their masters' will. They learned how to mock while seeming to flatter; how to lighten unending work with moments of spontaneity, song, intimacy, and relaxation; how to exploit whites' dependence on black field drivers and household servants; and how to play on the conflicts between their masters and white overseers. In short, they learned through constant experiment and struggle to preserve a core of dignity and self-respect. Sarah Gayle, the young wife of an Alabama governor, recorded in her diary the frustrations she felt over the "insubordination" of a slave named Hampton: "I never saw such a Negro in all my life before—he did not even pretend to regard a command of mine and treated me, and what I said, with the utmost contempt. He has often laughed in my face and told me that I was the only mistress he ever failed to please; on my saying he should try another soon, he said he could not be worsted and was willing to go."

Although slavery "worked" as an economic system, its fundamental conflict of interests created a highly unstable and violent society. The great sugar planters in Louisiana and cotton growers in the delta country of Mississippi, often employing more than one hundred slaves on a productive unit, tried to merge Christian paternalism with a kind of welfare capitalism. They provided professional medical care, offered monetary rewards for extra productivity, and granted a week or more of Christmas vacation. Yet these same plantations were essentially ruled by terror. Even the most humane and kindly masters knew that only the threat of violence could force gangs of field hands to work from dawn to dusk "with the discipline," as one contemporary observer put it, "of a regular trained army." Frequent public floggings reminded every slave of the penalty for inefficient labor, disorderly conduct, or refusal to accept the authority of a superior.

By 1860, the North and South had moved beyond the reach of compromise. The United States had originally emerged from an act of secession—from a final rejection of compromise with Britain. Even after independence had been won, Americans continued to perceive Britain as a conspiratorial power that threatened to hold back the nation's expansive energies. Jackson, for example, in his letter of 8 July 1844 to William Russell, expressed the typical Democrat view that only the annexation of Texas would "shut out all British and foreign influence from tampering with the Indians on our western frontiers and with our slaves in the South and West."

But despite the supposedly subversive links between Britain and its American abolitionist agents, America had continued to prosper and expand. The period from 1820 to 1860 witnessed a continuing extension of limits, an overleaping of boundaries of every kind. History seemed to confirm the people's wish for total self-determination. The American people, like the American individual, seemed to be free from the burdens of their past and free to shape their own character. The one problem that their ingenuity could not resolve was black slavery, which the founders had seen as an unwanted legacy of British greed. Ironically, the South increasingly came to regard black slavery as the necessary base upon which freedom must rest. For the North, a commitment to slavery's ultimate extinction, as Lincoln insisted, was the ultimate test of freedom. Each region detected a fatal change in the other—a betrayal of the principles and mission of the founders. Each feared that the other had become transformed into a despotic and conspiratorial "power" very similar to the original British enemy. And both shared a heritage of standing firm against despotism.

David Brion Davis is Sterling Professor of History at Yale University.

“Native Principles”

WHEN WALT WHITMAN depicted an “agitated and turbulent” America, the nation was nearing the end of the tumultuous four-decade era that preceded the Civil War. Optimism prevailed at the beginning of the period. In 1826, the great orator Daniel Webster declaimed: “It cannot be denied, but by those who would dispute against the sun, that with America, and in America, a new era commences in human affairs.” Indeed, the nation had entered a transformational period of economic growth, territorial expansion, and technological progress as well as a literary and artistic efflorescence. It had also embarked on an age of intense debate over its “native principles.”

America’s core principles were set forth in the Declaration of Independence (PL. 2), with Jefferson’s pronouncement that “all men are created equal”; the Constitution (PL. 1), which firmly established a free representative government; and the Bill of Rights, which enshrined individual liberties. In the 1820s, although there was general accord on the broad fundamentals of the republic’s essential texts, Americans disagreed on the application of the founding principles to the major social and political issues then emerging. Politicians, social and religious reformers, writers, and others offered competing visions of American democracy and how it ought to work.

In the brief essays that follow, as in the exhibition they accompany, these changing views of democracy and emerging voices of dissent are described largely through primary documents of the period. The letters, manuscripts, and other materials have been selected to illuminate one of the most convulsive periods in American history. For clarity, spelling and punctuation in the wide array of quotations have been modernized.

America
is not finished,
perhaps never will be;
now America is a
divine true sketch. . . .

Always America
will be agitated
and turbulent.
This day
it is taking shape,
not to be less so,
but to be more so,
capriciously, stormily,
on native principles,
with such vast
proportions
of parts.

WALT WHITMAN
“Letter to Ralph Waldo Emerson,”
in *Leaves of Grass* (1856)

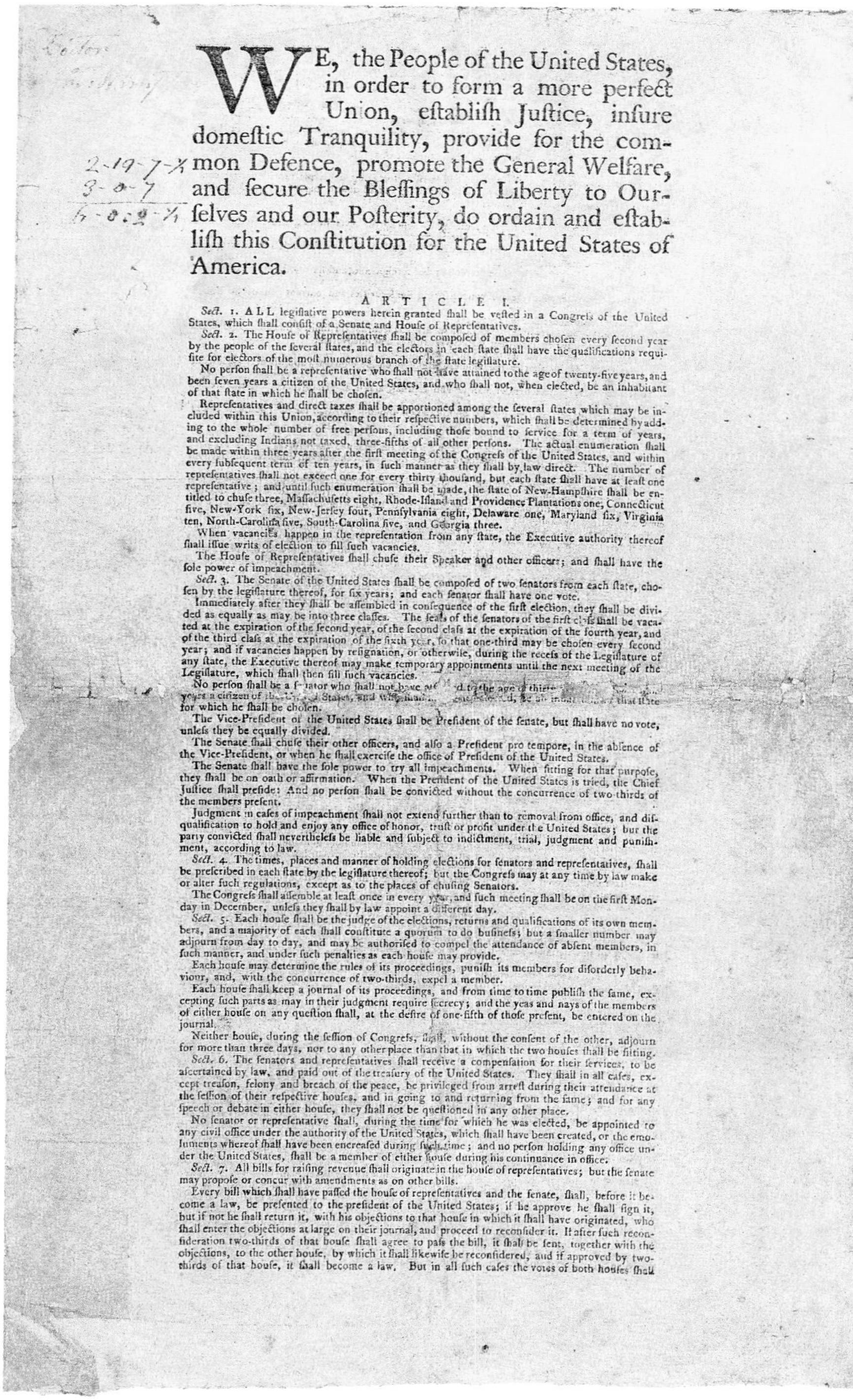

WE, the People of the United States, in order to form a more perfect Union, eſtabliſh Juſtice, inſure domeſtic Tranquility, provide for the common Defence, promote the General Welfare, and ſecure the Bleſſings of Liberty to Ourſelves and our Poſterity, do ordain and eſtabliſh this Conſtitution for the United States of America.

A R T I C L E I.

Sect. 1. ALL legiſlative powers herein granted ſhall be veſted in a Congreſs of the United States, which ſhall conſiſt of a Senate and Houſe of Repreſentatives.

Sect. 2. The Houſe of Repreſentatives ſhall be compoſed of members choſen every ſecond year by the people of the ſeveral ſtates, and the electors in each ſtate ſhall have the qualifications requiſite for electors of the moſt numerous branch of the ſtate legiſlature.

No perſon ſhall be a repreſentative who ſhall not have attained to the age of twenty-five years, and been ſeven years a citizen of the United States, and who ſhall not, when elected, be an inhabitant of that ſtate in which he ſhall be choſen.

Repreſentatives and direct taxes ſhall be apportioned among the ſeveral ſtates which may be included within this Union, according to their reſpective numbers, which ſhall be determined by adding to the whole number of free perſons, including thoſe bound to ſervice for a term of years, and excluding Indians not taxed, three-fifths of all other perſons. The actual enumeration ſhall be made within three years after the firſt meeting of the Congreſs of the United States, and within every ſubſequent term of ten years, in ſuch manner as they ſhall by law direct. The number of repreſentatives ſhall not exceed one for every thirty thouſand, but each ſtate ſhall have at leaſt one repreſentative; and until ſuch enumeration ſhall be made, the ſtate of New-Hampſhire ſhall be entitled to chuſe three, Maſſachuſetts eight, Rhode-Iſland and Providence Plantations one, Connecticut five, New-York ſix, New-Jerſey four, Pennſylvania eight, Delaware one, Maryland ſix, Virginia ten, North-Carolina five, South-Carolina five, and Georgia three.

When vacancies happen in the repreſentation from any ſtate, the Executive authority thereof ſhall iſſue writs of election to fill ſuch vacancies.

The Houſe of Repreſentatives ſhall chuſe their Speaker and other officers; and ſhall have the ſole power of impeachment.

Sect. 3. The Senate of the United States ſhall be compoſed of two ſenators from each ſtate, choſen by the legiſlature thereof, for ſix years; and each ſenator ſhall have one vote.

Immediately after they ſhall be aſſembled in conſequence of the firſt election, they ſhall be divided as equally as may be into three claſſes. The ſeats of the ſenators of the firſt claſs ſhall be vacated at the expiration of the ſecond year, of the ſecond claſs at the expiration of the fourth year, and of the third claſs at the expiration of the ſixth year, ſo that one-third may be choſen every ſecond year; and if vacancies happen by reſignation, or otherwiſe, during the receſs of the Legiſlature of any ſtate, the Executive thereof may make temporary appointments until the next meeting of the Legiſlature, which ſhall then fill ſuch vacancies.

No perſon ſhall be a ſenator who ſhall not have [illegible] to the age of thirty [illegible] years a citizen of the [illegible] States, and who [illegible] when elected, be an inhabitant [illegible] that ſtate for which he ſhall be choſen.

The Vice-Preſident of the United States ſhall be Preſident of the ſenate, but ſhall have no vote, unleſs they be equally divided.

The Senate ſhall chuſe their other officers, and alſo a Preſident pro tempore, in the abſence of the Vice-Preſident, or when he ſhall exerciſe the office of Preſident of the United States.

The Senate ſhall have the ſole power to try all impeachments. When ſitting for that purpoſe, they ſhall be on oath or affirmation. When the Preſident of the United States is tried, the Chief Juſtice ſhall preſide: And no perſon ſhall be convicted without the concurrence of two-thirds of the members preſent.

Judgment in caſes of impeachment ſhall not extend further than to removal from office, and diſqualification to hold and enjoy any office of honor, truſt or profit under the United States; but the party convicted ſhall nevertheleſs be liable and ſubject to indictment, trial, judgment and puniſhment, according to law.

Sect. 4. The times, places and manner of holding elections for ſenators and repreſentatives, ſhall be preſcribed in each ſtate by the legiſlature thereof; but the Congreſs may at any time by law make or alter ſuch regulations, except as to the places of chuſing Senators.

The Congreſs ſhall aſſemble at leaſt once in every year, and ſuch meeting ſhall be on the firſt Monday in December, unleſs they ſhall by law appoint a different day.

Sect. 5. Each houſe ſhall be the judge of the elections, returns and qualifications of its own members, and a majority of each ſhall conſtitute a quorum to do buſineſs; but a ſmaller number may adjourn from day to day, and may be authoriſed to compel the attendance of abſent members, in ſuch manner, and under ſuch penalties as each houſe may provide.

Each houſe may determine the rules of its proceedings, puniſh its members for diſorderly behaviour, and, with the concurrence of two-thirds, expel a member.

Each houſe ſhall keep a journal of its proceedings, and from time to time publiſh the ſame, excepting ſuch parts as may in their judgment require ſecrecy; and the yeas and nays of the members of either houſe on any queſtion ſhall, at the deſire of one-fifth of thoſe preſent, be entered on the journal.

Neither houſe, during the ſeſſion of Congreſs, ſhall, without the conſent of the other, adjourn for more than three days, nor to any other place than that in which the two houſes ſhall be ſitting.

Sect. 6. The ſenators and repreſentatives ſhall receive a compenſation for their ſervices, to be aſcertained by law, and paid out of the treaſury of the United States. They ſhall in all caſes, except treaſon, felony and breach of the peace, be privileged from arreſt during their attendance at the ſeſſion of their reſpective houſes, and in going to and returning from the ſame; and for any ſpeech or debate in either houſe, they ſhall not be queſtioned in any other place.

No ſenator or repreſentative ſhall, during the time for which he was elected, be appointed to any civil office under the authority of the United States, which ſhall have been created, or the emoluments whereof ſhall have been encreaſed during ſuch time; and no perſon holding any office under the United States, ſhall be a member of either houſe during his continuance in office.

Sect. 7. All bills for raiſing revenue ſhall originate in the houſe of repreſentatives; but the ſenate may propoſe or concur with amendments as on other bills.

Every bill which ſhall have paſſed the houſe of repreſentatives and the ſenate, ſhall, before it become a law, be preſented to the preſident of the United States; if he approve he ſhall ſign it, but if not he ſhall return it, with his objections to that houſe in which it ſhall have originated, who ſhall enter the objections at large on their journal, and proceed to reconſider it. If after ſuch reconſideration two-thirds of that houſe ſhall agree to paſs the bill, it ſhall be ſent, together with the objections, to the other houſe, by which it ſhall likewiſe be reconſidered, and if approved by two-thirds of that houſe, it ſhall become a law. But in all ſuch caſes the votes of both houſes ſhall

1. U.S. Constitution.
[Philadelphia]: Dunlap and Claypoole, [18 or 19 September 1787].

Gilder Lehrman Collection
GLC 258

This final version of the Constitution appeared within a few days of approval by the Constitutional Convention. There are two known copies of this early printing.

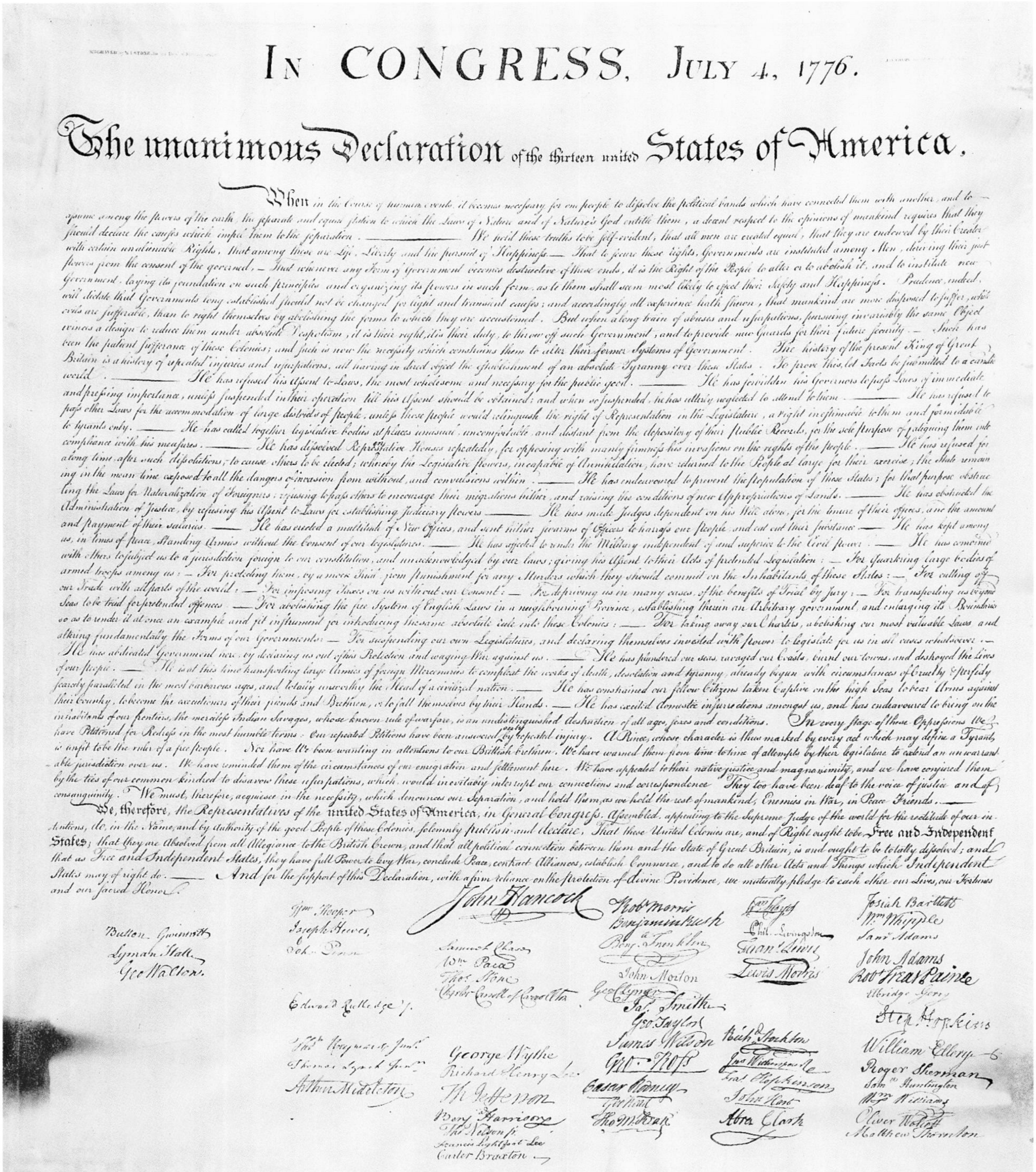

IN CONGRESS, JULY 4, 1776.

The unanimous Declaration of the thirteen united States of America,

When in the Course of human events, it becomes necessary for one people to dissolve the political bands which have connected them with another, and to assume among the powers of the earth, the separate and equal station to which the Laws of Nature and of Nature's God entitle them, a decent respect to the opinions of mankind requires that they should declare the causes which impel them to the separation. —— We hold these truths to be self-evident, that all men are created equal, that they are endowed by their Creator with certain unalienable Rights, that among these are Life, Liberty and the pursuit of Happiness. — That to secure these rights, Governments are instituted among Men, deriving their just powers from the consent of the governed, — That whenever any Form of Government becomes destructive of these ends, it is the Right of the People to alter or to abolish it, and to institute new Government, laying its foundation on such principles and organizing its powers in such form, as to them shall seem most likely to effect their Safety and Happiness. Prudence, indeed, will dictate that Governments long established should not be changed for light and transient causes; and accordingly all experience hath shewn, that mankind are more disposed to suffer, while evils are sufferable, than to right themselves by abolishing the forms to which they are accustomed. But when a long train of abuses and usurpations, pursuing invariably the same Object evinces a design to reduce them under absolute Despotism, it is their right, it is their duty, to throw off such Government, and to provide new Guards for their future security. — Such has been the patient sufferance of these Colonies; and such is now the necessity which constrains them to alter their former Systems of Government. The history of the present King of Great Britain is a history of repeated injuries and usurpations, all having in direct object the establishment of an absolute Tyranny over these States. To prove this, let Facts be submitted to a candid world. —— He has refused his Assent to Laws, the most wholesome and necessary for the public good. —— He has forbidden his Governors to pass Laws of immediate and pressing importance, unless suspended in their operation till his Assent should be obtained; and when so suspended, he has utterly neglected to attend to them. —— He has refused to pass other Laws for the accommodation of large districts of people, unless those people would relinquish the right of Representation in the Legislature, a right inestimable to them and formidable to tyrants only. —— He has called together legislative bodies at places unusual, uncomfortable, and distant from the depository of their Public Records, for the sole purpose of fatiguing them into compliance with his measures. —— He has dissolved Representative Houses repeatedly, for opposing with manly firmness his invasions on the rights of the people. —— He has refused for a long time, after such dissolutions, to cause others to be elected; whereby the Legislative powers, incapable of Annihilation, have returned to the People at large for their exercise; the State remaining in the mean time exposed to all the dangers of invasion from without, and convulsions within. —— He has endeavoured to prevent the population of these States; for that purpose obstructing the Laws for Naturalization of Foreigners; refusing to pass others to encourage their migrations hither, and raising the conditions of new Appropriations of Lands. —— He has obstructed the Administration of Justice, by refusing his Assent to Laws for establishing Judiciary powers. —— He has made Judges dependent on his Will alone, for the tenure of their offices, and the amount and payment of their salaries. —— He has erected a multitude of New Offices, and sent hither swarms of Officers to harrass our people, and eat out their substance. —— He has kept among us, in times of peace, Standing Armies without the Consent of our legislatures. —— He has affected to render the Military independent of and superior to the Civil power. —— He has combined with others to subject us to a jurisdiction foreign to our constitution, and unacknowledged by our laws; giving his Assent to their Acts of pretended Legislation: — For Quartering large bodies of armed troops among us: — For protecting them, by a mock Trial, from punishment for any Murders which they should commit on the Inhabitants of these States: — For cutting off our Trade with all parts of the world: — For imposing Taxes on us without our Consent: — For depriving us in many cases, of the benefits of Trial by Jury: — For transporting us beyond Seas to be tried for pretended offences — For abolishing the free System of English Laws in a neighbouring Province, establishing therein an Arbitrary government, and enlarging its Boundaries so as to render it at once an example and fit instrument for introducing the same absolute rule into these Colonies: — For taking away our Charters, abolishing our most valuable Laws, and altering fundamentally the Forms of our Governments: — For suspending our own Legislatures, and declaring themselves invested with power to legislate for us in all cases whatsoever. — He has abdicated Government here, by declaring us out of his Protection and waging War against us. —— He has plundered our seas, ravaged our Coasts, burnt our towns, and destroyed the lives of our people. —— He is at this time transporting large Armies of foreign Mercenaries to compleat the works of death, desolation and tyranny, already begun with circumstances of Cruelty & perfidy scarcely paralleled in the most barbarous ages, and totally unworthy the Head of a civilized nation. —— He has constrained our fellow Citizens taken Captive on the high Seas to bear Arms against their Country, to become the executioners of their friends and Brethren, or to fall themselves by their Hands. —— He has excited domestic insurrections amongst us, and has endeavoured to bring on the inhabitants of our frontiers, the merciless Indian Savages, whose known rule of warfare, is an undistinguished destruction of all ages, sexes and conditions. In every stage of these Oppressions We have Petitioned for Redress in the most humble terms: Our repeated Petitions have been answered only by repeated injury. A Prince, whose character is thus marked by every act which may define a Tyrant, is unfit to be the ruler of a free people. Nor have We been wanting in attentions to our Brittish brethren. We have warned them from time to time of attempts by their legislature to extend an unwarrantable jurisdiction over us. We have reminded them of the circumstances of our emigration and settlement here. We have appealed to their native justice and magnanimity, and we have conjured them by the ties of our common kindred to disavow these usurpations, which, would inevitably interrupt our connections and correspondence. They too have been deaf to the voice of justice and of consanguinity. We must, therefore, acquiesce in the necessity, which denounces our Separation, and hold them, as we hold the rest of mankind, Enemies in War, in Peace Friends. ——

We, therefore, the Representatives of the united States of America, in General Congress, Assembled, appealing to the Supreme Judge of the world for the rectitude of our intentions, do, in the Name, and by Authority of the good People of these Colonies, solemnly publish and declare, That these United Colonies are, and of Right ought to be Free and Independent States; that they are Absolved from all Allegiance to the British Crown, and that all political connection between them and the State of Great Britain, is and ought to be totally dissolved; and that as Free and Independent States, they have full Power to levy War, conclude Peace, contract Alliances, establish Commerce, and to do all other Acts and Things which Independent States may of right do. —— And for the support of this Declaration, with a firm reliance on the protection of divine Providence, we mutually pledge to each other our Lives, our Fortunes and our sacred Honor.

John Hancock

Button Gwinnett
Lyman Hall
Geo Walton.

Wm Hooper
Joseph Hewes,
John Penn

Edward Rutledge 1.
Thos Heyward Junr.
Thomas Lynch Junr.
Arthur Middleton

Samuel Chase
Wm. Paca
Thos. Stone
Charles Carroll of Carrollton

George Wythe
Richard Henry Lee
Th Jefferson
Benj. Harrison
Thos Nelson jr.
Francis Lightfoot Lee
Carter Braxton

Robt Morris
Benjamin Rush
Benja. Franklin
John Morton
Geo Clymer
Jas. Smith.
Geo. Taylor
James Wilson
Geo. Ross
Caesar Rodney
Geo Read
Tho M:Kean

Wm. Floyd
Phil. Livingston
Frans. Lewis
Lewis Morris

Richd. Stockton
Jno Witherspoon
Fras. Hopkinson
John Hart
Abra Clark

Josiah Bartlett
Wm. Whipple
Saml Adams
John Adams
Robt Treat Paine
Elbridge Gerry
Step. Hopkins
William Ellery
Roger Sherman
Saml Huntington
Wm. Williams
Oliver Wolcott
Matthew Thornton

2. Declaration of Independence.
Broadside. Washington, D.C.: W. J. Stone, [1823].

Gilder Lehrman Collection
GLC 154.02

In 1820, John Quincy Adams commissioned engraver William J. Stone to make facsimiles of the Declaration of Independence. Only 31 of the 200 that were made are known to survive.

3. [Thomas Jefferson]. Engraving by J. C. Buttre, from Daniel Webster's *Discourse in Commemoration of the Lives and Services of John Adams and Thomas Jefferson, Delivered in Faneuil Hall, Boston, August 2, 1826*. Boston: Cummings, Hilliard and Co., 1826.

Morgan Library
PML 125583

This engraving is after a portrait of Jefferson by Gilbert Stuart, painted from life and known as the "Edgehill Stuart." Exceptionally popular as an image on stamps and currency, it was also published in Daniel Webster's commemoration of Jefferson and John Adams, who died just hours apart on 4 July 1826.

The United States in 1820

The Missouri Compromise

IN 1820, the United States was a young, vigorous nation, rapidly expanding in population and domain. At the beginning of the constitutional republic's fourth decade, its inhabitants had multiplied from 3,929,214 in 1790 to 9,638,453, an increase of 150 percent. Located mostly along the East Coast, the postrevolutionary population did not foresee migration beyond the Appalachian Mountains. By 1800, however, the nation's boundaries extended to the Mississippi River. Then, with one bold act—Thomas Jefferson's Louisiana Purchase in 1803—the United States almost doubled in area, from 888,685 to 1,715,877 square miles, encompassing both states and territories. With the admission of Vermont, Kentucky, Tennessee, Ohio, Louisiana, Indiana, Mississippi, Illinois, and Alabama, the number of states had increased from thirteen to twenty-two by 1820 (PL. 4).

As the nation grew, political leadership passed from the aging founders to Henry Clay, John C. Calhoun, Daniel Webster, and other members of the subsequent generation. Several of the surviving founders viewed the politics of the era with puzzlement and skepticism. Writing in 1822 to America's staunch ally of the Revolution and his good friend the marquis de Lafayette, Thomas Jefferson professed disengagement from the current political scene. "My race is run," he stated. "On our affairs," he continued, "little can be expected from an octogenary, retired within the mountains, going nowhere, seeing nobody but in his own house and reading a single newspaper only and that chiefly for the sake of advertisements." Jefferson's further observations to Lafayette indicate, however, that he was not inattentive to the major issues of the day. His letter goes on to assess the current state of affairs in America.

> But the papers tell you there are no parties now. Republicans and Federalists forsooth are all amalgamated. This, my friend, is not so. The same parties exist now which existed before.... [Federalists] now call themselves Republicans. Like the fox pursued by the dogs, they take shelter in the midst of sheep. They see that monarchism is a hopeless wish in this country and are rallying anew to the next best point, a consolidated government. They are therefore endeavoring to break down the barriers of states' rights, provided by the Constitution, against a consolidation.

Commenting on likely issues of the upcoming 1824 presidential election, Jefferson assured Lafayette that states' rights "is the sentiment of the nation and will probably prevail if the principle of the Missouri question should not mingle itself with those of the election. Should it do so, all will be uncertain." Indeed, the "Missouri question," which resulted in the Missouri Compromise of 1820, was one of the most divisive issues yet confronted by the republic.

All these perplexities develop more and more—the dreadful fruitfulness of the original sin of the African trade.

JAMES MADISON

4. John Melish.
A Map of the United States with the Contiguous British and Spanish Possessions.
1823 ed., copyright 1820.

Gilder Lehrman Collection
GLC 4319

Melish's map shows the nation at the time of the Missouri Compromise.

In 1819, Missouri's application for admission as a state in which slavery would be legal precipitated bitter argument. Slavery had been a source of tension since the nation's founding. In 1787, the framers of the Constitution, after considerable debate and compromise, avoided mentioning slavery by name but included three provisions relating thereto. In Article I, Section 2, slaves ("all other persons") would be counted as three-fifths of "free persons" in determining Congressional representation; in Article I, Section 9, the slave trade ("importation of such persons as any of the States now existing shall think proper to admit") could not be prohibited by Congress before 1808; and in Article IV, Section 2, fugitive slaves ("person[s] held to service or labor in one State… escaping into another") had to be returned to their masters ("party to whom such service or labor is due").

A number of the delegates to the Constitutional Convention, including several slave owners, thought slavery to be morally wrong and incompatible with American ideals of human liberty. They nevertheless made concessions to produce a document that would be approved by delegates of diverse and rival interests. The ideal of a unified country prevailed over doubts about the morality of slavery. In 1786, a year before the drafting of the Constitution began, George Washington, one of the largest slaveholders in America, declared that among his first wishes for the new nation was "to see some plan adopted by which slavery in this country may be abolished by slow, sure, and imperceptible degrees."

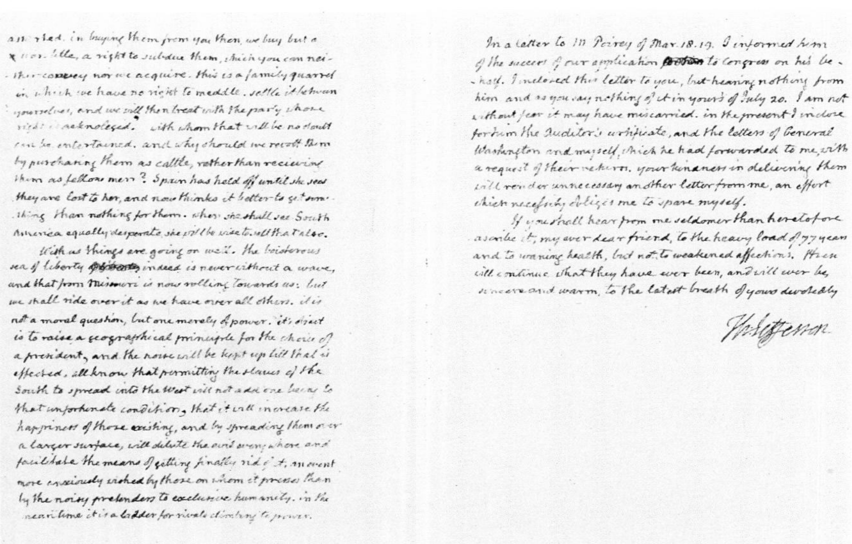
asserted. in buying them from you then, we buy but a [illegible] title, a right to subdue them, which you can neither convey nor we acquire. this is a family quarrel in which we have no right to meddle. settle it between yourselves, and we will then treat with the party whose right is acknoleged. with whom that will be no doubt can be entertained. and why should we revolt them by purchasing them as cattle, rather than recieving them as fellow men? Spain has held off until she sees they are lost to her, and now thinks it better to get something than nothing for them. when she shall see South America equally desperate, she will be wise to sell that also.

With us things are going on well. the boisterous sea of liberty ~~[illegible]~~ indeed is never without a wave, and that from Missouri is now rolling towards us: but we shall ride over it as we have over all others. it is not a moral question, but one merely of power. it's object is to raise a geographical principle for the choice of a president, and the noise will be kept up till that is effected. all know that permitting the slaves of the South to spread into the West will not add one being to that unfortunate condition, that it will increase the happiness of those existing, and by spreading them over a larger surface, will dilute the evil every where and facilitate the means of getting finally rid of it, an event more anxiously wished by those on whom it presses than by the noisy pretenders to exclusive humanity. in the mean time it is a ladder for rivals climbing to power.

In a letter to M. Poirey of Mar. 18. 19. I informed him of the success of our application ~~[illegible]~~ to Congress on his behalf. I inclosed that letter to you, but hearing nothing from him and as you say nothing of it in your's of July 20. I am not without fear it may have miscarried. in the present I inclose for him the Auditor's certificate, and the letters of General Washington and myself, which he had forwarded to me, with a request of their return. your kindness in delivering them will render unnecessary another letter from me, an effort which necessity obliges me to spare myself.

If you shall hear from me seldomer than heretofore ascribe it, my ever dear friend, to the heavy load of 77 years and to waning health, but not to weakened affections. these will continue what they have ever been, and will ever be, sincere and warm, to the latest breath of yours devotedly

Th: Jefferson

5. Thomas Jefferson. Autograph letter signed, dated Monticello, 26 December 1820, to the marquis de Lafayette.

Morgan Library
MA 54

Jefferson shared with Lafayette his personal view of the Missouri question. A firm advocate of states' rights, Jefferson favored the admission of Missouri as a slave state.

Progress and reason, Washington and many of his contemporaries believed, would bring about naturally the demise of slavery. They also thought that a constitutional ban on the slave trade as of 1808 would mean the end of American slavery. They were tragically mistaken, for, rather than waning, slavery proliferated. The 1790 census indicates that there were 697,624 slaves nationwide. Thirty years later, although several states had abolished slavery and others had provided for gradual emancipation, the number of slaves had more than doubled to 1,538,022. Most of the enslaved population was in the South, where the economy had become increasingly dependent on cotton. In 1819, when debate arose over Missouri's statehood, slavery had become a serious point of discord between the North and the South.

For abolitionist groups, the issue of Missouri's admission was fundamentally moral. The Pennsylvania Society for the Abolition of Slavery petitioned Congress to reject "firmly and unhesitatingly" Missouri's application for statehood on the basis of its legislative powers to "avert and remove evils" that were contrary to moral principle and the national interest. The society's petition ominously acknowledged the potential danger of the dispute over slavery in the territories—that ultimately the Union might be destroyed.

> Holding, as we do, the union of the states as the great basis of their prosperity and happiness, we shall be among the last of the members of this free nation to abandon it; and we shall wait until the heavy pressure of the evils, which might have

been prevented or remedied by the due and proper exercise of those powers, shall compel us to submit to its termination.

For most senators and representatives, the Missouri question was less a moral topic and more a contest of political strength between North and South. Between 1803 and 1819, Congress had admitted slave states and free states alternatively. With Alabama's admission as a slave state in December 1819, at the outset of congressional debates on the Missouri question, twenty-two states were divided equally between slave and free. The South sought two more senators from Missouri to redress the imbalance in the House of Representatives, which comprised 81 seats for slave states against 105 for free states. Writing to Lafayette about the crisis, Jefferson correctly observed, "It is not a moral question but one merely of power" (PL. 5).

Prominent in the opposition to the admission of Missouri as a slave state was Senator Rufus King of New York. In acknowledging the constitutional provision that three-fifths of the slave population be counted as free citizens in determining congressional representation, Senator King argued that "the disproportionate power and influence allowed to the slave-holding states was a necessary sacrifice to the establishment of the Constitution.... But the extension of this disproportionate power to the new states would be unjust and odious." Senator King's further argument that Congress had the authority to exclude slavery in a newly admitted state stirred advocates of states' rights. They objected, pointing out that if Congress declared slavery illegal in new states, it could do the same in existing ones.

Debate, often impassioned, ensued in the Senate and House from December 1819 until March 1820. On 1 March, the House rejected the bill passed by the Senate, and deadlock appeared certain until a conference of opponents who advocated compromise proposed a solution: admission of Maine as a free state, Missouri as a slave state, and, with the exception of Missouri, the exclusion of slavery from the Louisiana Territory above 36°30' north latitude.

Many politicians, Northern and Southern, hoped fervently that the divisiveness sparked by the Missouri issue would be temporary. Jefferson wrote optimistically to Lafayette, "The boisterous sea of liberty indeed is never without a wave, and that from Missouri is now rolling toward us; but we shall ride over it as we have over all others." His contemporary James Madison took a less sanguine view in his own letter to Lafayette: "All these perplexities develop more and more—the dreadful fruitfulness of the original sin of the African trade" (PL. 6).

Madison's somber view was more accurate than Jefferson's. As the United States expanded farther west, conflict over slavery in the territories became increasingly ferocious, even bloody, and sectional strife intensified.

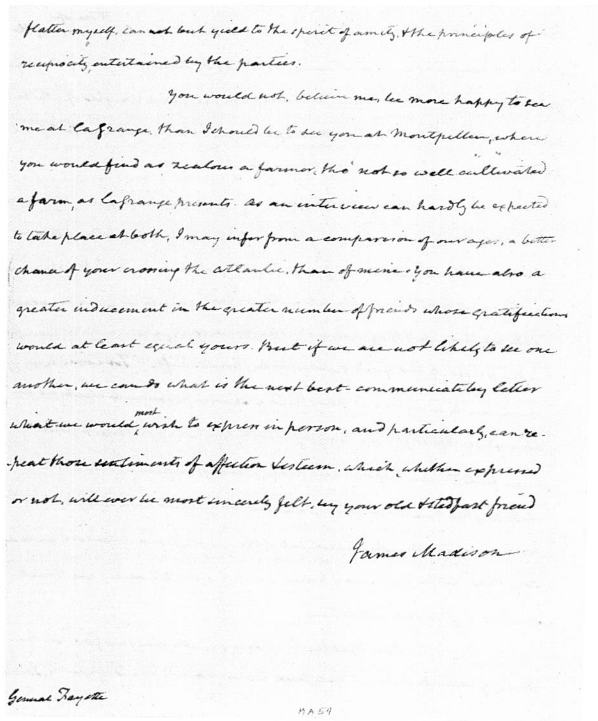

flatter myself, can not but yield to the spirit of amity, & the principles of reciprocity, entertained by the parties.

You would not, believe me, be more happy to see me at Lafrange, than I should be to see you at Montpellier, where you would find as zealous a farmer, tho' not so well cultivated a farm, as Lafrange presents. As an interview can hardly be expected to take place at both, I may infer from a comparison of our ages, a better chance of your crossing the Atlantic, than of mine. You have also a greater inducement in the greater number of friends whose gratifications would at least equal yours. But if we are not likely to see one another, we can do what is the next best - communicate by letter what we would most wish to express in person, and particularly, can repeat those sentiments of affection & esteem, which, whether expressed or not, will ever be most sincerely felt, by your old & stedfast friend

James Madison

General Fayette

MA 54

6. James Madison. Autograph letter signed, dated Montpelier, [Virginia], 25 November 1820, to the marquis de Lafayette.

Morgan Library
MA 54

Madison wrote to Lafayette that the debate over Missouri opened "the wider field" of the nation's treatment of free blacks, pointing out that most free states imposed "various disqualifications which degrade them from the rank and rights of white persons."

The Presidency of
Andrew Jackson

THE CENTER OF CONTROVERSY during much of his lifetime, Andrew Jackson continues to generate discussion over his presidency and notions of democracy. His legacy includes framing political debate as a contest between an elite minority and the majority of voters, strengthening the chief executive's power, acting resolutely in crisis to preserve the Union, and eliminating the national debt. Jacksonian democracy is rife with contradictions: broadened suffrage but limited to white males, greater opportunities for farmers and planters to acquire land but with the forced removal of Native Americans, advocacy of egalitarianism but with a determination to keep the issue of slavery out of politics.

Born in South Carolina in 1767, Jackson was barely a teenager when he was taken prisoner by the British during the Revolutionary War. After the war, he undertook the study of law in North Carolina. In 1788, when he was twenty-one, he was appointed public prosecutor for the western district of North Carolina, which became the state of Tennessee in 1796. The shrewd, ambitious Jackson thrived professionally and financially in the frontier environment of Nashville. By 1804, he was a successful businessman and the owner of a 420-acre plantation. Named the Hermitage by Jackson, the estate eventually encompassed 1,200 acres. Like Washington, Jefferson, Madison, and Monroe—four of his six presidential predecessors—Jackson was a southerner and a slave owner. When he was elected president in 1828, the Hermitage was worked by ninety-five slaves.

Jackson entered the American political landscape as a military hero, renowned for his leadership of troops against the Creek nation in 1813–14 and in 1815 against the British in the Battle of New Orleans, the decisive engagement of the War of 1812 (PL. 7). His perseverance earned him the nickname "Old Hickory" from his troops. The traits that helped Jackson achieve military triumphs—an abundance of self-confidence and the ability to focus relentlessly on vanquishing his foe—provoked trouble in civilian life. The survivor of several duels, he had the reputation of a hothead, ever ready to resort to violence in a disagreement.

> **If I go
> into office,
> it shall be by the
> unsolicited will
> of the people,
> and I shall not envy
> the man
> who gets there
> in any other way.**
>
> ANDREW JACKSON

7. [Andrew Jackson]. Engraving by James B. Longacre, after a painting by Thomas Sully. From an extra-illustrated copy of John Trumbull's *Autobiography and Reminiscences*. New York: [Wiley & Putnam], 1841–73.

Morgan Library
PML 18084

Andrew Jackson sat for Thomas Sully in Philadelphia in 1819. That Sully painted this portrait specifically to be engraved and sold attests to the great popularity of the "Hero of New Orleans."

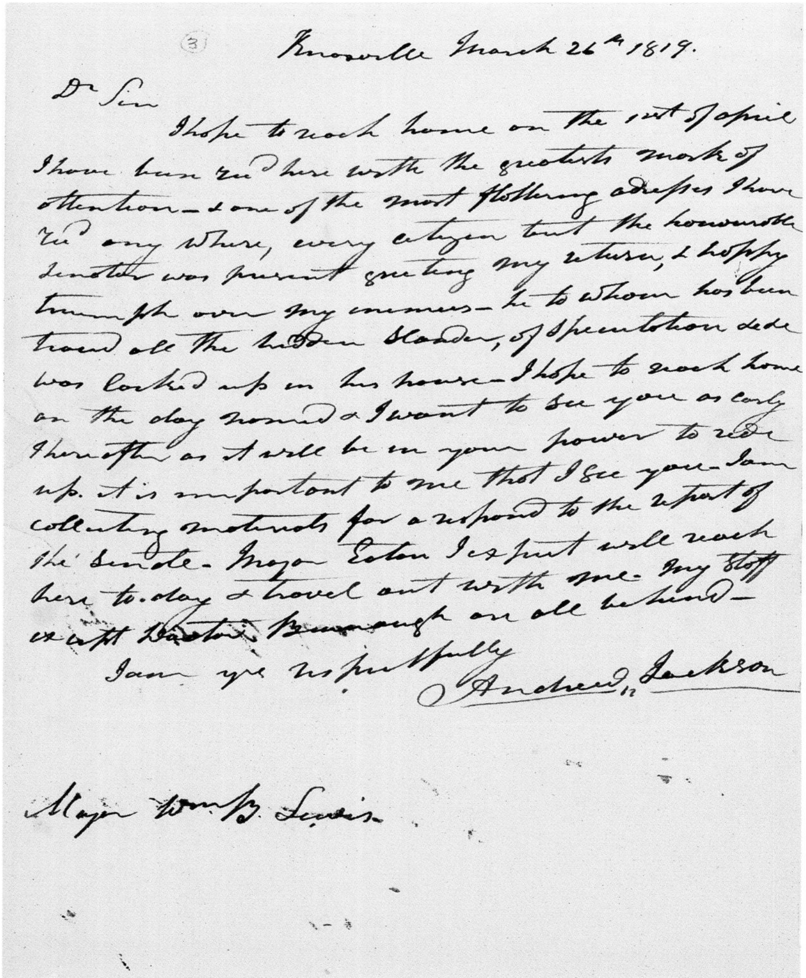

(3)

Knoxville March 26th 1819.

Dr Sir

I hope to reach home on the 1st of April
I have been recd here with the greatest mark of
attention — & one of the most flattering addresses I have
recd any where, every citizen but the honourable
senator was present greeting my return, & happy
triumph over my enemies — he to whom has been
traced all the hidden slander, of speculation &c &c
was locked up in his house — I hope to reach home
on the day named & I want to see you as early
thereafter as it will be in your power to ride
up. it is important to me that I see you — I am
collecting materials for a respond to the report of
the senate — Major Eaton I expect will reach
here to.day & travel out with me — my staff
except Doctor Bronaugh are all behind —

I am yr respectfully
Andrew Jackson

Major Wm B. Lewis

8. Andrew Jackson. Autograph letter signed, dated Knoxville, 26 March 1819, to Major William B. Lewis.

Morgan Library
MA 811

Andrew Jackson's letters to his friend and adviser Major William B. Lewis reveal a shrewd politician, ever mindful of his opponents.

Jackson's pride and combativeness toward enemies, whom he often perceived to be conspiring against him, are well documented in his correspondence. In 1819, relishing the defeat of a congressional effort to censure him for military actions during the First Seminole War (1817–18), he wrote to his friend Major William B. Lewis about the extraordinary public acclaim that greeted him along the way from Washington to Nashville (PL. 8).

> I have been received [in Nashville] with the greatest marks of attention—and one of the most flattering addresses I have received anywhere. Every citizen but the honorable senator [John Williams of Tennessee] was present, greeting my return and happy triumph over my enemies. He to whom has been traced all the hidden slander, of speculation, etc., was locked up in his house.

The Election of 1824

In 1824, encouraged by Major Lewis and other trusted allies in Nashville, Jackson sought the presidency. His candidacy was viewed with alarm by a number of America's most influential politicians. In addition to having reservations about Jackson's character and personal history, some political leaders saw danger in electing so dedicated a military man as president. In 1827, Henry Clay, speaker of the House of Representatives in 1824, recalled his unease about Jackson in a letter to the marquis de Lafayette.

> I could not think it proper to vote for General Jackson, who [*sic*] I believed to be incompetent, and whose election, as he had no claim other than one founded upon exclusive military pretension, I believed would be injurious to the republic, especially in this early stage of its existence.

As the 1824 presidential campaign proceeded, Clay, Jackson, Secretary of the Treasury William Crawford, and Secretary of State John Quincy Adams became the four candidates most likely to be elected. Clay, like many political observers, thought it "certain that the election will come into the House of Representatives" (PL. 9). Not only were there four strong candidates, there was also in effect a dual method of choosing presidential electors: by popular vote in eighteen of the twenty-four states and by state legislatures in the other six. In such circumstances, chances of one candidate receiving the required majority of electoral votes were slim.

In the election, Jackson was the beneficiary of a broadened suffrage. Though still limited to white males, in 1824 voting rights had been extended to increased numbers by the trend among states to eliminate property-holding requirements. Jackson received 42 percent of the popular vote and the largest number of electoral votes (ninety-nine); Adams was second with 32 percent of the popular vote and eighty-four electoral votes; Crawford and Clay were third and fourth. As Clay predicted, with no candidate receiving a majority of electoral votes, the choice of president fell to the House of Representatives.

Intense political bargaining ensued in Washington during January 1825. Jackson, who had the plurality of popular and electoral votes, assessed the situation for Major Lewis in Nashville.

> It was stated to me yesterday that if I was elected, it would be against the whole cabinet influence, combined with that of the speaker [Clay]. If this is true, and success is secure, it [would be] the greater triumph of principle over intrigue and management.

"If I go into office," Jackson continued, in a strong statement of his political philosophy, "it shall be by the unsolicited will of the people, and I shall not envy the man who gets there in any other way."

When the House vote was taken a month later, Adams, supported by Clay, emerged the victor. Jackson's advocates were furious, claiming that Clay had entered into a "corrupt bargain" with Adams by exchanging his endorsement for the position of secretary of state. The accusation appeared in print as an anonymous letter in a Philadelphia newspaper, the *Columbian Observer*. The author was identified as Pennsylvania congressman George Kremer, whose previously undistinguished career led supporters of Adams and Clay to suspect him to be the unwitting tool of Jacksonians. Jackson, incensed at his defeat,

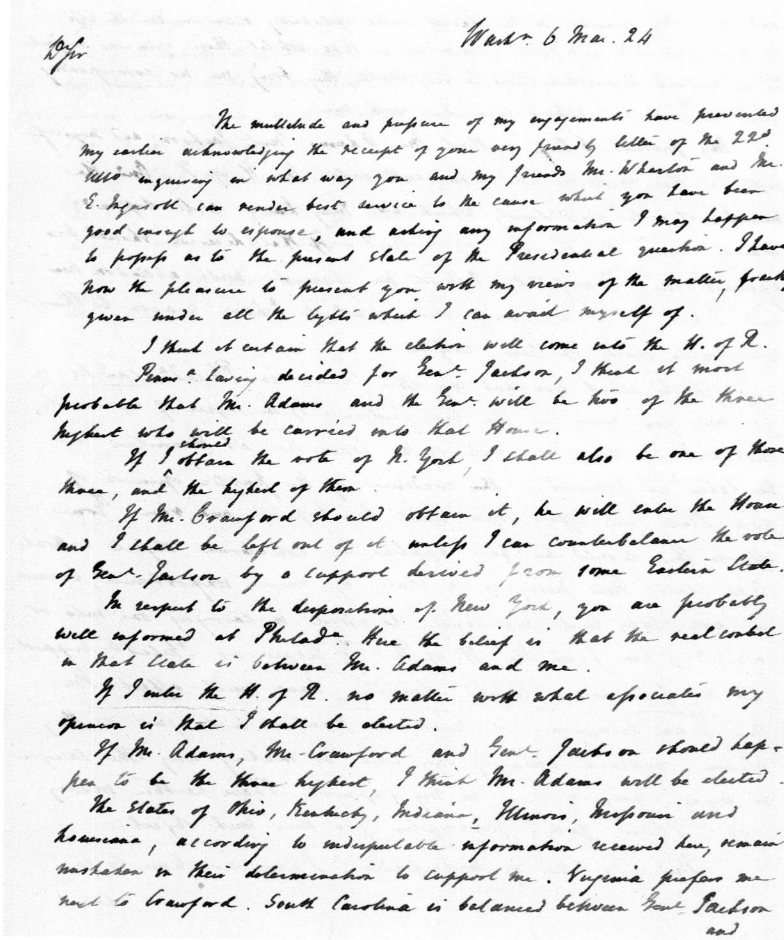

Washn. 6 Mar. 24

Dr Sir

The multitude and pressure of my engagements have prevented my earlier acknowledging the receipt of your very friendly letter of the 22d. ult. enquiring in what way you and my friends Mr. Wharton and Mr. E. Ingersoll can render best service to the cause which you have been good enough to espouse, and asking any information I may happen to possess as to the present state of the Presidential question. I have now the pleasure to present you with my views of the matter, frankly given under all the lights which I can avail myself of.

I think it certain that the election will come into the H. of R.

Penna. having decided for Genl. Jackson, I think it most probable that Mr. Adams and the Genl. will be two of the three highest who will be carried into that House.

If I ^should obtain the vote of N. York, I shall also be one of those three, and the highest of them.

If Mr. Crawford should obtain it, he will enter the House and I shall be left out of it unless I can counterbalance the vote of Genl. Jackson by a support derived from some Eastern State.

In respect to the dispositions of New York, you are probably well informed at Philada. Here the belief is that the real contest in that State is between Mr. Adams and me.

If I enter the H. of R. no matter with what associates my opinion is that I shall be elected.

If Mr. Adams, Mr. Crawford and Genl. Jackson should happen to be the three highest, I think Mr. Adams will be elected.

The States of Ohio, Kentucky, Indiana, Illinois, Missouri and Louisiana, according to indisputable information received here, remain unshaken in their determination to support me. Virginia prefers me next to Crawford. South Carolina is balanced between Genl. Jackson and

9. Henry Clay.
Autograph letter signed, dated Washington, [D.C.], 6 March 1824, to J. D. Godman.

Gilder Lehrman Collection
GLC 1028

Though correctly predicting that the election would go to the House of Representatives, speaker and presidential candidate Henry Clay misjudged his own chances: "If I enter the H[ouse] of R[epresentatives], no matter with what associates, my opinion is that I shall be elected." Fourth in the electoral vote, Clay ultimately supported John Quincy Adams, giving rise to charges by Jacksonians of a "corrupt bargain."

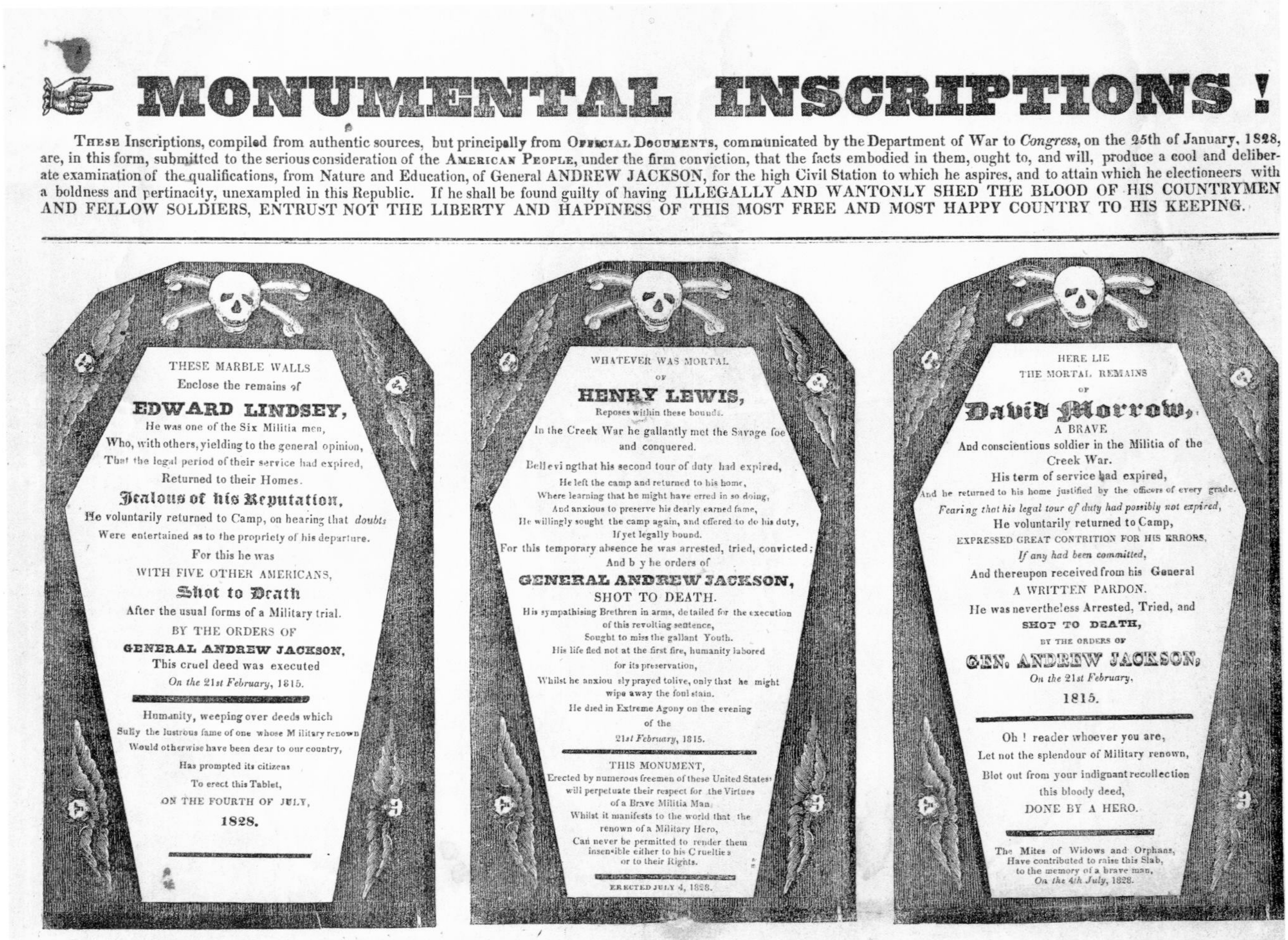

MONUMENTAL INSCRIPTIONS!

These Inscriptions, compiled from authentic sources, but principally from Official Documents, communicated by the Department of War to *Congress*, on the 25th of January, 1828, are, in this form, submitted to the serious consideration of the American People, under the firm conviction, that the facts embodied in them, ought to, and will, produce a cool and deliberate examination of the qualifications, from Nature and Education, of General ANDREW JACKSON, for the high Civil Station to which he aspires, and to attain which he electioneers with a boldness and pertinacity, unexampled in this Republic. If he shall be found guilty of having ILLEGALLY AND WANTONLY SHED THE BLOOD OF HIS COUNTRYMEN AND FELLOW SOLDIERS, ENTRUST NOT THE LIBERTY AND HAPPINESS OF THIS MOST FREE AND MOST HAPPY COUNTRY TO HIS KEEPING.

THESE MARBLE WALLS
Enclose the remains of
EDWARD LINDSEY,
He was one of the Six Militia men,
Who, with others, yielding to the general opinion,
That the legal period of their service had expired,
Returned to their Homes.
Jealous of his Reputation,
He voluntarily returned to Camp, on hearing that *doubts*
Were entertained as to the propriety of his departure.
For this he was
WITH FIVE OTHER AMERICANS,
Shot to Death
After the usual forms of a Military trial.
BY THE ORDERS OF
GENERAL ANDREW JACKSON,
This cruel deed was executed
On the 21st February, 1815.

Humanity, weeping over deeds which
Sully the lustrous fame of one whose Military renown
Would otherwise have been dear to our country,
Has prompted its citizens
To erect this Tablet,
ON THE FOURTH OF JULY,
1828.

WHATEVER WAS MORTAL
OF
HENRY LEWIS,
Reposes within these bounds.
In the Creek War he gallantly met the Savage foe
and conquered.
Bellevingthat his second tour of duty had expired,
He left the camp and returned to his home,
Where learning that he might have erred in so doing,
And anxious to preserve his dearly earned fame,
He willingly sought the camp again, and offered to do his duty,
If yet legally bound.
For this temporary absence he was arrested, tried, convicted;
And b y he orders of
GENERAL ANDREW JACKSON,
SHOT TO DEATH.
His sympathising Brethren in arms, detailed for the execution
of this revolting sentence,
Sought to miss the gallant Youth.
His life fled not at the first fire, humanity labored
for its preservation,
Whilst he anxiou sly prayed tolive, only that he might
wipe away the foul stain.
He died in Extreme Agony on the evening
of the
21st February, 1815.

THIS MONUMENT,
Erected by numerous freemen of these United States,
will perpetuate their respect for the Virtues
of a Brave Militia Man;
Whilst it manifests to the world that the
renown of a Military Hero,
Can never be permitted to render them
insensible either to his Cruelties
or to their Rights.

ERECTED JULY 4, 1828.

HERE LIE
THE MORTAL REMAINS
OF
David Morrow,
A BRAVE
And conscientious soldier in the Militia of the
Creek War.
His term of service had expired,
And he returned to his home justified by the officers of every grade.
Fearing that his legal tour of duty had possibly not expired,
He voluntarily returned to Camp,
EXPRESSED GREAT CONTRITION FOR HIS ERRORS,
If any had been committed,
And thereupon received from his General
A WRITTEN PARDON.
He was nevertheless Arrested, Tried, and
SHOT TO DEATH,
BY THE ORDERS OF
GEN. ANDREW JACKSON,
On the 21st February,
1815.

Oh! reader whoever you are,
Let not the splendour of Military renown,
Blot out from your indignant recollection
this bloody deed,
DONE BY A HERO.

The Mites of Widows and Orphans,
Have contributed to raise this Slab,
to the memory of a brave man,
On the 4th July, 1828.

10. *Monumental Inscriptions.*
Broadside. [N.p., 1828].

Gilder Lehrman Collection
GLC 1825

The 1828 presidential contest between John Quincy Adams and Andrew Jackson was marked by slanderous accusations from both sides. This broadside listed men Jackson had ordered executed during the 1813–14 war against the Creek.

forwarded the *Columbian Observer* to Major Lewis. "I am told," he wrote, "Mr. Kremer's exposé is strong and will carry conviction everywhere of the corruption of Clay and others. I enclose the paper that you may have it republished in such papers in Nashville as you deem best." Jackson's fine political instincts were at work. He concluded correctly that his public popularity would be strengthened by the portrayal of his opponents as corrupt bargainers who had thwarted the will of the people.

The Election of 1828

Andrew Jackson's second run for the presidency was marked by a particularly tumultuous campaign. To deflate Jackson's reputation as a war hero, supporters of the incumbent Adams portrayed the "Hero of New Orleans" as a bloodthirsty tyrant. A "coffin handbill" alleged that Jackson had brutally executed six young soldiers for minor offenses during the Creek War (PL. 10). Jackson contended that the militiamen had been guilty of mutiny and desertion. To attack his personal morality, opponents depicted him as an adulterer. Scurrilous rumors circulated about the circumstances of his marriage to Rachel Donelson Robards, whose divorce from

Lewis Robards was not actually final on the date that she and Jackson claimed to have been married. Jackson responded indignantly to the conjecture surrounding his relationship with Rachel (PL. 11). To a Pennsylvania supporter, he wrote:

> All the slander that wickedness can suggest and falsehood invent have been leveled against me and my family by the panderers of power and competition. This will recoil upon its own head. Truth is mighty and will ultimately prevail, and when it does, I feel release from the multiplied shafts of slander.

As hostile newspaper articles and campaign materials appeared, Jackson's well-organized Nashville Central Committee quickly distributed statements to refute each new alleged violation of morality and judgment. His forces in New York, Philadelphia, and Boston similarly published retorts to opposition attacks (PL. 12).

11. [Rachel Jackson]. Miniature attributed to Mary Catherine Strobel. Watercolor on ivory.

Gilder Lehrman Collection
GLC 2793.19

This miniature was painted after Rachel Jackson's death and given by Andrew Jackson to Mary Eastin Polk, her great-niece.

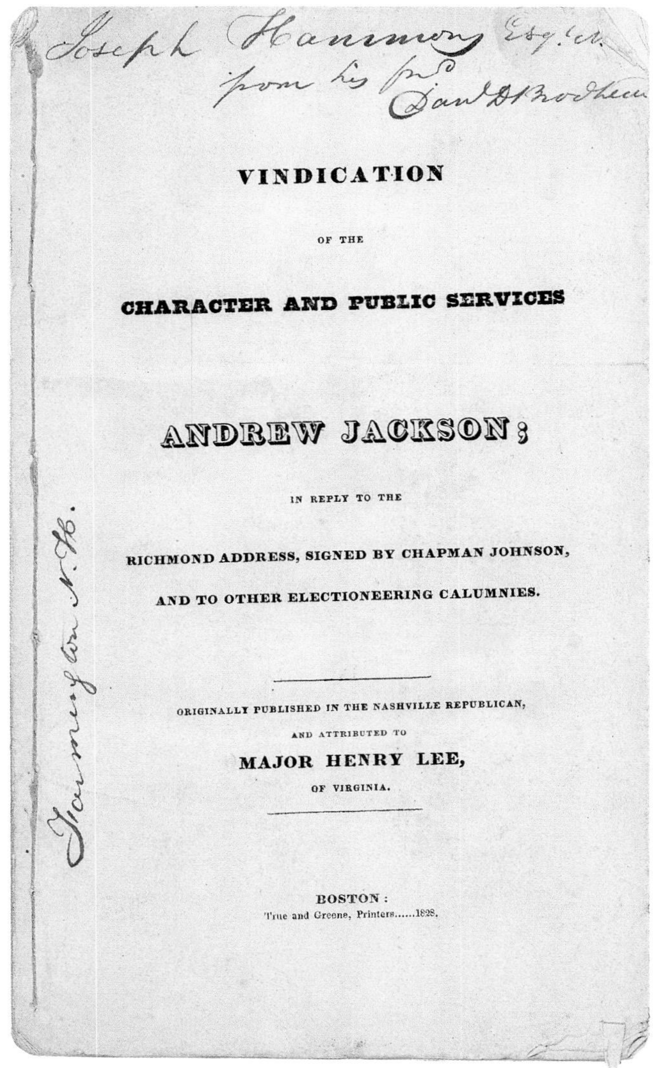

VINDICATION

OF THE

CHARACTER AND PUBLIC SERVICES

OF

ANDREW JACKSON;

IN REPLY TO THE

RICHMOND ADDRESS, SIGNED BY CHAPMAN JOHNSON,

AND TO OTHER ELECTIONEERING CALUMNIES.

ORIGINALLY PUBLISHED IN THE NASHVILLE REPUBLICAN,

AND ATTRIBUTED TO

MAJOR HENRY LEE,

OF VIRGINIA.

BOSTON:
True and Greene, Printers......1828.

12. Henry Lee. *A Vindication of the Character and Public Services of Andrew Jackson; in Reply to the Richmond Address, Signed by Chapman Johnson, and to Other Electioneering Calumnies.* Boston: True and Greene, 1828.

Gilder Lehrman Collection
GLB 100

Henry Lee worked closely with Andrew Jackson during the 1828 campaign and was the author of this pamphlet refuting charges against the war hero.

With the lively campaign, two rather than four principal candidates, and better organized political parties, voter participation in 1828 tripled that of the previous election. Jackson won with 647,292 ballots, which represented 56 percent of the popular vote. John C. Calhoun of South Carolina was elected vice president. For the president-elect, the thrill of victory was tempered by personal loss. One month after the election, his wife, Rachel, died. Jackson blamed her sudden physical decline on the opposition for having made their private lives a campaign issue.

Rotation of Officeholders

After Jackson's inauguration, political adversaries quickly seized opportunities to depict him as the tyrant whom they had long feared. One of President Jackson's first acts was to recall William Henry Harrison as minister to Colombia. Harrison, an appointee of Adams and staunch ally of Clay, wrote from Bogotá, "If [Andrew Jackson] could do it, rely upon it that the bodies of his political foes would not only be removed from their offices, but heads from their bodies as fast as ever took place in the time of Nero or Robespierre." Clay, evaluating Jackson's administration after its first year, expressed alarm to George C. Washington, nephew of the first president.

> Nothing appears to be solid and safe.... [P]ublic offices and honors are distributed often among the most worthless.... [S]urely there is enough to fill every patriot bosom with the most awful apprehensions.

During his first year in office, Jackson had, in fact, replaced slightly over 9 percent of federal officeholders. Though he installed more of his own appointees than had any previous president, Jackson did not employ the practice wholesale, as Harrison, Clay, and others implied. The new president claimed that his system of rotation would ensure integrity in government and lessen the influence of entrenched blocs. In his first message to Congress in December 1829, Jackson declared:

> Corruption in some and in others a perversion of correct feelings and principles divert government from its legitimate ends and make it an engine for the support of the few at the expense of the many.... I cannot but believe that more is lost by the long continuance of men in office than is generally to be gained by their experience.

During the balance of his two terms, Jackson's application of the system of rotation never matched the pace of his first year. Overall, he replaced less than 20 percent of officeholders on political grounds.

The Nullification Controversy

In 1832, Jackson confronted the deepest crisis of his two terms and most serious threat yet to the Union. His former vice president, John C. Calhoun, was a principal opponent. Their simmering feud had come to a head in 1831, when Calhoun—still vice president at the time—published a pamphlet about the Seminole War controversy of 1818–19. The president was angered by the public airing of a matter about which he was exceptionally sensitive and especially by Calhoun's unauthorized disclosure of several of Jackson's letters. Martin Van Buren succeeded Calhoun for Jackson's second term, and Calhoun was elected to the Senate.

The crisis began as a dispute over tariffs. South Carolina asserted that progressively higher tariffs imposed by Congress to protect American manufacturers actually harmed the state's cotton growers. Senator Calhoun, on behalf of his constituents, argued that, constitutionally, South Carolina had the right to declare a federal law null and void within its borders. In November, a South Carolina state convention nullified the tariff acts of 1828 and 1832 and declared that a federal attempt to enforce the acts within the state would justify secession.

Jackson maintained that states' rights, which he advocated, extended neither to nullification of federal law nor secession. To that effect, he issued a proclamation to the people of South Carolina on 10 December 1832 (PL. 13). Artfully combining high-minded suasion with the threat of force, Jackson depicted the Union as a supreme value and expressed his firm resolve to preserve it. He warned:

> Disunion by armed force is treason. Are you really ready to incur its guilt?… On your unhappy state will inevitably fall all the evils of the conflict you force upon the government of your country. It cannot accede to the mad project of disunion, of which you would be the first victims. Its first magistrate cannot, if he would, avoid the performance of his duty.

Extolling the benefits of the United States, he finally appealed to the national pride of the state's citizens.

> Consider the extent of its territory, its increasing and happy population, its advance in arts which render life agreeable and the sciences which elevate the mind!… Behold it as the asylum where the wretched and oppressed find a refuge and support! Look on this picture of happiness and honor and say—we, too, are citizens of America.… On your undivided support of your government depends the decision of the great question it involves, whether your sacred Union will be preserved, and the blessing it secures to us one people shall be perpetuated.

Jackson skillfully balanced determination to use force with the support of lower tariffs. A compromise tariff bill, formulated by Clay and endorsed by Calhoun, resolved the crisis. South Carolina rescinded its ordinance of nullification in March 1833. Several months later, Clay recalled, "I distinctly saw that if nothing were done to preserve [the American system] at the last session, we should, at the next, witness its entire destruction or a civil war." Massachusetts senator Daniel Webster, writing to a friend, predicted future assaults on the Union (PL. 14):

> The contest is far from ended.… If I do not mistake, the question of paramount importance in our affairs is likely to be, for some time to come, the preservation of the Union or its dissolution.

The Bank War

Another major controversy of Jackson's presidency was the rechartering of the Second Bank of the United States. The matter of a central bank had been the subject of political debate since the establishment of the first Bank of the

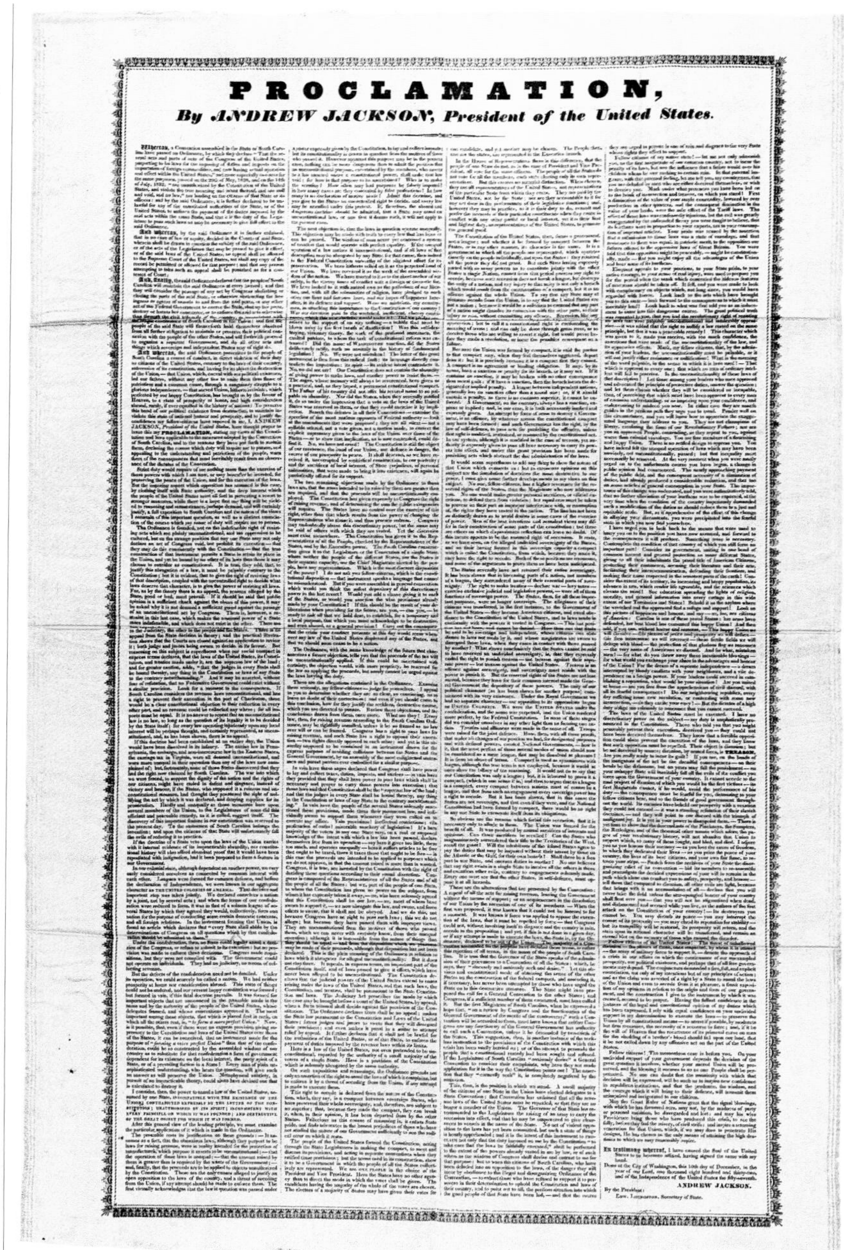

PROCLAMATION,

By ANDREW JACKSON, President of the United States.

13. Andrew Jackson. *Proclamation, by Andrew Jackson, President of the United States.* Broadside, on silk. New York: G. F. Hopkins, 10 December 1832.

Gilder Lehrman Collection
GLC 1895

Andrew Jackson's response to South Carolina's threatened secession firmly established his determination to fight any rebellious activity.

United States in 1791. Originally proposed by Alexander Hamilton, the Bank of the United States had been opposed by Jeffersonians, who viewed it as an unconstitutional instrument of federal control. The first bank operated until the expiration of its charter in 1811.

The Second Bank of the United States was established in 1816. Its constitutionality was upheld by the Supreme Court under Chief Justice John Marshall, notably in McCulloch v. Maryland in 1819 and Osborn v. Bank of the United States in 1824 (PL. 15). Nevertheless, the bank remained a potent political issue. For many, it represented a conflict between the commercial power of the Northeast and the agrarian interests of the South and West.

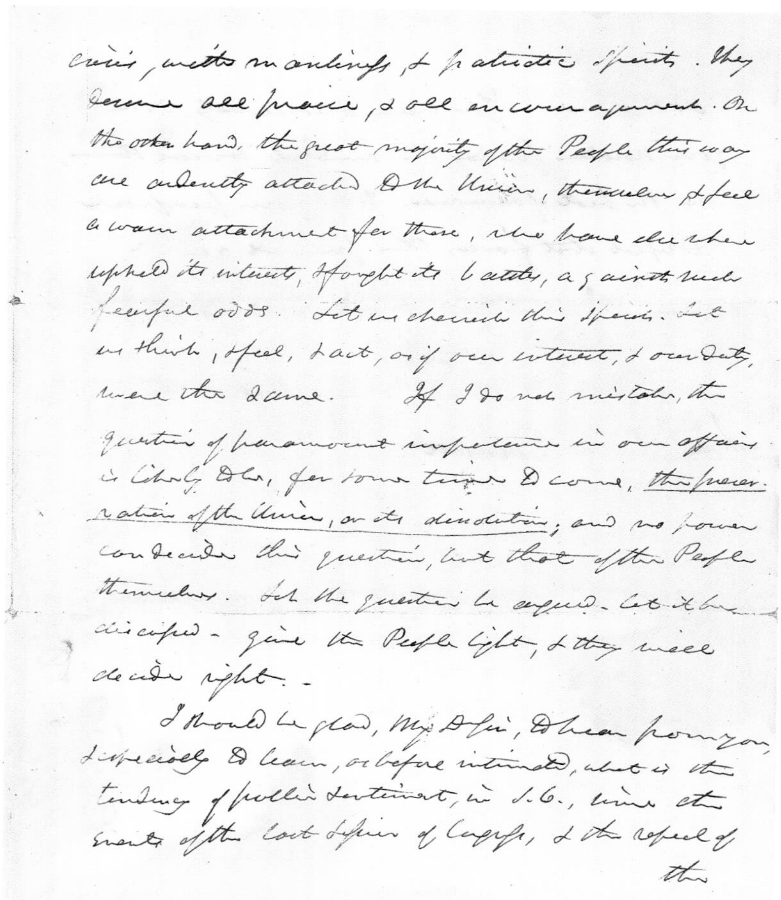

crisis, with manliness, & patriotic spirit. They
deserve all praise, & all encouragement. On
the other hand, the great majority of the People this way
are ardently attached to the Union, themselves, & feel
a warm attachment for those, who have else where
upheld its interests, & fought its battles, against such
fearful odds. Let us cherish this spirit. Let
us think, & feel, & act, as if our interest, & our duty,
were the same. If I do not mistake, the
question of paramount importance in our affairs
is likely to be, for some time to come, the preservation of the Union, or its dissolution; and no power
can decide this question, but that of the People
themselves. Let the question be argued—let it be
discussed—give the People light, & they will
decide right.—

I should be glad, My Dear Sir, to hear from you
especially to learn, as before intimated, what is the
tendency of public sentiment, in S.C., since the
events of the last session of Congress, & the repeal of
the

14. Daniel Webster. Autograph letter signed, dated Boston, 7 May 1833, to Joel Poinsett.

Morgan Library
MA 2123

Throughout his political career, Daniel Webster applied his great oratorical gift toward his ardent support of the Union.

The bank became an issue in the 1832 presidential campaign when Clay, advocate of the bank and the National-Republican candidate, persuaded Nicholas Biddle, the bank's president, to apply early for renewal of its charter. After the House and Senate passed the bill for rechartering, Jackson responded with a veto. Jackson's veto was a milestone in the strengthening of the presidency. His predecessors had vetoed bills on the grounds of constitutionality. In his veto message, Jackson argued that the president, as direct representative of the people's interests, could also take into account the social and economic consequences of a bill. Jackson set a precedent. Henceforth, the legislative branch would need to consider the president's viewpoint as well as a bill's constitutionality when drafting legislation. There were too few votes in the Senate to override his veto, and the bank would have to reapply for rechartering.

Jackson regarded his 1832 election victory a mandate to curtail the power of the bank and thus diminish its chances of being rechartered in 1836. He began to remove federal funds and deposit them in selected state banks. This measure was highly controversial within his own cabinet. Two secretaries of the treasury were replaced before Jackson appointed Roger B. Taney, who already was serving in the cabinet as attorney general. Taney issued the first order to begin removing funds in September 1833. Though denied Senate confirmation as treasury secretary, Taney was allowed to oversee the removal of deposits. Prominent congressional opponents to Jackson's policy included Tennessee representative Davy Crockett, who declared, "Never was the money of Rome more complete in the hands of Caesar than the whole purse of the nation is at this time in the hands of our President Jackson."

Hoping to demonstrate the need for a central bank, Biddle responded by restricting loans and taking other steps to precipitate a financial crisis. His was a Pyrrhic victory, however, for the ensuing economic disruption only confirmed, for many, the perils of a central bank. In Jackson's view, any financial problems caused by his own actions would be temporary. He was confident not only of the economic wisdom but also the political soundness of his stand against the bank. In the face of fierce congressional opposition, he declared confidently in 1834:

> The [financial] panic is fast subsiding, and like other panics must end in leaving society in a more pure state.... Fear or faint not...the tyrant is chained and must expire at the end of its charter.

The Bank of the United States ceased to be a national institution when its charter expired in 1836. Reestablished as a commercial bank in Pennsylvania, it failed in 1841.

In addition to preventing the rechartering of the Bank of the United States, Jackson realized, during his second term, one of his most important economic goals: elimination of the national debt. In 1835 and 1836, there was no public debt, a situation unreplicated in any previous or subsequent administration (PL. 16).

Jackson's Farewell Address

In the fall of 1836, as his second term neared its end, Jackson decided to follow George Washington's precedent of issuing a farewell address to the American people (PL. 18). To draft the speech, Jackson tapped Supreme Court Chief Justice Taney, who, as attorney general, had helped write the message accompanying the veto of the bank recharter in 1832. The final text touched on a wide range of Jacksonian themes. Jackson could not resist allusions to past political battles, warning that "the planter, the farmer, the mechanic, and the laborer"—those whom he deemed "the bone and sinew of country"—were in danger of "losing their fair influence in government.... The mischief springs," he asserted, "from the power which the moneyed interest derives from a paper currency which they are able to control,

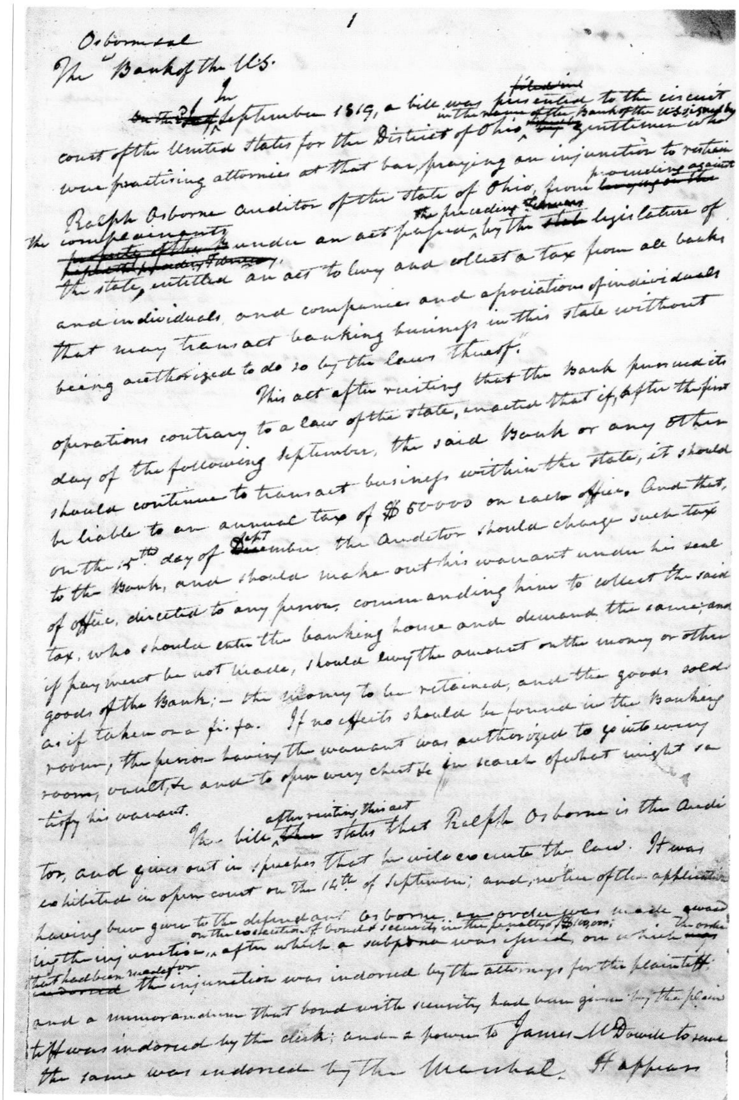
1
Osborn et al
The Bank of the U.S.
In September 1819, a bill was filed in the name of the Bank of the U.S. signed by in the circuit
court of the United States for the District of Ohio, gentlemen who
were practising attornies at that bar, praying an injunction to restrain
Ralph Osborne auditor of the state of Ohio, from proceeding against
the complainants under an act passed by the preceding legislature of
the state, entitled "an act to levy and collect a tax from all banks
and individuals, and companies and associations of individuals
that may transact banking business in this state without
being authorized to do so by the laws thereof."
This act after reciting that the bank pursued its
operations contrary to a law of the state, enacted that if, after the first
day of the following September, the said Bank or any other
should continue to transact business within the state, it should
be liable to an annual tax of $50000 on each office. And that,
on the 15th day of Sept the Auditor should charge such tax
to the Bank, and should make out his warrant under his seal
of office, directed to any person, commanding him to collect the said
tax, who should enter the banking house and demand the same; and
if payment be not made, should levy the amount on the money or other
goods of the Bank; — the money to be retained, and the goods sold
as if taken on a fi. fa. If no effects should be found in the banking
room, the person having the warrant was authorized to go into every
room, vault, &c and to open every chest &c in search of what might sa-
tisfy his warrant.
The bill after reciting this act states that Ralph Osborne is the Auditor, and gives out in speeches that he will execute the law. It was
exhibited in open court on the 14th of September; and, notice of the application
having been given to the defendant Osborne, an order was made award-
ing the injunction, on the execution of bond & security in the penalty of $100,000; after which a subpoena was issued, on which the order
that had been made for the injunction was indorsed by the attorneys for the plaintiff.
and a memorandum that bond with security had been given by the plaintiff was indorsed by the clerk; and a power to James McDowell to serve
the same was indorsed by the Marshal. It appears

15. John Marshall.
[*Osborn v. the Bank of the U.S.*]. Autograph manuscript, [Washington], 1824.

Gilder Lehrman Collection
GLC 3653

John Marshall, chief justice of the Supreme Court, consistently vexed Andrew Jackson with his decisions, particularly those relative to Native Americans and the Bank of the United States. This manuscript is of an 1824 decision favoring the bank.

from the multitude of corporations with exclusive privileges."

The principal theme of the speech, though, was Jackson's reverence for the Union.

> We have now lived almost fifty years under the Constitution framed by the sages and patriots of the Revolution.... Our constitution is no longer a doubtful experiment.... Experience, the unerring test of all human undertakings, has shown the wisdom and foresight of those who framed it and has proved that in the Union of the states there is a sure foundation for the brightest hopes of freedom and for the happiness of the people. At every hazard and by every sacrifice this Union must be preserved.

Jackson closed with a touching valediction.

> My own race is nearly run.... I thank God that my life has been spent in a land of liberty and that He has given me a heart to love my country with the affection of a son.

Jackson was succeeded by his protégé, Martin Van Buren. He retired to the Hermitage, where he died in 1845 (PL. 17).

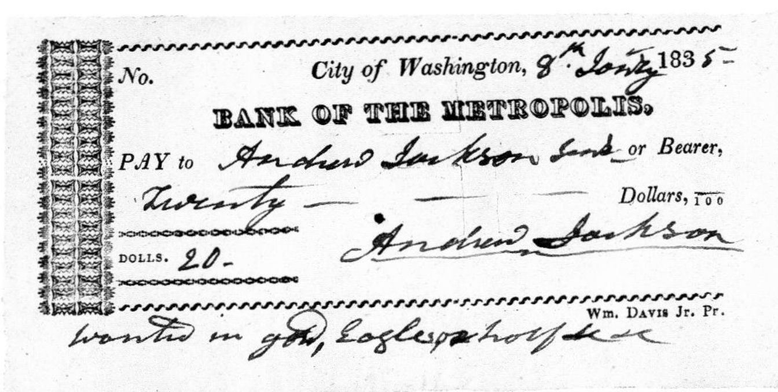
No. City of Washington, 8th Jany 1835

BANK OF THE METROPOLIS.

PAY to Andrew Jackson Junr or Bearer,

Twenty — Dollars, 100

DOLLS. 20. Andrew Jackson

Wm. Davis Jr. Pr.

wanted in gold, Eagles

16. Andrew Jackson.
Check signed, dated Washington, D.C., 8 January 1835, to Andrew Jackson, Jr.

Gilder Lehrman Collection
GLC 1994.01

On the day the national debt was paid, Jackson, a staunch opponent of paper money, wrote this check to his son, specifying that it be redeemed for hard currency.

17. [Andrew Jackson].
Funeral ribbon. [New York], 1845.

Morgan Library
MA 6035

Andrew Jackson's death in 1845, eight years after he left the presidency, plunged the nation into mourning. Eulogies and memorials came from all corners of the country as well as from voices once hostile to his administration.

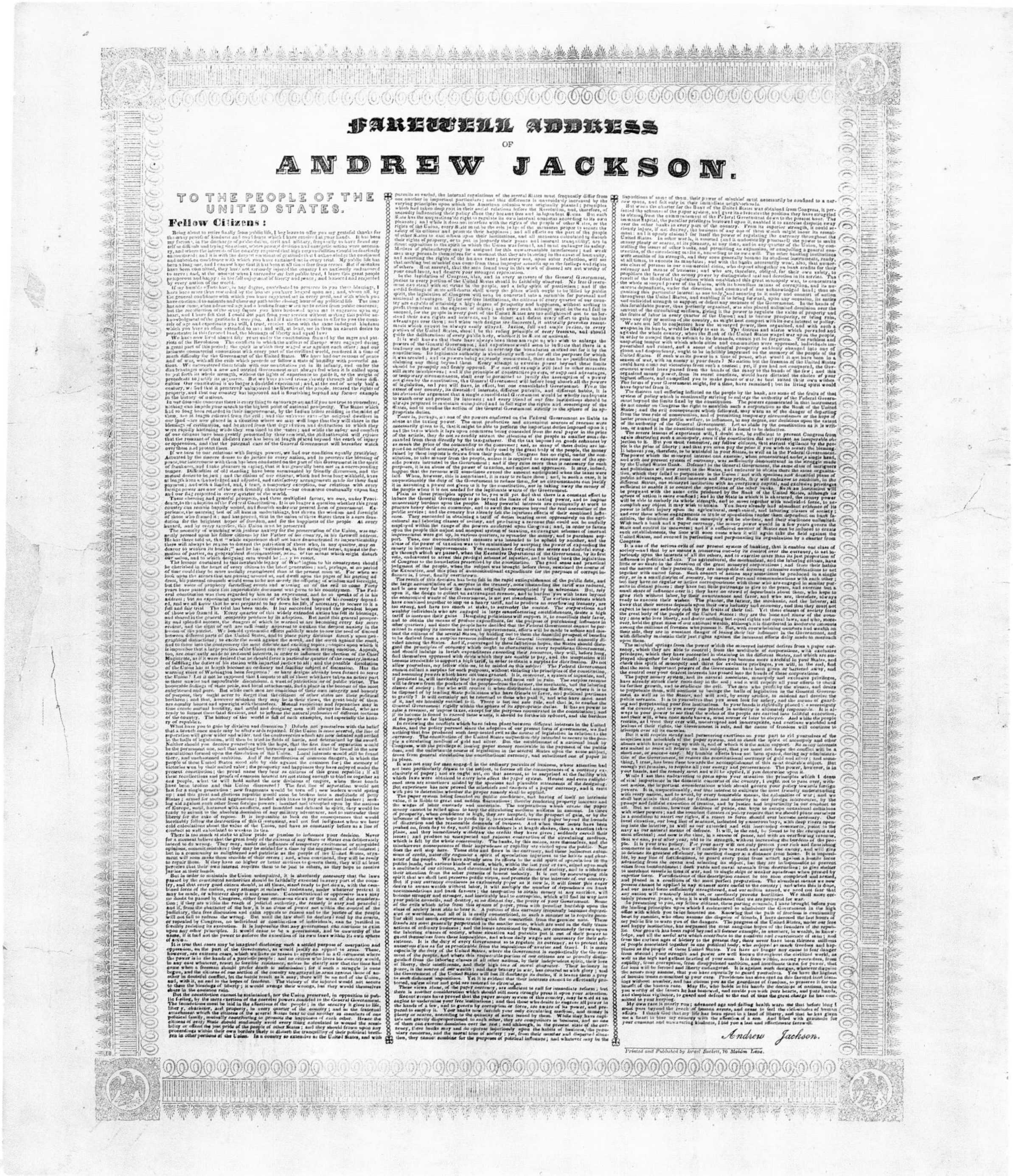

FAREWELL ADDRESS

OF

ANDREW JACKSON.

TO THE PEOPLE OF THE UNITED STATES.

Fellow Citizens:

Andrew Jackson.

Printed and Published by Israel Sackett, 76 Maiden Lane.

18. Andrew Jackson. *Farewell Address of Andrew Jackson*. Broadside. [New York]: Israel Sackett, [1837].

Gilder Lehrman Collection
GLC 3680

Andrew Jackson's farewell address was the first made by a president since George Washington.

Removal of Native Americans

The government consider it a very important object to introduce among the several Indian nations within the United States the arts of civilization.

HENRY DEARBORN, secretary of war

THE ECONOMIC DEVELOPMENT and territorial expansion that so greatly benefited whites from 1820 to 1860 brought tragedy to the Native American population. This was particularly true after 1830, when President Jackson authorized the coerced removal of Native Americans who occupied land east of the Mississippi River to settlements in the West. Before 1820, government policy recognized Native American rights. As stated in the Northwest Ordinance of 1787: "The utmost good faith shall always be observed toward the Indians; their lands and property shall never be taken from them without their consent, and in their property, rights, and liberty, they shall never be invaded or disturbed, unless in just and lawful wars authorized by Congress."

This assurance was granted by a generation that regarded Native American culture worthy of serious study. In his *Notes on the State of Virginia* (1785), Thomas Jefferson wrote respectfully of Native Americans (PL. 19). Like many of his contemporaries, Jefferson was particularly fascinated by the abundance of Native American languages and compiled, in the course of his life, vocabularies of some forty tribes.

Jefferson and the other founders tended to be assimilationists. Though they respected Native American civilization, they believed it to be less developed than their own. They thought that with education, Native Americans could be integrated into white society. This became government policy under George Washington and was administered by Henry Knox, Washington's secretary of war who was the official responsible for Native American affairs. In 1803, Henry Dearborn, Jefferson's secretary of war, outlined a federal program.

The government consider it a very important object to introduce among the several Indian nations within the United States the arts of civilization—to induce the men to engage in agriculture and the raising of stock and to convince the women of the benefits they would derive from a knowledge of the domestic arts and manufactures.

I have the pleasure to inform you that we have obtained by cession from the Cherokees and Chickasaws all their claim south of the Tennessee.

ANDREW JACKSON to James Monroe

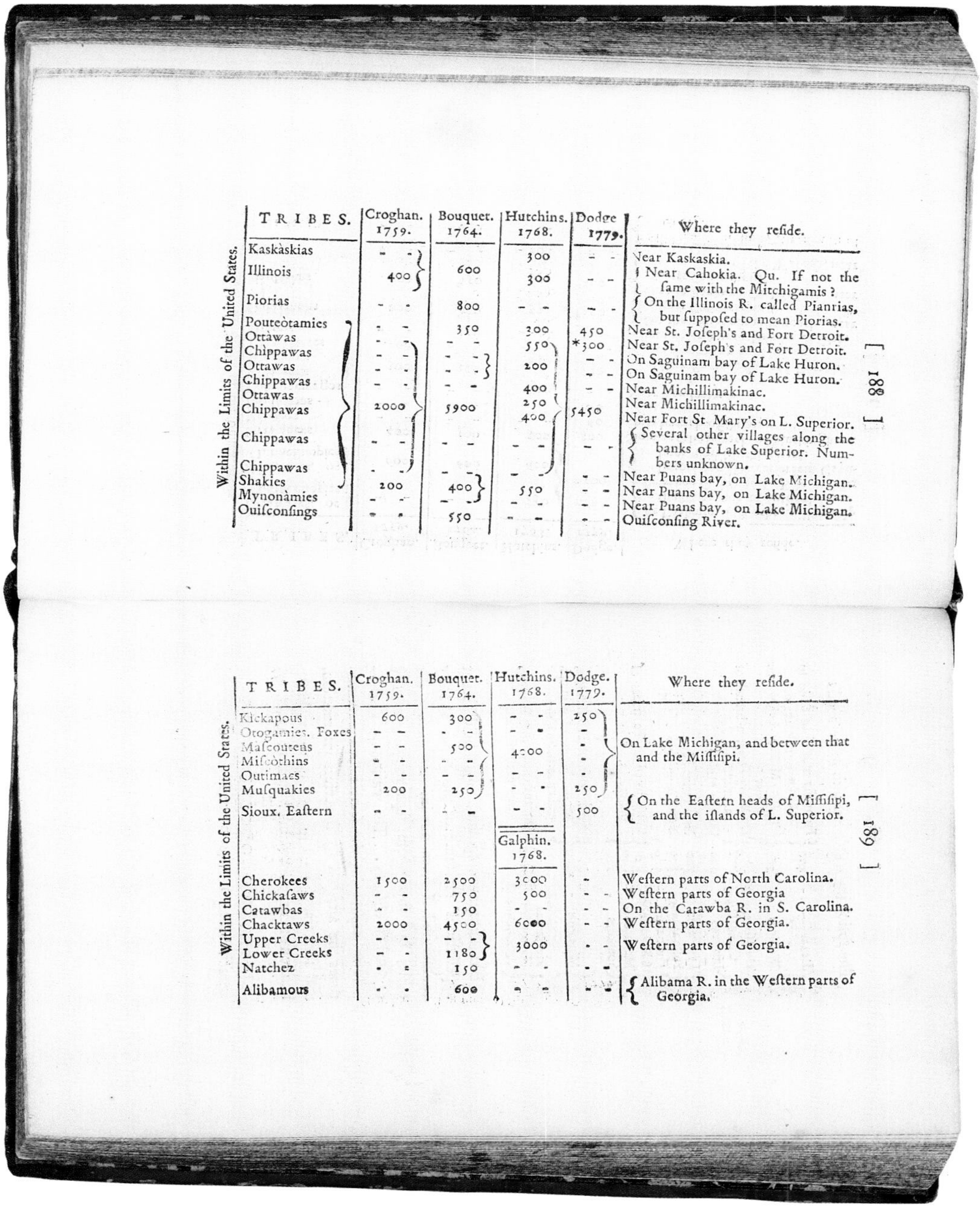

[188]

Within the Limits of the United States.

TRIBES.	Croghan. 1759.	Bouquet. 1764.	Hutchins. 1768.	Dodge 1779.	Where they reſide.
Kaskàskias	- -		300	- -	Near Kaskaskia.
Illinois	400	600	300	- -	Near Cahokia. Qu. If not the ſame with the Mitchigamis ?
Piorias	- -	800	- -	- -	On the Illinois R. called Pianrias, but ſuppoſed to mean Piorias.
Pouteòtamies	- -	350	300	450	Near St. Joſeph's and Fort Detroit.
Ottàwas	- -	- -	550	*300	Near St. Joſeph's and Fort Detroit.
Chìppawas	- -	- -	200	- -	On Saguinam bay of Lake Huron.
Ottawas	- -	- -		- -	On Saguinam bay of Lake Huron.
Chippawas	- -	- -	400	- -	Near Michillimakinac.
Ottawas			250		Near Michillimakinac.
Chippawas	2000	5900	400	5450	Near Fort St Mary's on L. Superior.
Chippawas	- -	- -	- -	- -	Several other villages along the banks of Lake Superior. Numbers unknown.
Chippawas	- -	- -	- -		
Shakies	200	400		- -	Near Puans bay, on Lake Michigan.
Mynonàmies	- -	- -	550	- -	Near Puans bay, on Lake Michigan.
Ouiſconſings	- -	550	- -	- -	Near Puans bay, on Lake Michigan.
				- -	Ouiſconſing River.

[189]

Within the Limits of the United States.

TRIBES.	Croghan. 1759.	Bouquet. 1764.	Hutchins. 1768.	Dodge. 1779.	Where they reſide.
Kickapous	600	300	- -	250	On Lake Michigan, and between that and the Miſſiſipi.
Otogamies. Foxes	- -	- -	- -	-	
Maſcoutens	- -	500	4000	-	
Miſcòthins	- -	- -		-	
Outimacs	- -	- -	- -	-	
Muſquakies	200	250	- -	250	
Sioux. Eaſtern	- -	- -	- -	500	On the Eaſtern heads of Miſſiſipi, and the iſlands of L. Superior.
			Galphin. 1768.		
Cherokees	1500	2500	3000	-	Weſtern parts of North Carolina.
Chickaſaws	- -	750	500	- -	Weſtern parts of Georgia
Catawbas	- -	150	- -	- -	On the Catawba R. in S. Carolina.
Chacktaws	2000	4500	6000	- -	Weſtern parts of Georgia.
Upper Creeks	- -	- -	3000	- -	Weſtern parts of Georgia.
Lower Creeks	- -	1180			
Natchez	- -	150	- -	- -	
Alibamous	- -	600	- -	- -	Alibama R. in the Weſtern parts of Georgia.

19. Thomas Jefferson. *Notes on the State of Virginia.* Paris: privately printed by Phillipe Denis Pierres, 1785.

Morgan Library
PML 3734

Thomas Jefferson's chapter on Native Americans in his *Notes on the State of Virginia* included this statistical chart of tribes showing their diminishing numbers since 1607. He attributed this to "spirituous liquor, the smallpox, war, and an abridgement of territory."

Assimilation became less likely during the War of 1812, when several tribes were recruited as allies by the British. In a letter to his friend Baron von Humboldt in 1813, Jefferson reported the demise of his "benevolent plan" for the Native Americans. "They would have mixed their blood with ours," he wrote, "and been amalgamated and identified with us within no distant period of time." While blaming the British for enticing the Native Americans to side with them, he offered a chilling prediction.

> They [the British] seduced the greater part of the tribes within our neighborhood to take up the hatchet against us, and the cruel massacres they [Native Americans] have committed on the women and children of our frontiers taken by surprise will oblige us now to pursue them to extermination or drive them to new seats beyond our reach.

Camp near Fort Williams april 25th 1814

My Love I have the pleasure to inform you that I reached this place on my return from the Junction of the Coosee and Tallapoosee, and of course on my return home — The creeks are conquered, some submitting unconditionally, and others whose crimes are great flying towards pensacola, to save them from the destruction of the sword, and meeting death by the hand of famine — You will receive this by the hands of Col. Carroll, for the particulars of our last excursion, I refer you — I shall be necessarily detained here untill the 28th when I hope to be able to take up the line of march for Tennessee — I shall be detained in Huntsville some short time settling my publick accpts and signing the abstracts — from which place I will write you, and be able to say to you on what day I shall reach Nashville and at which place I shall expect the pleasure of meeting you — I regret extremely your indisposition, but am happy to hear of your returning health — kiss my little andrew with you — with compliments to all friends, and best wishes for your recovering health I bid you adieu —

Andrew Jackson

20. Andrew Jackson. Autograph letter signed, dated Camp near Fort Williams, 25 April 1814, to Rachel Jackson.

Gilder Lehrman Collection GLC 522

During the War of 1812, Andrew Jackson led a volunteer militia to victory over the Creek. In this letter to his wife, Rachel, he triumphantly declared, "The Creeks are conquered."

The War of 1812 brought millions of acres of Native American lands into the possession of the United States. As both a military leader and tough negotiator, Andrew Jackson secured a large portion of these acquisitions. In 1814, Creek who had been warring with whites in the Southeast were defeated by Jackson and his forces and signed a treaty ceding much of their land to the United States (PL. 20). In 1816, Jackson was the dominant member of a government commission negotiating treaties with the Cherokee, Chickasaw, and Choctaw. Combining persuasion, offers of government reimbursement, and, at times, bribery, General Jackson and his colleagues gained further significant cessions of territory. To James Monroe, then a presidential candidate, Jackson reported:

> I feel happy that... extensive fertile country west of the county of Madison and north of the Tennessee, which at once opens a free intercourse to, and defense for, the lower country, is acquired. In a political point of view, its benefits are incalculable. We will now have good roads, kept up and supplied by the industry of our own citizens and our frontier defended by a strong population.

Settlers rushed to occupy the newly available land. Though some people continued to advocate assimilation, Andrew Jackson and many more believed that the "incalculable benefits" of national development could be realized only with the removal of Native Americans to the West.

In 1829, when he assumed the presidency, Jackson's views became official policy. At his initiation, Congress passed the Indian Removal Act in 1830, which empowered the president to negotiate with tribes for the exchange of their lands for payment and a grant of land west of the Mississippi. In 1834, Congress designated an Indian territory in what is now Oklahoma (PL. 21). Tribes were never offered a choice in the matter. Resistance was met with military force. In Georgia, Cherokee, who had established a nation with its own constitution, used

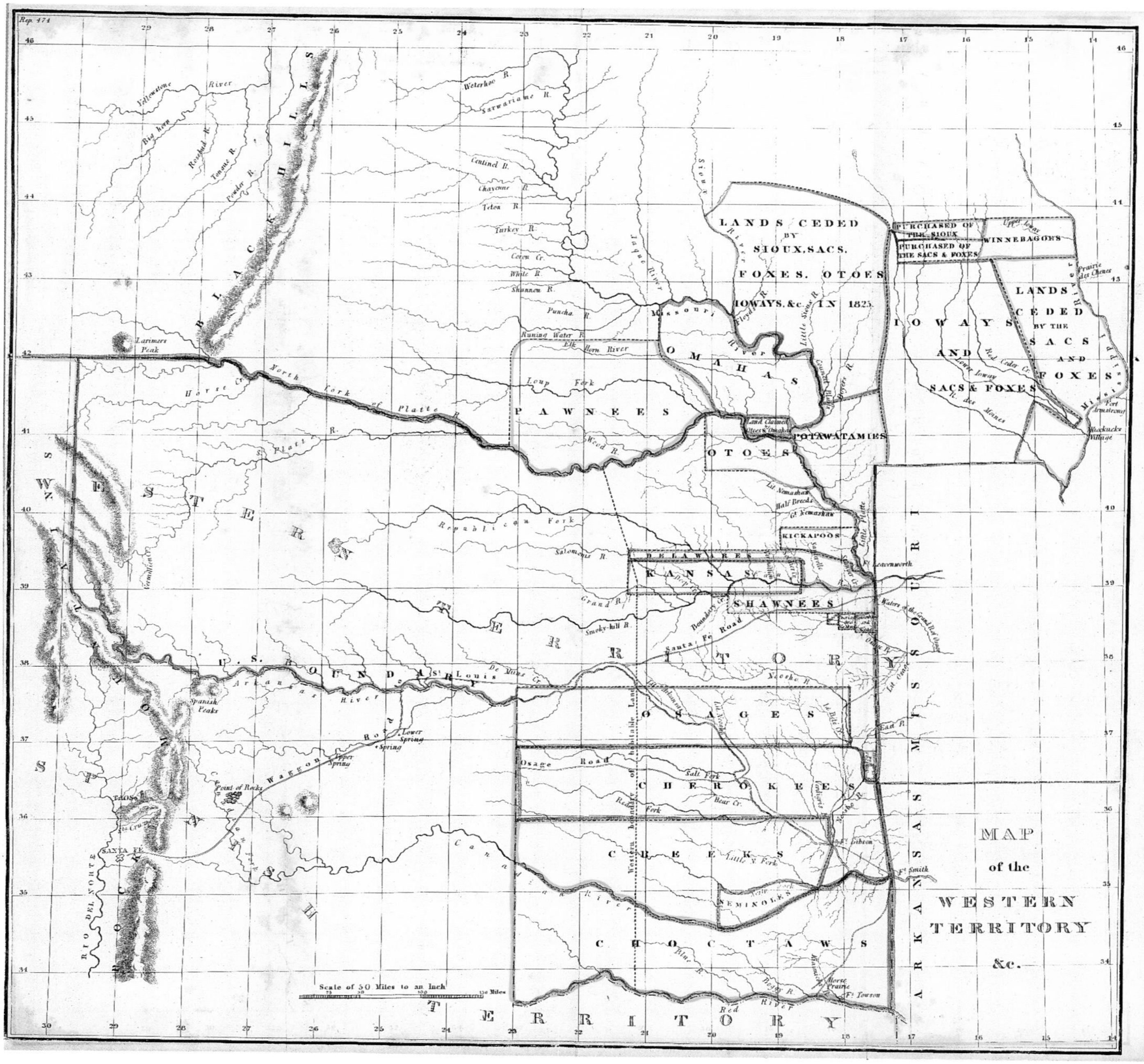

21. U.S. Congress.
House of Representatives, Committee on Indian Affairs. Report no. 474, 23d Congress, 1st session, *Regulating the Indian Department*. To accompany bills H.R. nos. 488, 489, and 490. [Washington]: Gales and Seaton, 1834.

Gilder Lehrman Collection
GLC 4132

In 1834, Congress proposed a reorganization of the Indian Department. This map indicates territory west of the Mississippi to which tribes were removed.

SUPPLEMENT TO THE PICAYUNE.

BILLY BOWLEGS

AND THE FLORIDA WAR.

The air of romance which attaches to the native children of our forests, it matters not to what tribe they may belong, has induced us to furnish our readers with a faithful portrait of Billy Bowlegs, the last King of the Everglades.

Since 1835 the Florida Indians have occupied a large share of public attention, and almost fabulous sums have been expended by the United States Government in a useless endeavor to drive them from their island homes among the morasses and lagoons in the interior of the country. The first hostilities originated in the opposition of the Mecasukians and most of the Chiefs of the Seminole nation to the execution of the treaty of Payne's Landing. It was stipulated in this treaty that the Seminoles should surrender their lands to the United States and emigrate west of the Mississippi, in consideration of a certain sum of money which was to be paid them on their arrival at the banks of the river. About the time that preparations for their removal were completed, John Hext, an influential Chief, who had favored the movement, died, and Osceola became the controlling spirit of the Mecasukians. From that period the minds of the Mecasukians and of the Seminoles were inflamed against the whites, and active outrages became frequent. The most disastrous of these was the massacre of Major Dade's command, consisting of two companies of Artillery, on the 28th of December, 1835.

STEVENS ENGR FROM A PHOTOGRAPH BY J. H. CLARK.

From the date of this massacre, the war was continued under Gen. Clinch, Brig. Gen. Call, Gen. Gaines, Col. Twiggs, Gen. Scott, Gen. Jessup, and Gen. Taylor, till 1839, when Gen. Macomb, Commander-in-Chief of the Army, invited the Indian Chiefs to a conference, and such arrangements were entered into as induced him to believe that the war would speedily be terminated. His hopes, however, proved to be ill-founded. Shortly after the conference, and in violation of its provisions, trains, travellers and plantations were attacked. Lieut. Col. Harney, at Charlotte Harbor, was surprised while asleep, and of thirty dragoons who were with him only six escaped. Harney saved his life by rushing out from the rear of his tent without waiting to dress himself, then running for several miles and swimming to a fishing boat.

This surprise was effected by two hundred and fifty Seminoles, under the command of Billy Bowlegs, and it was indeed the first time that the hero of our sketch appeared in any prominent position as a leader of his savage followers. When in this city a few days since, somebody asked Billy if he knew Gen. Harney. He replied, with a drunken swagger, "O, yes—I make him run like h—l, one time!"

The reply is curiously illustrative of the fact that savages more readily acquire the vices than the virtues of civilization.

Shortly after the Harney surprise, the Legislature of Florida made provision for the employment of bloodhounds to track the Indians to their lurking places, and thirty animals of approved breed were imported from Cuba. But among the waters of the Everglades they proved wholly useless, and the Government was saved the reproach of outdoing the savages themselves in savage strategy.

In 1840 Gen. Taylor obtained permission to retire from the command in Florida, and Gen. Armistead succeeded him. During that year and the following, when Col. Worth had the chief command, skirmishes were frequent and the forty-seven thousand square miles of territory occupied in part by the Indians were kept in a constant state of alarm. During 1842 a number of chiefs were invited to a feast and were made prisoners while partaking of it. Another chief, with eighteen warriors, was decoyed on board of a vessel and secured, and great numbers of the Indians, being thus deprived of their leaders, surrendered and consented to emigrate.

At this period Billy Bowlegs and other chiefs from the South, among whom was the venerable Sam Jones, "the Fisherman," came in to negotiate a treaty of peace. But Billy proved to be more wary than any of his peers.

"With side-long, never-ceasing glance,
By doubt and cunning marked at once,"

he was cautious about placing himself in the power of the whites, and for a considerable time he kept the attention of the government officers engaged by his rude but skillful diplomacy. Col. Worth, deceived by appearances and hollow promises, proclaimed the war over in April, 1842, but no sooner had he resigned the command, which was assumed by Col. Vose, than guerrilla conflicts broke out afresh on the part of the Indians. In these movements Bowlegs had the credit of being the chief agent and director, and it is certain that he resisted large promises of reward in case he induced his people to emigrate.

Conference after conference was had, and Billy, by his frequent intercourse with the whites, acquired quite a fluent use of the English and Spanish languages. Indeed, he pretended to be quite a *savant* among the redskins of the Everglades, and it is said that he obtained the prettiest of his two wives by means of a fraud founded on his educational assumptions.

It appears that one of the braves of his tribe had a young and pretty wife, who attracted the attention of Billy, much in the same manner that the psalmist king of old was attracted by the beauteous wife of his servant Uriah. Nor does the parallel end in mere "passional attraction." Each compassed the death of a husband for the accomplishment of an unhallowed purpose, and in no respect does the case of the savage appear worse than that of the psalmist.

As the story runs Billy pretended to have received a letter informing him that the husband of the pretty squaw was about to betray the Seminoles to the whites, and he at once preferred against him the charge of being a traitor. The brave indignantly denied the charge, but Billy showed the letter which he had received, and read from it, in English, the most convincing proofs against the culprit. Thereupon the surprised brave questioned Billy's ability to read. But Billy replied, that he was willing to have his skill in reading and writing English, put to the severest test, and if a letter which he would write in the presence of the chiefs of the nation, were not immediately understood by the officers of the neighboring Fort, he would himself stand impeached and allow the prosecution to fall.

And Billy, with his wicked foresight, knew what he was about. When at the Fort a few days previously he asked the officer in charge to write what he would dictate, and, the officer consenting, he had written, "I, Billy Bowlegs, King of the Seminoles, can read and write the English language." Billy then told the officer that he wanted to play a joke off on some of his people and if any of them came to the Fort with a letter bearing his autograph, to read or translate it in the words which had just been written.

So when a messenger was sent with Billy's letter the officer at once understood and read it as per previous agreement, and the result was the conviction and execution of the pretty squaw's husband. Then Billy comforted the pretty squaw and she became his wife.

After Col. Worth was brevetted Brigadier General and returned to the command, innumerable petty treaties and hollow truces were agreed to by Billy, until finally, during Mr. Fillmore's occupancy of the Presidential Chair, he was induced by Gen. Blake to pay a visit to the great White Chief at Washington.

So Billy, with a few of his chosen braves, made his first tour through the white man's territory, and manifested the usual indifference of the Indian stoic, whenever evidences of the white man's skill were presented for his admiration. The steamboat was pretty good, but he preferred the canoes of the Everglades; and the locomotive went pretty fast, but he had a little black pony that would beat it.

When taken into the Presidential presence, he observed to Mr. Fillmore, "You, big Chief, and I'm King of the Seminoles: Let there be friendship between us."

After he had become tired of Washington, Gen. Blake took him to New York, which he acknowledged was considerable of a village. One day he was shown the principal harbor defences, and he observed of the guns, that they might do very well there, but they would not be worth a rush among the Everglades.

On his return to Florida he expressed his willingness to emigrate, and a friend of ours who spent an evening with him in the quarters of Gen. Childs at Tampa Bay, informs us that he conducted himself in the presence of the ladies with marked propriety.

But Billy's promises to emigrate were not fulfilled, though repeated time and again to Capt. Casey, the Indian Agent at Tampa Bay. Every year his warriors were becoming less in number, and his predatory power and prestige were consequently diminished.

The last of Billy's outrages which attracted much attention, occurred about two years ago. It was the attack and massacre of a party with two wagons, under command of Lieut. Hartsuff, between Fort Deynard and Fort Simon Drum. The party was surprised on a palmetto hummock, and all were killed with the exception of the Lieutenant, who, single handed, kept the Indians for some time at bay, he firing from the shelter of a wagon, while two of his wounded companions kept his weapons loaded. At length, however, he was wounded in the right arm and breast, and, concluding to give up the unequal contest, he ran for a neighboring thicket, where there was a pond of water surrounded by a tall growth of rushes. Into this pond he crawled and lay down in the water; and though pursued by the Indians and called upon by Billy to come out and surrender, he managed to escape the notice of his savage foes, who left him to his fate about the time that a new danger began to threaten him in the shape of a hungry alligator. Two days afterwards he was found by a party from Fort Simon Drum, in an almost dying condition.

The recent agreement with Billy to emigrate was never ratified by the venerable Sam Jones, who declared that two wagon loads of money would not induce him to leave. On the morning of the 4th inst., Col. Rector left Fort Myers in charge of Billy and the rest of the voluntary emigrants and captives, numbering in all one hundred and sixty-five.

According to Billy's statement, there were left in the country three parties of Indians—one known as the boatmen, consisting of twelve warriors and a boy; the second, Sam Jones's party, consisting of seventeen warriors and their families; and the third, the Tallahassees, numbering about eight warriors, with their families. The boatmen Billy left with great reluctance, for he asserts that they would have emigrated willingly if they could only have been found.

Billy and his followers arrived at the Barracks below the city of New Orleans on the 14th inst., on the steamer Gray Cloud; and for a few days the last King of the Everglades was lionized by the wonder-mongers of the Crescent City. But he defeated most of the arrangements which were made on his behalf by his continual drunkenness, and his tendency to beg was rather inclined to moderate the admiration of his visitors.

Ere this, Billy has arrived at his new home in the Indian territory west of Arkansas; and the contest with the Florida Indians, which lasted for twenty-three years, and cost the United States Government, directly and indirectly, a hundred millions of dollars, may now be considered as at an end.

Our portrait of Billy is a faithful copy from real life. Though by no means handsome, the features indicate the keen, cunning and determined warrior; and the dress, which is profusely ornamented with silver, betrays rude evidences of royal vanity.

NEW ORLEANS, Sunday, May 30, 1858.

legal maneuvers to forestall expulsion (PL. 23). In 1838, under coercion by federal troops, some 16,000 Cherokee began the journey on what came to be called the Trail of Tears. As much as a quarter of the Cherokee population may have died from the harsh conditions encountered along the way. In order to oust the Seminole from Florida, the Second Seminole War, which cost the United States 1,500 lives and $30 million, was waged from 1835 to 1842. One contingent, led by Billy Bowlegs, resisted removal until 1858 (PL. 22).

Despite the resistance of the Cherokee and Seminole, as well as the efforts of some whites, organized opposition to the removal policy never took firm hold. During congressional debate over the Indian Removal Act in 1829, Joseph Evarts, as secretary of the American Board of Commissioners for Foreign Missions, encouraged church members to write to their senators and representatives on behalf of Native Americans. The letter-writing campaign did not prevent passage of the act in 1830. In literature, Lydia Maria Child's and John Neal's stories explicitly condemning removal were unusual among fictional depictions of Native Americans.

The estimated total of Native Americans forced from their lands ranges as high as 100,000. Alexis de Tocqueville, who observed the initial stages of removal in 1831, poignantly expressed their plight in *Democracy in America*.

> The ruin of these tribes began from the day when the Europeans landed on their shores; it has proceeded ever since, and we are now witnessing its completion. They seem placed by Providence amid the riches of the New World only to enjoy them for a season; they were there merely to wait till others came.

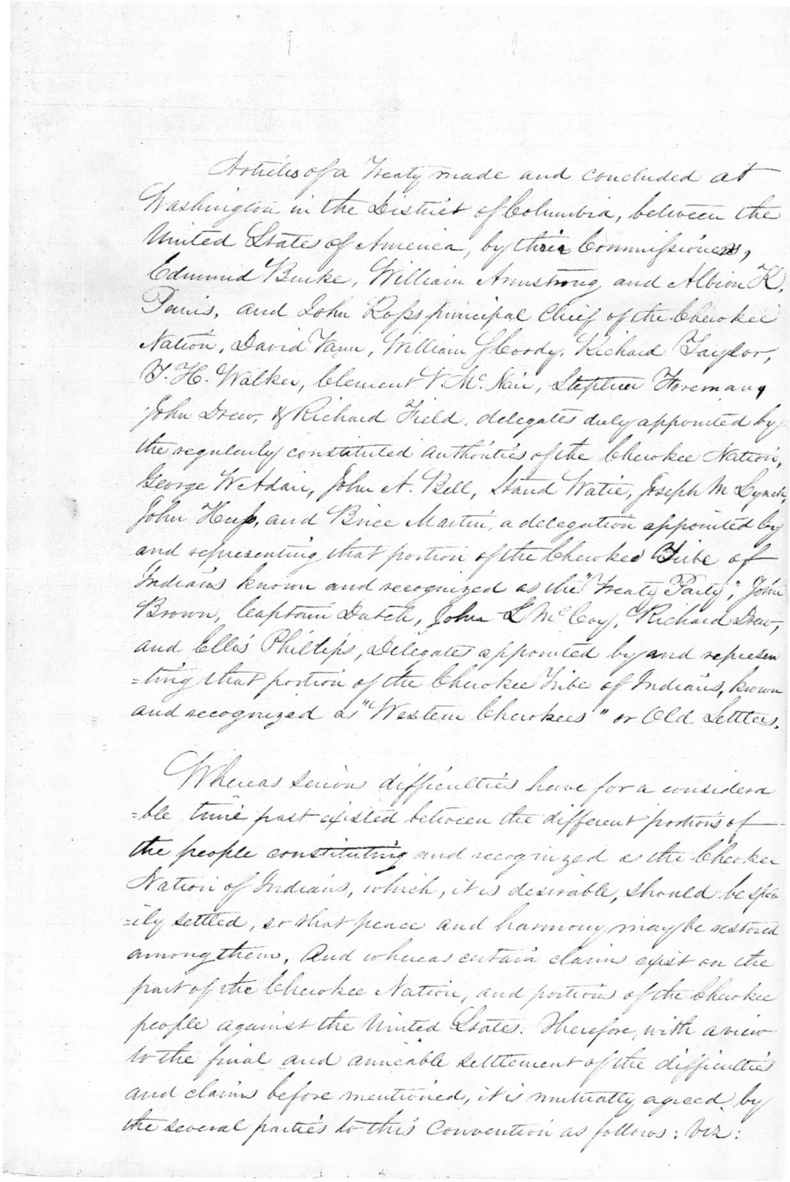

Articles of a Treaty made and concluded at Washington in the District of Columbia, between the United States of America, by three Commissioners, Edmund Burke, William Armstrong, and Albion K. Parris, and John Ross principal Chief of the Cherokee Nation, David Vann, William S. Coody, Richard Taylor, T. H. Walker, Clement V. McNair, Stephen Foreman, John Drew, & Richard Field, delegates duly appointed by the regularly constituted authorities of the Cherokee Nation; George W. Adair, John A. Bell, Stand Watie, Joseph M. Lynch, John Huss, and Brice Martin, a delegation appointed by and representing that portion of the Cherokee Tribe of Indians known and recognized as the "Treaty Party;" John Brown, Captain Dutch, John L. McCoy, Richard Drew, and Ellis Phillips, Delegates appointed by and representing that portion of the Cherokee Tribe of Indians, known and recognized as "Western Cherokees" or Old Settlers.

Whereas serious difficulties have for a considerable time past existed between the different portions of the people constituting and recognized as the Cherokee Nation of Indians, which, it is desirable, should be speedily settled, so that peace and harmony may be restored among them; And whereas certain claims exist on the part of the Cherokee Nation, and portions of the Cherokee people against the United States: Therefore, with a view to the final and amicable settlement of the difficulties and claims before mentioned, it is mutually agreed by the several parties to this Convention as follows: viz:

23. [*U.S. Treaty with Cherokee Nation*].
Manuscript, Washington, D.C., 6 August 1846.

Gilder Lehrman Collection
GLC 1233.5

Dissent within the Cherokee tribe over forced relocation led to prolonged internal warfare. Peace was finally achieved with the treaty of 1846.

22. *The Times-Picayune, New Orleans.* *Picayune Supplement.*
New Orleans, 30 May 1858.

Gilder Lehrman Collection
GLC 4201

The Seminole and the United States engaged in three long and costly wars during the first half of the nineteenth century. In the third (1855–58), Billy Bowlegs was a formidable Seminole leader.

An Age of Reform

AS TOCQUEVILLE OBSERVED, mid-nineteenth-century Americans zealously pursued the reform of society. Through a remarkable array of secular and religious activities, they sought to abolish slavery, obtain equal rights for women, eradicate drunkenness, convert sinners, and otherwise better their world. This activity was fueled by the belief of many that society actually could be improved. For some reformers, this optimistic outlook was confirmed by their direct experience of the era's progress, made manifest by technological innovation, improved transportation, and expanded economic opportunities in new urban centers and western territories.

In the prevailing spirit of dynamism and creativity, education was a particular focus of reform. Horace Mann's efforts in the 1830s and 1840s to increase funding and improve standards for public schools in Massachusetts set the pattern for public education throughout the nation. In 1821, Emma Willard founded the nation's first high school for women in New York, and, in 1836, Mary Lyon established the first permanent college for women, Mount Holyoke Female Seminary. Thomas H. Gallaudet and Samuel Gridley Howe revamped methods for teaching the deaf and blind. Responding to the propensity for self-improvement, Josiah Holbrook, in 1826, organized a lyceum for adult education in Millbury, Massachusetts. By 1834, there was a lyceum circuit of some 3,000 towns providing receptive audiences for many of the nation's most renowned speakers.

Amid the progress that instilled optimism, however, coexisted conditions that provoked anxiety. Many citizens who were sensitive to society's flaws and inequities joined antislavery groups, temperance unions, and a host of other such associations founded to cure social ills. Among the countless reform initiatives of the period, six particularly influential movements were revivalism, Mormonism, utopianism, temperance, abolitionism, and women's rights.

> [T]he political activity that pervades the United States must be seen in order to be understood. No sooner do you set foot upon American ground than you are stunned by a kind of tumult; a confused clamor is heard on every side, and a thousand simultaneous voices demand the satisfaction of their social wants.
>
> ALEXIS DE TOCQUEVILLE
> *Democracy in America*

24. *The Camp Meeting at Sing Sing, New York, August, 1859.*
Engraving from *Harper's Weekly*, 10 September 1859.

Gilder Lehrman Collection
GLC 1733

Revivals included intense preaching, group prayer, and, often, worshipers whose religious fervor drove them to convulsions.

Revivalism

In the 1820s, a religious revival began to sweep the United States. In Ohio, Pennsylvania, New York, and Massachusetts, Charles Grandison Finney, a Presbyterian preacher, swayed enormous crowds toward repentance. Over the next four decades, Finney and other evangelicals tapped the religious fervor of individuals of all social classes. Camp meetings throughout the country provided the venue for fiery preaching and highly demonstrative emotional conversions (PL. 24). In *The Domestic Manners of the Americans* (1832), English visitor Frances Trollope described a camp meeting in Indiana at which 2,000 souls listened and reacted to the gospel. She was amazed by the sights and sounds of worshipers "ceasing not to call in every variety of tone, on the name of Jesus, accompanied with sobs, groans, and a sort of low howling inexpressibly painful to listen to."

Tocqueville reported, in *Democracy in America*, that established New England churches were integral to American evangelicalism. He surmised that in sending missionaries to the nation's western regions, the churches were motivated as much by civic as by religious duty. The evangelical impulse in America, he theorized, sprang from a unique commingling of religious and republican ideals. "Americans," he wrote, "combine the notions of Christianity and of liberty so intimately in their minds that it is impossible to make them conceive the one without the other." Tocqueville also noted a tendency of Americans to intertwine religious faith and material well-being. "If you converse with these missionaries of Christian civilization," he added, "you will be surprised to hear them speak so often of the goods of this world and to meet a politician where you expected to find a priest."

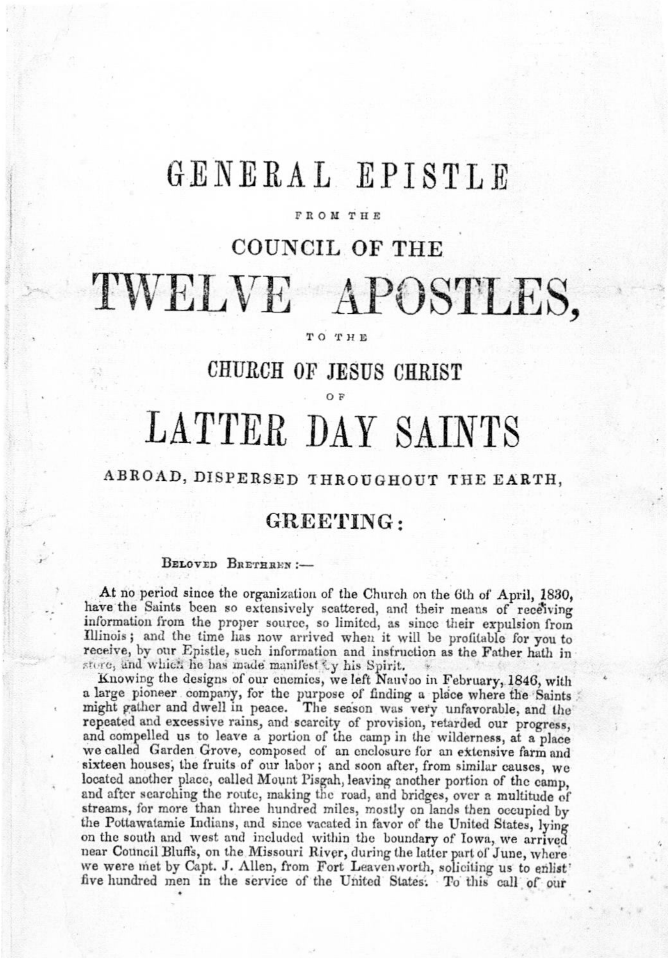

GENERAL EPISTLE

FROM THE

COUNCIL OF THE

TWELVE APOSTLES,

TO THE

CHURCH OF JESUS CHRIST

OF

LATTER DAY SAINTS

ABROAD, DISPERSED THROUGHOUT THE EARTH,

GREETING:

BELOVED BRETHREN:—

At no period since the organization of the Church on the 6th of April, 1830, have the Saints been so extensively scattered, and their means of receiving information from the proper source, so limited, as since their expulsion from Illinois; and the time has now arrived when it will be profitable for you to receive, by our Epistle, such information and instruction as the Father hath in store, and which he has made manifest by his Spirit.

Knowing the designs of our enemies, we left Nauvoo in February, 1846, with a large pioneer company, for the purpose of finding a place where the Saints might gather and dwell in peace. The season was very unfavorable, and the repeated and excessive rains, and scarcity of provision, retarded our progress, and compelled us to leave a portion of the camp in the wilderness, at a place we called Garden Grove, composed of an enclosure for an extensive farm and sixteen houses, the fruits of our labor; and soon after, from similar causes, we located another place, called Mount Pisgah, leaving another portion of the camp, and after searching the route, making the road, and bridges, over a multitude of streams, for more than three hundred miles, mostly on lands then occupied by the Pottawatamie Indians, and since vacated in favor of the United States, lying on the south and west and included within the boundary of Iowa, we arrived near Council Bluffs, on the Missouri River, during the latter part of June, where we were met by Capt. J. Allen, from Fort Leavenworth, soliciting us to enlist five hundred men in the service of the United States. To this call of our

25. [Brigham Young]. *General Epistle from the Council of the Twelve Apostles, to the Church of Jesus Christ of Latter Day Saints Abroad, Dispersed Throughout the Earth.* [N.p., 1848].

Gilder Lehrman Collection
GLC 4149

Brigham Young published this letter to inform Mormons of plans to establish a new settlement in Utah.

The Mormons

In an era that offered many options for the gratification of Americans' religious impulses, a new religion emerged in upstate New York. Its doctrine was based on the Bible and *The Book of Mormon*. Published in 1830, *The Book of Mormon* was a collection of revelations that Joseph Smith claimed to have experienced during the previous decade. Smith recruited converts primarily from rural areas and, in 1834, founded the Church of Jesus Christ of Latter-day Saints.

The Mormons' rejection of alcohol and tobacco and their advocacy of hard work were values shared by many of their contemporaries. The insistence that their doctrine was based on divine revelation along with their self-sufficient communities, in which outsiders were not welcome, set Mormons apart and alienated the populace. As they emigrated westward in pursuit of their ideal of a religious state, Mormons continually encountered hostility from surrounding communities. In 1839, Smith and 12,000 to 15,000 of his followers settled in Illinois, where they established Nauvoo and began construction of a temple. Upon being attacked in print by dissenting Mormons in 1844, Smith ordered the destruction of their press. He and his brother Hyram were jailed in Carthage, Illinois, where they were lynched by a mob that included members of the state militia.

Under the leadership of Brigham Young, a large contingent of Mormons emigrated farther westward in search of a safe place to settle. In 1847, Young issued a *General Epistle from the Council of the Twelve Apostles* to Mormons all over the world, urging them to join a new community in Great Salt Lake Valley. There, he assured them, Mormons would be "far removed from those who have been their oppressors" (PL. 25). In 1849, Young and his followers established the provisional state of Deseret, with its own army and Young as its governor. When Congress established the Utah Territory in 1850, Young retained the governorship by federal appointment. Although Mormons asserted their loyalty to the Constitution, their independent, church-regulated government and Young's 1852 public proclamation of the doctrine of polygamy engendered fear and outrage among other settlers. President Buchanan removed Young as governor and sent 2,500 troops to enforce federal law in 1857. The troops were eventually withdrawn, but federal disputes with the church continued until negotiations with Mormon leaders made Utah statehood possible in 1896.

Utopianism

While Mormons and other religious groups formed communities based on sacred principles, many individuals were attracted to communities based on secular ideals. From the 1820s through the 1840s, Robert Owen's New Harmony, Indiana, John Humphrey Noyes's Oneida, New York, and other communities offered alternative

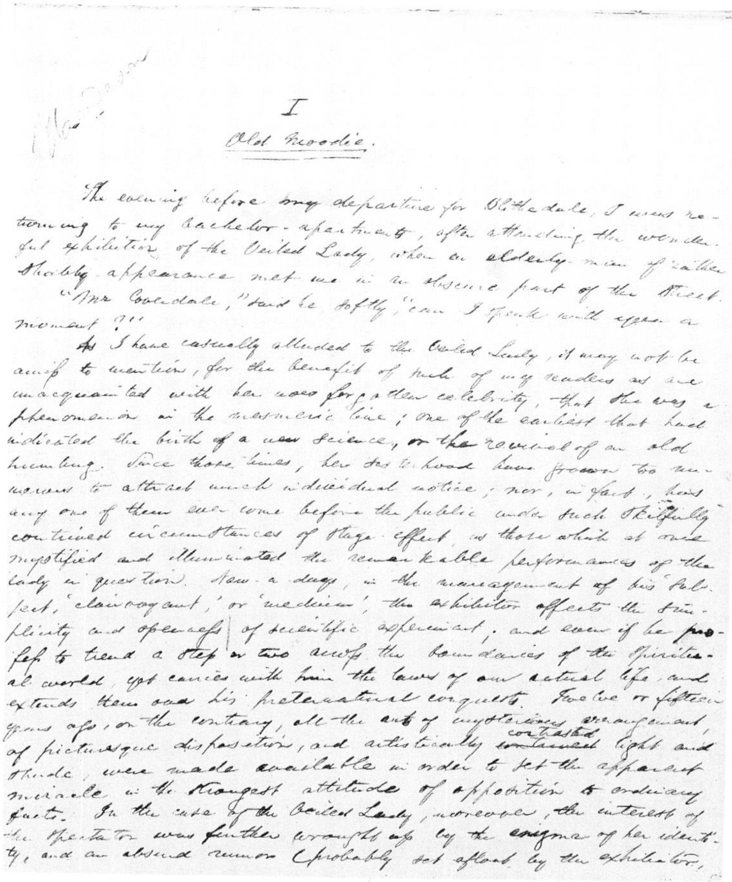
I

Old Moodie.

The evening before my departure for Blithedale, I was returning to my bachelor-apartments, after attending the wonderful exhibition of the Veiled Lady, when an elderly-man of rather shabby appearance met me in an obscure part of the street.

"Mr. Coverdale," said he softly, "can I speak with you a moment?"

As I have casually alluded to the Veiled Lady, it may not be amiss to mention, for the benefit of such of my readers as are unacquainted with her now forgotten celebrity, that she was a phenomenon in the mesmeric line; one of the earliest that had indicated the birth of a new science, or the revival of an old humbug. Since those times, her sisterhood have grown too numerous to attract much individual notice; nor, in fact, has any one of them ever come before the public under such skilfully contrived circumstances of stage-effect, as those which at once mystified and illuminated the remarkable performances of the lady in question. Now-a-days, in the management of his 'subject,' 'clairvoyant,' or 'medium,' the exhibitor affects the simplicity and openness of scientific experiment; and even if he profess to tread a step or two across the boundaries of the spiritual world, yet carries with him the laws of our actual life, and extends them over his preternatural conquests. Twelve or fifteen years ago, on the contrary, all the arts of mysterious arrangement, of picturesque disposition, and artistically contrasted light and shade, were made available in order to set the apparent miracle in the strongest attitude of opposition to ordinary facts. In the case of the Veiled Lady, moreover, the interest of the spectator was further wrought up by the enigma of her identity, and an absurd rumor (probably set afloat by the exhibitor,

26. Nathaniel Hawthorne. *The Blithedale Romance.* Autograph manuscript signed, [1852].

Morgan Library MA 573

After a sojourn at Brook Farm, Hawthorne expressed a skeptical, ironic view of utopian communities in *The Blithedale Romance.*

economic and social arrangements to dissenters who wanted to avoid the selfishness and materialism they perceived in society. One of the most prominent utopian communities was Brook Farm, founded in 1841 in West Roxbury, Massachusetts, by Boston transcendentalist George Ripley. Based on a cooperative economic system, Brook Farm provided a simple way of life that emphasized cultural pursuits. Nathaniel Hawthorne's six-month residence there became the basis of his novel *The Blithedale Romance* (PL. 26). Beset with debts and other calamities, Brook Farm disbanded in 1847. By the 1850s, widespread enthusiasm for utopian communities had waned.

27. "Ancient and Modern Republic." Lithograph by A. Descotes, after A. Hervieu, from Frances Trollope's *The Domestic Manners of Americans*. London: Whittaker, Treavler, and Co., 1832.

Morgan Library
PML 9317

This engraving illustrates English traveler Frances Trollope's disdainful depiction of what she terms typical American "*reposoires*, which as you pass them, blast the sense for a moment, by reeking forth the fumes of whiskey and tobacco."

The Temperance Movement

Rather than withdrawing into separate religious or secular communities, many Americans addressed society's problems directly. The temperance movement attracted reformers who identified excessive drinking as the principal cause of family violence, poverty, and the general breakdown of morality. Per capita consumption of alcohol was, indeed, much higher in the mid-nineteenth century than it is now, and public drunkenness was more common. Frances Trollope considered America to be an "alcoholic republic," asserting that hard drinking was more prevalent here than in any other nation (PL. 27). Among the hundreds of temperance organizations were the American Temperance Union, which in 1831 had over 170,000 members in over 2,000 local chapters; the Washingtonian Society, which sought to reform alcoholics primarily from the working class; and

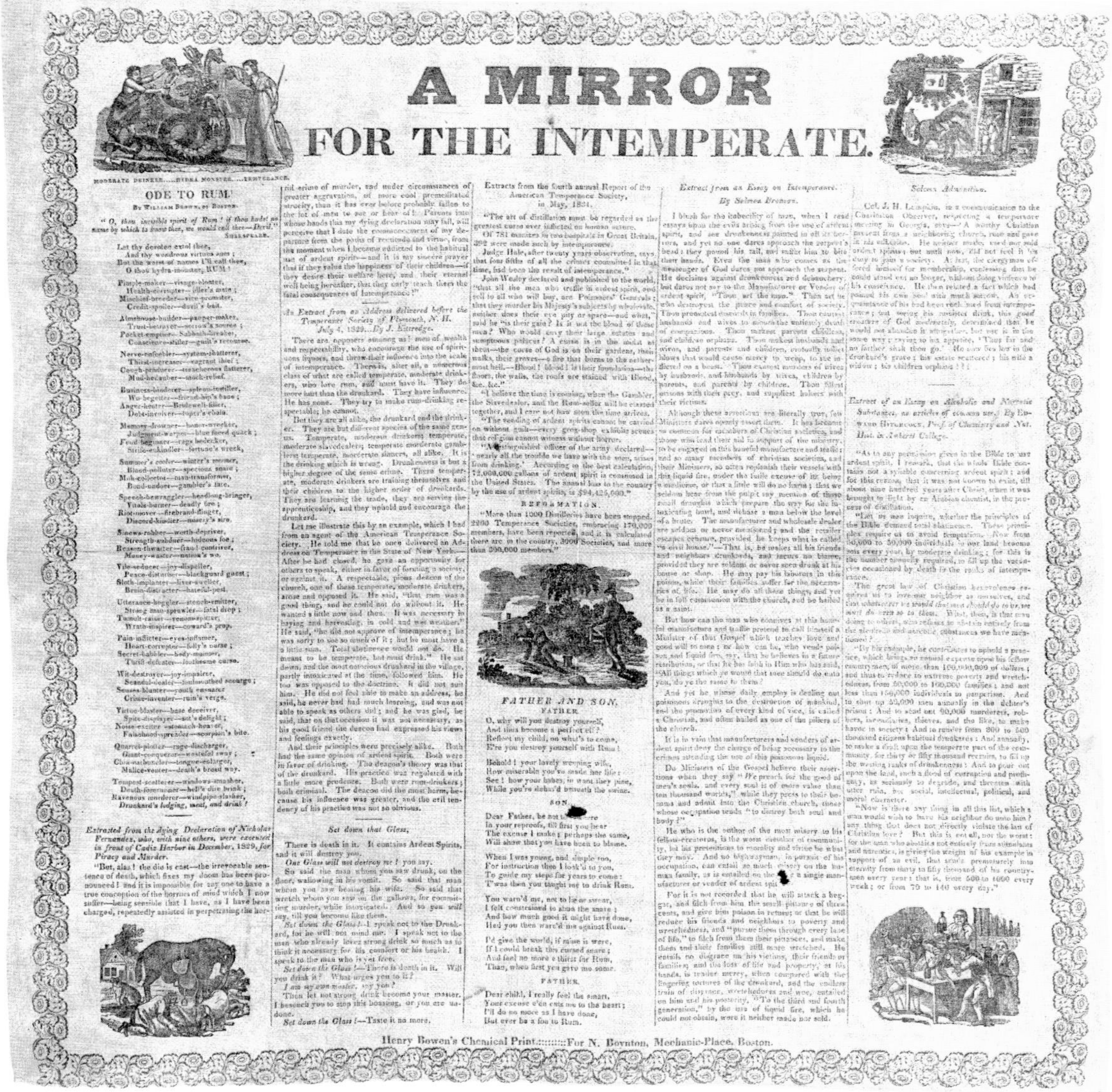

A MIRROR FOR THE INTEMPERATE.

ODE TO RUM.

FATHER AND SON.

Henry Bowen's Chemical Print:::::::For N. Boynton, Mechanic-Place, Boston.

28. *A Mirror for the Intemperate.*
Broadside, on silk. Boston: N. Boynton, [1831].

Gilder Lehrman Collection
GLB 200

Temperance publications often inventoried alcohol's evils. Here, hard drink is condemned as "wit-destroyer, youth ensnarer," among other villainies.

the Women's Temperance Army, which focused on the detrimental effects of alcoholism on family life (PL. 28).

Temperance advocates promulgated their messages through rallies, a plethora of printed matter, and testimonials from eminent individuals. Edward C. Delavan, a wine merchant and benefactor of the movement, was particularly successful in obtaining signatures of American political leaders, including presidents, on petitions urging young men to refrain from alcohol. While some reformers opposed hard liquor only and accepted limited consumption of beer and wine, others advocated the prohibition of all alcoholic beverages. Through the efforts of crusading businessman Neal Dow, the state of Maine passed a law in 1851 that outlawed the manufacture and sale of intoxicating liquor. Vermont and Rhode Island followed with their own laws. By 1855, thirteen of the thirty-one states had "Maine laws."

SLAVE MARKET OF AMERICA.
THE WORD OF GOD.
"ALL THINGS WHATSOEVER YE WOULD THAT MEN SHOULD DO TO YOU, DO YE EVEN SO TO THEM, FOR THIS IS THE LAW AND THE PROPHETS."
"AND THEY SIGHED BY REASON OF THE BONDAGE, AND THEY CRIED, AND THEIR CRY CAME UP UNTO GOD BY REASON OF THE BONDAGE, AND GOD HEARD THEIR GROANING."
"THUS SAITH THE LORD, EXECUTE JUDGMENT IN THE MORNING, AND DELIVER HIM THAT IS SPOILED OUT OF THE HANDS OF THE OPPRESSOR, LEST MY FURY GO OUT LIKE FIRE, AND BURN THAT NONE CAN QUENCH IT, BECAUSE OF THE EVIL OF YOUR DOINGS."
THE DECLARATION OF AMERICAN INDEPENDENCE.
"WE HOLD THESE TRUTHS TO BE SELF-EVIDENT;—THAT ALL MEN ARE CREATED EQUAL; THAT THEY ARE ENDOWED BY THEIR CREATOR WITH CERTAIN UNALIENABLE RIGHTS; THAT AMONG THESE ARE LIFE, LIBERTY, AND THE PURSUIT OF HAPPINESS."
THE CONSITUTION OF THE UNITED STATES.
"THE CITIZENS OF EACH STATE SHALL BE ENTITLED TO ALL THE PRIVILEGES AND IMMUNITIES OF CITIZENS OF THE SEVERAL STATES." Article 4, Section 2.
"CONGRESS SHALL MAKE NO LAW ABRIDGING THE FREEDOM OF SPEECH OR OF THE PRESS, OR OF THE RIGHT OF THE PEOPLE PEACEABLY TO ASSEMBLE, AND TO PETITION THE GOVERNMENT FOR A REDRESS OF GRIEVANCES."—Article 1. Amendment.
"CONGRESS SHALL HAVE POWER TO EXERCISE EXCLUSIVE LEGISLATION, IN ALL CASES WHATSOEVER, OVER SUCH DISTRICT (NOT EXCEEDING TEN MILES SQUARE) AS MAY, BY CESSION OF PARTICULAR STATES AND THE ACCEPTANCE OF CONGRESS, BECOME THE SEAT OF GOVERNMENT OF THE UNITED STATES."—Article 1, Section 8.
CONSTITUTIONS OF THE STATES.
"EVERY CITIZEN MAY FREELY SPEAK, WRITE, AND PUBLISH HIS SENTIMENTS ON ALL SUBJECTS, BEING RESPONSIBLE FOR THE ABUSE OF THAT LIBERTY." Constitutions of Maine, Connecticut, New-York, Pennsylvania, Delaware, Ohio, Indiana, Illinois, Tennessee, Louisiana, Alabama, Mississippi, and Missouri.
"THE FREEDOM OF THE PRESS IS ONE OF THE GREAT BULWARKS OF LIBERTY, AND THEREFORE OUGHT NEVER TO BE RESTRAINED."—North Carolina.
"THE LIBERTY OF THE PRESS OUGHT TO BE INVIOLABLY PRESERVED."—Maryland.
"THE FREEDOM OF THE PRESS IS ONE OF THE GREAT BULWARKS OF LIBERTY, AND CAN NEVER BE RESTRAINED BUT BY DESPOTIC GOVERNMENTS."—Virginia. Other States nearly the same.
DISTRICT OF COLUMBIA.
"THE LAND OF THE FREE."
THE RESIDENCE OF 7000 SLAVES.
"THE HOME OF THE OPPRESSED."
READING OF THE DECLARATION OF INDEPENDENCE.
PART OF WASHINGTON CITY.
CAPITOL OF THE UNITED STATES. "Hail Columbia."
RIGHT TO INTERFERE.
PUBLIC PRISONS IN THE DISTRICT.
Built by Congress with $15,000 of the People's money; perverted from the purposes for which they were built, and used by Slaveholders for the confinement of refractory Slaves, by licensed Slave-dealers as depots for their victims, and by kidnappers for the imprisonment of Free Americans, seized and sold to pay their jail fees!
JAIL IN ALEXANDRIA.
JAIL IN WASHINGTON,—SALE OF A FREE CITIZEN TO PAY HIS JAIL FEES!
VIEW OF THE INTERIOR OF THE JAIL IN WASHINGTON.—FANNY JACKSON.
FACTS.
FACTS.
FACTS.
NOTICE.
PRIVATE PRISONS IN THE DISTRICT, LICENSED AS SOURCES OF PUBLIC REVENUE.
"For a license to trade or traffic in slaves for profit, whether as agent or otherwise, four hundred dollars;"—the Register to "deposit all monies received from taxes imposed by this act to the credit of the Canal Fund." Act to provide a revenue for the Canal Fund, approved July 28, 1831. City Laws, p. 249.
SLAVE HOUSE OF J. W. NEAL & CO.
VIEW OF A SECTION OF ALEXANDRIA, WITH A SLAVE SHIP RECEIVING HER CARGO OF SLAVES.
FRANKLIN & ARMFIELD'S SLAVE PRISON.
"CASH FOR 200 NEGROES."
"JOSEPH W. NEAL & CO."
"ALEXANDRIA AND NEW-ORLEANS PACKETS."
"FRANKLIN & ARMFIELD."
"CASH FOR 400 NEGROES."
"FRANKLIN & ARMFIELD."
People of the United States, Congress alone possess the constitutional power to legislate for the District of Columbia; yet one hundred and sixty-three of your representatives are striving to perpetuate in the Capital of your Republic this system of robbery, cruelty and despotism. House of Representatives, 8th February 1836.—Certain petitions and resolutions respecting the Abolition of Slavery in the District of Columbia were referred to a Select Committee with instructions to report, "THAT IN THE OPINION OF THIS HOUSE CONGRESS OUGHT NOT IN ANY WAY TO INTERFERE WITH SLAVERY IN THE DISTRICT OF COLUMBIA." Yeas 163—Nays 47.—The following are the Yeas:
Published by the American Anti-Slavery Society, 144 Nassau-street, New-York, 1836.

29. *Slave Market of America.*

Broadside. New York: American Anti-Slavery Society, 1836.

Gilder Lehrman Collection
GLC 4557

Slavery in the nation's capital was vigorously condemned by abolitionists until it was eliminated in 1850.

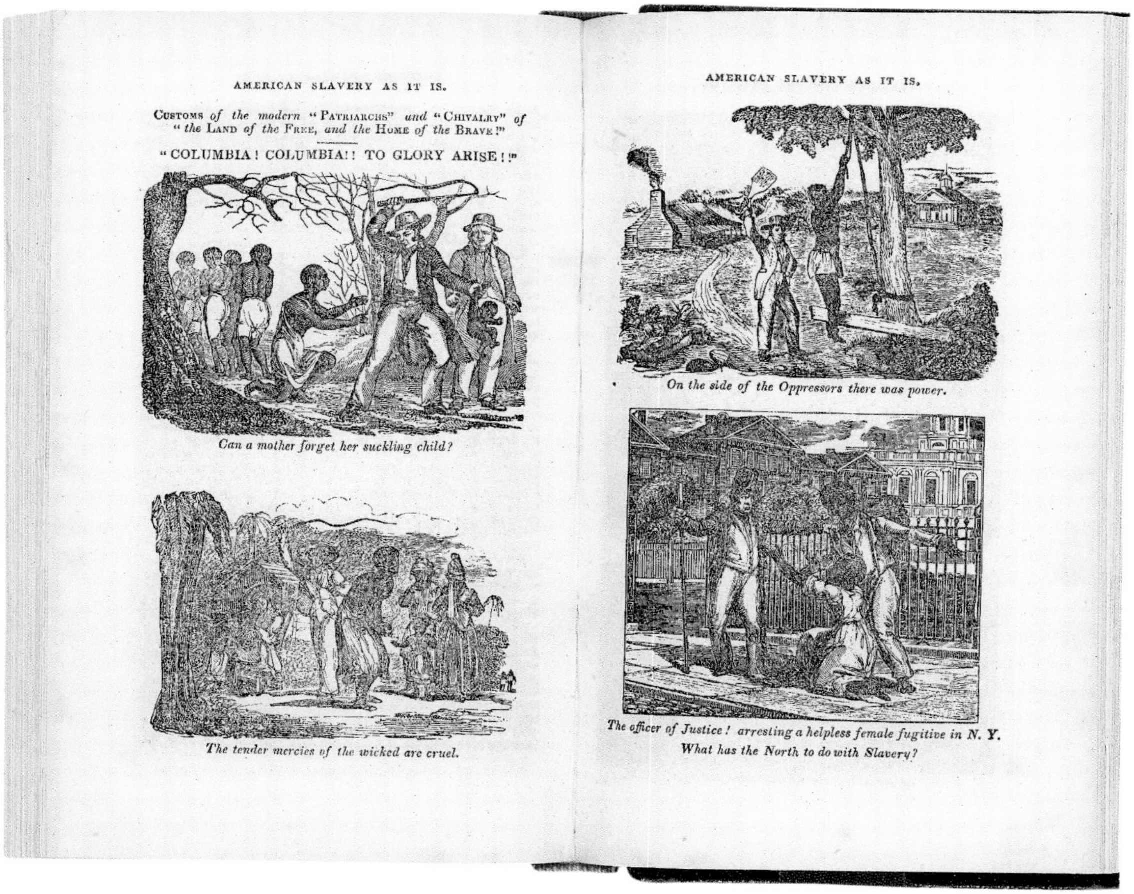

AMERICAN SLAVERY AS IT IS.
CUSTOMS of the modern "PATRIARCHS" and "CHIVALRY" of "the LAND of the FREE, and the HOME of the BRAVE!"
"COLUMBIA! COLUMBIA!! TO GLORY ARISE!"
Can a mother forget her suckling child?
The tender mercies of the wicked are cruel.
AMERICAN SLAVERY AS IT IS.
On the side of the Oppressors there was power.
The officer of Justice! arresting a helpless female fugitive in N. Y.
What has the North to do with Slavery?

30. *The Legion of Liberty! And Force of Truth, Containing the Thoughts, Words, and Deeds, of Some Prominent Apostles, Champions, and Martyrs.*
10th edition. New York: American Anti-Slavery Society, 1847.

Morgan Library Archives

The American Anti-Slavery Society used its publications to depict "American Slavery as It Is."

Abolitionism

Organized efforts to abolish American slavery began before the Revolutionary War, when Quakers in Pennsylvania and New Jersey began disciplining members who held slaves. By the 1780s, Quakers throughout the North had adopted a policy of "disunion" from slave-holding members. After the Revolution, slavery became increasingly entrenched in the South. Although somewhat diminished by legislation and private manumissions, it was still practiced in the North in 1820. Several states had policies of gradual emancipation. In 1817, for example, the New York legislature voted to abolish slavery completely after ten years. A similar law was not passed in Connecticut until 1848. Antislavery groups proliferated accordingly during the first two decades of the century. By 1827, there were at least 130 such organizations proposing a range of measures that included expatriation, gradual emancipation, and immediate abolition.

In the 1830s, abolitionists were consolidated by William Lloyd Garrison, a deeply religious Massachusetts Baptist. In 1829, Garrison had joined Quaker journalist Benjamin Lundy in Baltimore to edit a newspaper, *The Genius of Universal Emancipation*. Garrison's printed denunciation of a slave trader led to his being jailed for libel. Imprisonment deepened Garri-

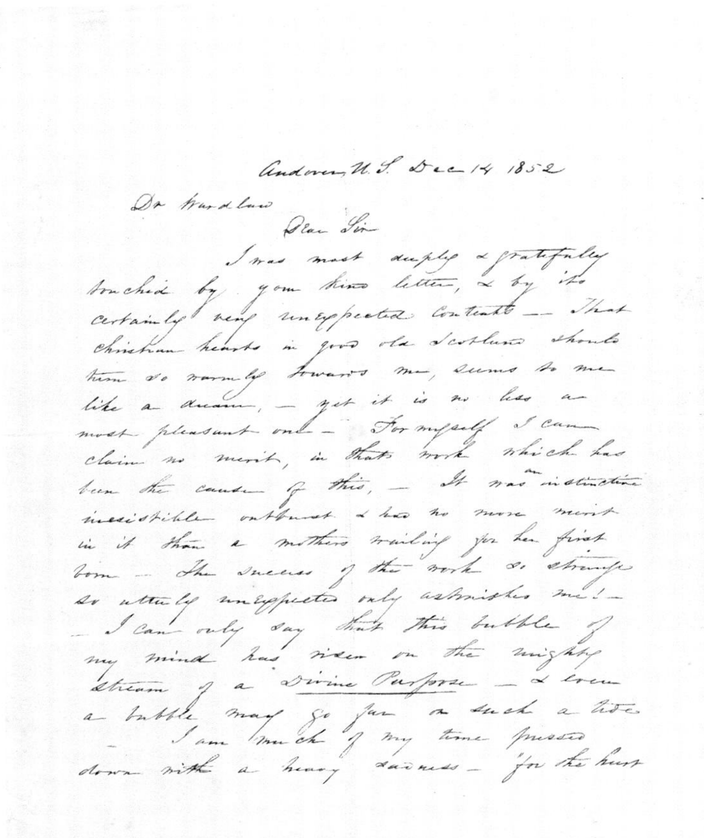
Andover, U. S. Dec 14 1852

Dr Wardlaw

Dear Sir

I was most deeply & gratefully touched by your kind letter, & by its certainly very unexpected contents — That Christian hearts in good old Scotland should turn so warmly towards me, seems to me like a dream, — yet it is no less a most pleasant one — For myself I can claim no merit, in that work which has been the cause of this, — It was an instinctive irresistible outburst & has no more merit in it than a mothers wailing for her first born — The success of the work so strange so utterly unexpected only astonishes me! — — I can only say that this bubble of my mind has risen on the mighty stream of a Divine Purpose — & even a bubble may go far on such a tide — I am much of my time pressed down with a heavy sadness — for the hurt

31. Harriet Beecher Stowe.
Autograph letter signed, dated Andover, [Massachusetts], 14 December 1852, to Dr. Ralph Wardlaw.

Gilder Lehrman Collection
GLC 4631

Uncle Tom's Cabin was translated into at least forty languages, and Harriet Beecher Stowe became immensely popular abroad, particularly in the United Kingdom. In this letter, Stowe grants a Scottish abolitionist group's request for a speaking engagement.

son's resolve. After returning to Massachusetts, he established his own newspaper, *The Liberator*, in 1831 and, in 1833, founded the American Anti-Slavery Society (PL. 32).

Garrison and other abolitionists were masters of propaganda (PL. 30). Their rallies featured the rousing oratory of many of the era's greatest preachers and songs that celebrated the escapes of Harriet Tubman and other fugitive slaves. Hundreds of thousands of pamphlets that vividly illustrated slavery's horrors were disseminated throughout the country. In the South, these publications were feared for their potential to incite slave rebellion. In 1835, President Jackson recommended a law prohibiting the distribution of abolitionist publications through the mail. Although the bill failed in the Senate, some Southern postmasters took it upon themselves to intercept abolitionist tracts. Abolitionists also flooded Congress with petitions calling for the end of slavery in the District of Columbia (PL. 29). The House of Representatives responded, in 1836, by passing a "gag rule," which forbade even the discussion of antislavery petitions.

Literature was another weapon in the abolitionist arsenal. Testimonies of the slave experience were published by Frederick Douglass, Harriet Jacobs, and others who had escaped to the North. John Greenleaf Whittier and Henry Wadsworth Longfellow were prominent among antislavery poets. The most widely read condemnation of slavery was Harriet Beecher Stowe's *Uncle Tom's Cabin*, published in 1852 and the first American novel to sell over a million copies. Though Stowe never participated in organized abolition activity, her abilities as a storyteller galvanized abolitionists and converted many Northerners to the cause (PL. 31). In 1853, she published a nonfiction work, *A Key to Uncle Tom's Cabin*, which she described as "containing all the facts and documents which confirm the story—both darker and sadder and more painful to write than the fiction." It, too, was immensely popular, with 90,000 copies sold in the month following publication.

Stowe wrote *Uncle Tom's Cabin* in response to the Fugitive Slave Act of 1850, whereby Congress authorized federal commissioners to arrest slaves who escaped to the North and return them to their masters (PL. 33). Hiding a fugitive slave or otherwise interfering with an arrest was punishable by a fine of $1,000 or imprisonment. Residents of free states who greatly resented compliance in the return of runaway slaves used legal maneuvers and, at times, physical attacks to prevent slave owners from capturing escapees. Among New England's most vigorous opponents of the law was

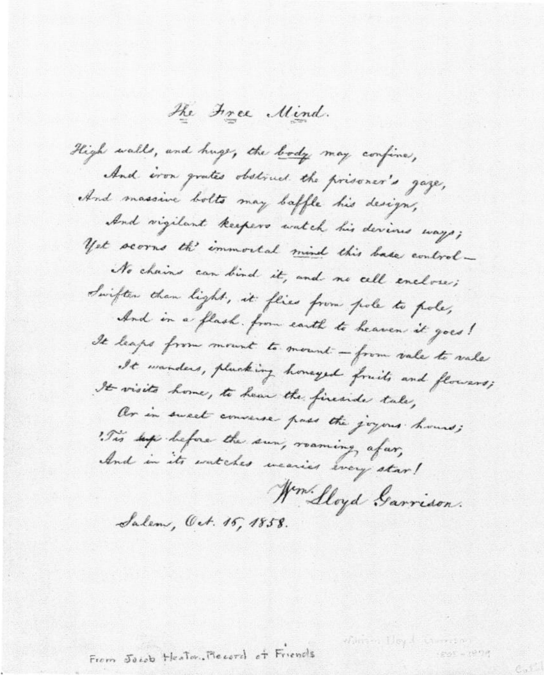

The Free Mind.

High walls, and huge, the body may confine,
And iron grates obstruct the prisoner's gaze,
And massive bolts may baffle his design,
And vigilant keepers watch his devious ways;
Yet scorns th' immortal mind this base control—
No chains can bind it, and no cell enclose;
Swifter than light, it flies from pole to pole,
And in a flash from earth to heaven it goes!
It leaps from mount to mount—from vale to vale
It wanders, plucking honeyed fruits and flowers;
It visits home, to hear the fireside tale,
Or in sweet converse pass the joyous hours;
'Tis up before the sun, roaming afar,
And in its watches wearies every star!

Wm. Lloyd Garrison.

Salem, Oct. 16, 1858.

32. William Lloyd Garrison. "The Free Mind." Autograph manuscript signed, Salem, [Massachusetts], 16 October 1858.

Morgan Library
MA 6036

Radical abolitionist William Lloyd Garrison promoted the antislavery cause through journalism, lectures, and poetry.

Henry David Thoreau, who joined other abolitionists in assisting the flight of fugitive slaves to Canada.

Many Northerners objected to the tenacity and growing militancy of abolitionists. In 1850, Daniel Webster of Massachusetts complained to fellow senators, "No drumhead in the longest day's march was ever more incessantly beaten and smitten than public sentiment in the North has been every month and day and hour by the din and roll and rub-a-dub of abolition writers and abolition lecturers." Northern antiabolitionists often disrupted rallies. In 1860, at a memorial for John Brown at Tremont Temple, Boston, they heckled Frederick Douglass. Pandemonium ensued, and Douglass and other abolitionists were ejected by city police (PL. 34).

Read and Ponder THE FUGITIVE SLAVE LAW!

Which disregards all the ordinary securities of PERSONAL LIBERTY, which tramples on the Constitution, by its denial of the sacred rights of Trial by Jury, *Habeas Corpus*, and Appeal, and which enacts, that the Cardinal Virtues of Christianity shall be considered, in the eye of the law, as CRIMES, punishable with the severest penalties,—*Fines and Imprisonment.*

***Freemen of Massachusetts*, R E M E M B E R, That Samuel A. Elliott of Boston, voted for this law, that Millard Filmore, our whig President *approved* it and the Whig Journals of Massachusetts sustain them in this iniquity.**

SECTION 1. That persons who have been, or may hereafter be, appointed Commissioners, in virtue of any act of Congress, by the Circuit Courts of the United States, and who in consequence of such appointments, are authorized to exercise the powers that any justice of the peace or other magistrate of any of the United States may exercise in respect to offenders for any crime or offence against the United States, by arresting, imprisoning or bailing the same under and by virtue of the thirty third section of the act of the fourth of September seventeen hundred and eighty-nine, entitled "An act to establish judicial courts of the United States," shall be and are hereby authorized and required to exercise and discharge all the powers and duties conferred by this act.

SEC. 2 And be it further enacted. That the Superior Court of each organized Territory of the United States shall have the same power to appoint commissioners to take acknowledgments of bail and affidavits and to take depositions of witnesses in civil causes which is now possessed by the circuit court of the United States; and all commissioners who shall hereafter be appointed for such purposes by the superior court of any organized Territory of the United States, shall possess all the powers and exercise all the duties conferred by law upon the commissioner appointed by the circuit courts of the United States for similar purposes, and shall moreover exercise and discharge all the powers and duties conferred by this act.

SEC. 3. And be it further enacted, That the circuit courts of the United States, and the superior courts of each organized Territory of the United States, shall, from time to time, enlarge the number of commissioners with a view to afford reasonable facilities to reclaim fugitives from labor, and to the prompt discharge of the duties imposed by this act.

SEC. 4. And be it further enacted, That the commissioners above named shall have concurrent jurisdiction with the judges of the circuit and district courts of the United States, in their respective circuits and districts within the several States, and with the judges of the territories, severally and collectively, in term time and vacation; and shall grant certificates to such claimants, upon satisfactory proof being made with authority to take and remove such fugitives from service or labor, under the restrictions herein contained, to the State or Territory from which such persons may have escaped or fled

SEC. 5. And be it further enacted, that it shall be the duty of all marshalls and deputy marshalls to obey and execute all warrants and precepts issued under the provisions of this act, when to them directed; and should any marshall or deputy marshall refuse to receive such warrant or other process when tendered, or to use all proper means diligently to execute the same, he shall, on conviction thereof, be fined in the sum of $1,000, to the use of such claimant, on motion of the claimant, by the circuit or district court for the district of such marshall; and after arrest of such fugitive by said marshall, or his deputy, or whilst at any time in his custody under the provisions under this act, should such fugitive escape, whether with or without the assent of such marshall or his deputy, such marshall shall be liable on his official bond to be prosecuted for the benefit of such claimant for the full value of the service or labor of said fugitive, in the State, Territory or district whence he escaped; and the better to enable the said commissioners, when thus appointed, to execute their duties faithfully and efficiently; in conformity with the requirements of the Constitution of the United States and of this act, they are hereby authorized and empowered, within their counties respectively, to appoint, in writing under their hands, any one or more suitable persons, from time to time, to execute all such warrants and other process as may be issued by them in the lawful performance of their respective duties, with authority to such commissioners or the persons to be appointed by them to execute process as aforesaid, to summon and to call to their aid the bystanders or posse comitatus of the proper county, when necessary to insure a faithful observance of the clause of the constitution referred to, in conformity with the provisions of this act; and ALL GOOD CITIZENS are hereby commanded to aid and assist in the prompt and efficient execution of this law whenever their services may be required, as aforesaid for that purpose; and said warrant shall run and be executed by said officers anywhere in the State, within which they are issued.

SEC. 6. And be it further enacted. That when a person held to service or labor in any State or Territory of the United States has heretofore or shall hereafter escape into another State or Territory of the United States, the person or persons to whom such service or labor may be due, or his, her, or their agent or attorney, duly authorized, by power of attorney, in writing, acknowledged and certified under the seal of some legal officer or court of the State or Territory in which the same may be executed, may pursue and reclaim such fugitive person, either by procuring a warrant from some one of the courts judges or commissioners aforesaid, of the proper circuit, district, or county, for the apprehension of such fugitive from service or labor, or by seizing and arresting such fugitive, where the same can be done without process, and by taking, or causing such person to be taken, forthwith before such court, judge or commissioner, whose duty it shall be to hear and determine the case of such claimant in a SUMMARY MANNER; and upon satisfactory proof being made, by disposition or affidavit, in writing, to be taken and certified by such court, judge, or commissioner, or by other satisfactory testimony, duly taken and certified by some court, magistrate, justice of peace, or other legal officer authorized to administer an oath and take depositions under the laws of the State or Territory from which such persons owing a service or labor may have escaped, with a certificate of such magistracy or other authority, as aforesaid, with the seal of the proper court or officer thereto attached, which seal shall be SUFFICIENT TO ESTABLISH THE COMPETENCY OF THE PROOF, AND WITH PROOF, ALSO BY AFFIDAVIT, of the identity of the person whose service or labor is claimed to be due as aforesaid that the person so arrested does in fact owe service or labor to the person, or persons claiming him or her, in the State or Territory from which such fugitive may have escaped as aforesaid, and that said person escaped to make out and deliver to such claimant, his or her agent or attorney a certificate setting forth the substantial facts as to the service or labor due from such fugitive to the claimant, and of his or her escape from the State or Territory in which such service or labor was due, to the State or Territory in which he or she was arrested with authority to such claimant or his or her agent or attorney, to use such reasonable force and restraint as may be necessary, under the circumstances of the case, to take and remove such fugitive person back to the State or Territory from whence he or she may have escaped as aforesaid. IN NO TRIAL OR HEARING UNDER THIS ACT SHALL THE TESTIMONY OF SUCH ALLEDGED FUGITIVE BE ADMITTED IN EVIDENCE; and the certificates in this and the first section mentioned, shall be conclusive of the right of the person or persons in whose favor granted, to remove such fugitive to the State or Territory from which he escaped, and shall prevent all molestation of said person or persons by any process issued by any court, judge, magistrate, or other persons whomsoever.

SEC. 7. And be it further enacted, That any person who shall knowingly and willingly obstruct, hinder or prevent such claimant, his agent, or attorney, or any person or persons lawfully assisting him, her, or them from arresting such a fugitive from service or labor, either with or without process, as aforesaid; or shall rescue, or attempt to rescue, such fugitive from service or labor, from the custody of such claimant, his or her agent or attorney, or other person or persons lawfully assisting as aforesaid when so arrested, pursuant to the authority herein given and declared; or shall aid, abet, or assist such a person so owing service or labor as aforesaid, directly or indirectly to escape from such claimant, his agent or attorney, or other person or persons legally authorized as aforesaid; or SHALL HARBOR or CONCEAL such fugitive, so as to prevent the discovery and arrest of such person, after notice or knowledge of the fact that such person, was a fugitive from service or labor as aforesaid, shall, for either of said offences be subject to a fine not exceeding one thousand dollars, and imprisonment not exceeding six months, by indictment and conviction before the district court of the United States for the district in which such offence may have been committed, or before the proper court of criminal jurisdiction, if committed within any one of the organized territories of the United States; and shall moreover forfeit and pay, by way of civil damages to the party injured by such illegal conduct, the sum of ONE THOUSAND DOLLARS FOR EACH FUGITIVE SO LOST, as aforesaid to be recovered by action of debt, in any of the district or territorial courts aforesaid, within whose jurisdiction the said offence may have been committed.

SEC. 8. And be it further enacted, That the marshalls, their deputies, and the clerks of said district and territorial courts, shall be paid for their services the like fees as may be allowed to them for similar services in other cases, and where such services are rendered exclusively in the arrest, custody and delivery of the fugitive to the claimant, his or her agent or attorney, or where such supposed fugitive may be discharged out of custody for the want of sufficient proof as aforesaid, then such fees are to be paid in the whole by such claimant, his agent or attorney; and in all cases where the proceedings are before a commissioner, he shall be entitled to a fee of ten dollars in full for his services in each case, upon the delivery of said certificate to the claimant, his or her agent or attorney; or a fee of five dollars in cases where proof shall not in the opinion of such commissioner, warrant such certificate and delivery, inclusive of all services incident to such arrest and examination, to be paid, in either case, by the claimant, his or her agent or attorney. The person or persons authorized to execute the process to be issued by such commissioners for the arrest and detention of fugitives from service or labor, aforesaid, shall also be entitled to a fee of five dollars each for each person he or they may arrest and take before any such commissioners as aforesaid, at the instance and request of such claimant, with such other fees as may be deemed reasonable by such other additional services as may be necessarily performed by him or them; such as attending at the examination, keeping the fugitive in custody, and providing him with food and lodging during his detention, and until the final determination of such commissioner; and in general for performing such other duties as may be required by such claimant, his or her attorney or agent, or commissioner in the premises, such fees to be made up in conformity with the fees usually charged by the officers of the courts of justice within the proper district or county, as near as may be practicable, and paid by such claimants, their agents or attorneys, whether such supposed fugitive from service or labor, be ordered to be delivered to such claimants by the final determination of such commissioners or not.

SEC. 9. And be it further enacted, That upon affidavit made by the claimant of such fugitive his agent or attorney, after such certificate has been issued, that he has reason to apprehend that such fugitive will be rescued by force from his or their possession before he can be taken beyond the limits of the State in which the arrest is made, it shall be the duty of the officer making the arrest, to retain such fugitive in his custody, and to remove him to the State whence he fled, and there to deliver him to said claimant, his agent or attorney. And to this end the officer aforesaid is hereby authorized and required to employ so many persons as he may deem necessary, to overcome such force, and to retain them in his service so long as circumstances may require. The said officer and his assistants, while so employed, to receive the same compensation, and to be allowed the same expenses as are now allowed by law for transportation of criminals, to be certified by the judge of the district within which the arrest is made, and PAID OUT OF THE TREASURY OF THE UNITED STATES.

SEC. 10. And be it further enacted, That when any person held to service or labor in any State or Territory, or in the District of Columbia, shall escape therefrom, the party to whom such service or labor shall be due, his, her, or their agent or attorney may apply to any court of record therein, or judge thereof in vacation, and make satisfactory proof to such court of the escape aforesaid, and that the person escaping owed service or labor to such party. Whereupon the court shall cause a record to be made of the matters so proved, and also a general description of the person so escaping, with such convenient certainty as may be, and a transcript of such record authenticated by attestation of clerk and seal of the said court being produced in any other State, Territory or District in which the person so escaping may be found, and being exhibited to any judge, commissioner or other officer authorized by the law of the United States to cause persons escaping from service or labor to be delivered up, shall be held and taken to be full and conclusive evidence of the fact of escape, and that the service or labor of the person escaping is due to the party in such record mentioned. And upon the production by the said party of other and further evidence, if necessary, either oral or by affidavit, in addition to what is contained in the said record of the identity of the person escaping, he or she shall be delivered to the claimant. And the said court, commissioner, judge or other person authorized by this act to grant certificates to claimants of fugitives shall upon the production of the record, and other evidences aforesaid, grant to such claimant a certificate of his right to take any person identified and proved to be oweing service or labor as aforesaid, which certificate shall authorize such claimant to seize or arrest and transport such persons to the State or Territory from which he escaped, Provided,

That nothing herein contained shall be construed as requiring the production as a transcript of such record as evidence as aforesaid. But in its absence the claim shall be heard and determined upon other satisfactory proof, competent in law.

HOWELL COBB,
Speaker of the House of Representatives.
WILLIAM R. KING,
President of the Senate protempore.
Approved September 18, 1850.
MILLARD FILLMORE.

PRINTED AND FOR SALE AT THE SPY OFFICE.

33. Read and Ponder the Fugitive Slave Law! Broadside. [Boston]: printed and for sale at *The Spy* office, [1850].

Gilder Lehrman Collection
GLC 1862

To those opposed to slavery, the most odious provision of the Compromise of 1850 was the fugitive slave clause, which required all citizens to assist in the capture and detention of runaway slaves.

788
HARPER'S WEEKLY.
[DECEMBER 15, 1860.
EXPULSION OF NEGROES AND ABOLITIONISTS FROM TREMONT TEMPLE, BOSTON, MASSACHUSETTS, ON DECEMBER 3, 1860.—[SEE PAGE 787.]

34. ***Expulsion of Negroes and Abolitionists from Tremont Temple, Boston, Massachusetts, on December 3, 1860.*** Engraving from *Harper's Weekly*, 15 December 1860.

Gilder Lehrman Collection
GLC 1733

Depicted here is the 1860 attack by Northern antiabolitionists on Frederick Douglass at a memorial for John Brown.

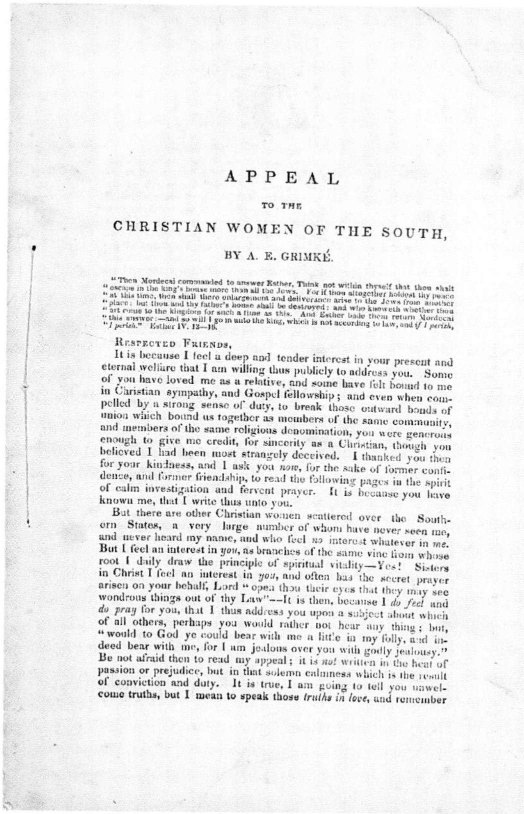

APPEAL

TO THE

CHRISTIAN WOMEN OF THE SOUTH,

BY A. E. GRIMKÉ.

"Then Mordecai commanded to answer Esther, Think not within thyself that thou shalt "escape in the king's house more than all the Jews. For if thou altogether holdest thy peace "at this time, then shall there enlargement and deliverance arise to the Jews from another "place: but thou and thy father's house shall be destroyed: and who knoweth whether thou "art come to the kingdom for such a time as this. And Esther bade them return Mordecai "this answer:—and so will I go in unto the king, which is not according to law, and *if I perish*, "*I perish*." Esther IV. 13—16.

Respected Friends,

It is because I feel a deep and tender interest in your present and eternal welfare that I am willing thus publicly to address you. Some of you have loved me as a relative, and some have felt bound to me in Christian sympathy, and Gospel fellowship; and even when compelled by a strong sense of duty, to break those outward bonds of union which bound us together as members of the same community, and members of the same religious denomination, you were generous enough to give me credit, for sincerity as a Christian, though you believed I had been most strangely deceived. I thanked you then for your kindness, and I ask you *now*, for the sake of former confidence, and former friendship, to read the following pages in the spirit of calm investigation and fervent prayer. It is because you have known me, that I write thus unto you.

But there are other Christian women scattered over the Southern States, a very large number of whom have never seen me, and never heard my name, and who feel *no* interest whatever in *me*. But I feel an interest in *you*, as branches of the same vine from whose root I daily draw the principle of spiritual vitality—Yes! Sisters in Christ I feel an interest in *you*, and often has the secret prayer arisen on your behalf, Lord "open thou their eyes that they may see wondrous things out of thy Law"—It is then, because I *do feel* and *do pray* for you, that I thus address you upon a subject about which of all others, perhaps you would rather not hear any thing; but, "would to God ye could bear with me a little in my folly, and indeed bear with me, for I am jealous over you with godly jealousy." Be not afraid then to read my appeal; it is *not* written in the heat of passion or prejudice, but in that solemn calmness which is the result of conviction and duty. It is true, I am going to tell you unwelcome truths, but I mean to speak those *truths in love*, and remember

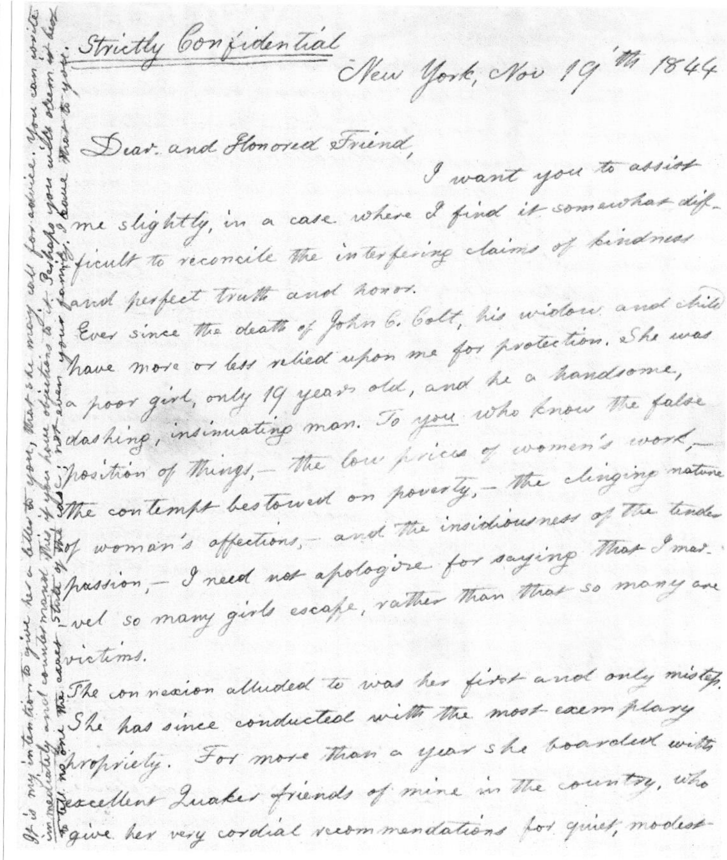

Strictly Confidential

New York, Nov 19th 1844

Dear and Honored Friend,

I want you to assist
me slightly, in a case where I find it somewhat difficult to reconcile the interfering claims of kindness
and perfect truth and honor.
Ever since the death of John C. Colt, his widow and child
have more or less relied upon me for protection. She was
a poor girl, only 19 years old, and he a handsome,
dashing, insinuating man. To you who know the false
position of things,— the low prices of women's work,—
the contempt bestowed on poverty,— the clinging nature
of woman's affections,— and the insidiousness of the tende
passion,— I need not apologize for saying that I mar-
vel so many girls escape, rather than that so many are
victims.
The connexion alluded to was her first and only mistep.
She has since conducted with the most exemplary
propriety. For more than a year she boarded with
excellent Quaker friends of mine in the country, who
give her very cordial recommendations for quiet, modest-

It is my intention to give her a letter to you, that she may call for advice. You can write immediately and countermand this, if you have objections to it. Perhaps you will deem it best to tell no one the exact state of the case; not even your family. I leave that to you.

35. Angelina Emily Grimké.
Appeal to the Christian Women of the South. [New York: American Anti-Slavery Society, 1836].

Gilder Lehrman Collection
GLB 243

Angelina Grimké wrote this pamphlet, hoping to convince Southern mothers and daughters to use their influence to bring about the end of slavery. Her writings were burned publicly in the South, and she would have been arrested had she returned to South Carolina, her home state.

36. Lydia Maria Child.
Autograph letter signed, dated New York, 19 November 1844, to John Pierpont.

Morgan Library
MA 1756

Lydia Maria Child, an advocate of women's rights, wrote to fellow abolitionist the Reverend John Pierpont to plead the case of a young woman in need.

The movement itself was periodically beset by divisiveness. Many abolitionists were offended by Garrison's renunciation and public burning of the Constitution in 1854. The movement also split over the roles of black abolitionists and women. Frederick Douglass, William Wells Brown, and other black abolitionists, many of whom had been slaves and all of whom had experienced discrimination, were periodically at odds with Garrison and other white leaders over the most effective means of ending slavery. Douglass increasingly urged stronger action than did his white colleagues. To put forth his views, he founded his own abolitionist newspaper, *The North Star*.

The most divisive issue within the American Anti-Slavery Society was the participation of women. In 1840, when Abigail Kelley Foster was elected a member of the society's business committee, a contingent of males withdrew to form the American and Foreign Anti-Slavery Society. The American Anti-Slavery Society also featured women prominently as speakers at rallies, a radical step in a nation where women were generally not allowed to lecture publicly before mixed audiences of men and women.

Two of the society's best-known proselytizers were Angelina and Sarah Grimké, who had rejected their upbringing as daughters of a wealthy South Carolina slave owner (PL. 35). To those hostile to outspoken women abolitionists, Angelina Grimké declared: "American women have to do with [abolition] not only because it is moral and religious, but because it is political, inasmuch as we are citizens of the republic."

Such divisions did not significantly weaken the movement, and abolitionism had long-lasting effects on the nation. Abolitionists kept the issue of slavery in the territories at the forefront of political discussion. Black abolitionists, despite their patronization by many of their white allies, developed their own leadership and laid the groundwork for civil rights efforts after emancipation. For women's rights activists, the movement provided important training in organization and tactics.

The Women's Rights Movement

In 1848, two abolition activists, Lucretia Mott and Elizabeth Cady Stanton, organized the first women's rights convention in the United States. Mott and Stanton had met in London eight years previously, where both had been denied admission on the basis of gender to the World's Antislavery Conference. The convention at Seneca Falls, New York, drew 240 attendees and challenged male dominance with a Declaration of Sentiments modeled on the Declaration of Independence. Among the 40 men at the meeting was Frederick Douglass, whose support helped narrowly pass a controversial proposal for woman suffrage.

Suffrage, though, did not become the focus of women's rights activists until after the Civil War. Debate during the first decades of the movement centered on women's entry into the public sphere and economic issues, such as the right to own property. A staunch advocate of gender equality was writer Lydia Maria Child, whose *History of the Condition of Women in Various Ages and Nations* was published in 1835. Her view of women's plight is expressed privately in a letter seeking assistance for a needy young woman abandoned by her husband (PL. 36). She wrote to the Reverend John Pierpont in 1844:

> To you who know the false positions of things—the low prices of women's work—the contempt bestowed on poverty—the clinging nature of woman's affections—and the insidiousness of the tender passion, I need not apologize for saying that I marvel so many girls escape, rather than that so many are victims.

A close friend of Child was Margaret Fuller, a leading figure in transcendentalism. Fuller, in *Woman in the Nineteenth Century* (1845), argued that collective action was the most effective means of combating men's deliberate subordination of women. Regarding the opposition that she and other women's rights activists encountered, Fuller wrote, in a passage published posthumously in *Memoirs of Margaret Fuller Ossoli* (1852):

> It demands some valor to lift one's head amidst the shower of public squibs, private sneers, anger, scorn, [and] derision called out by the demand that women should be put on a par with their brethren legally and politically; that they should hold property not by permission but by right; and that they should take an active part in all great movements.

Through the 1850s, collective activity was represented by the national women's conventions that followed the Seneca Falls meeting (PL. 37). At the same time, Stanton, Susan B. Anthony, and others worked individually within their states on legislative reform. With so much overlapping of the leadership in the women's rights and antislavery movements, women's issues were subordinated to abolitionism until after the Civil War.

372
HARPER'S WEEKLY.
[JUNE 11, 1859.
Yᴱ MAY SESSION OF Yᴱ WOMAN'S RIGHTS CONVENTION—Yᴱ ORATOR OF Yᴱ DAY DENOUNCING Yᴱ LORDS OF CREATION.

37. *The May Session of the Woman's Rights Convention.* Engraving from *Harper's Weekly*, 11 June 1859.

Gilder Lehrman Collection
GLC 1733

The Seneca Falls meeting of 1848 precipitated local and national conventions to advance the cause of women's rights.

American Literature Comes of Age

AT THE TIME that politicians and reformers were reexamining the nature of democracy in an evolving republic, American writers were seeking a voice appropriate to their young nation. Laments about the state of American writing abounded in literary magazines and book reviews. The United States had come of age politically; Americans now craved a comparable cultural awakening. During the early decades of the nineteenth century, Washington Irving and James Fenimore Cooper emerged as the first American writers to be widely read and admired in an international context. Although these authors and their successors were hardly harmonious in their articulation of a national identity, as a group they conveyed the energy and variety of the American experience. By the time of the Civil War, American imaginative writing had undergone a renaissance.

Even as a student at Harvard, Henry David Thoreau was musing on the future of American writing. In a forensic exercise entitled "Advantages and Disadvantages of Foreign Influence on American Literature," written in 1836 for his rhetoric professor, Edward Tyrrel Channing, Thoreau acknowledged New Englanders' debt to British literature.

> We of New England are a peculiar people; we whistle, to be sure, our national tune, but the character of our literature is not yet established; ours is still in the gristle, and is yet receiving those impressions from the parent literature of the mother country, which are to mould its character.... We are, as it were, but colonies. True, we have declared our independence and gained our liberty, but we have dissolved only the political bands which connected us with Great Britain. Though we have rejected her tea, she still supplies us with food for the mind.

Still, Thoreau foresaw a declaration of American literary independence that would mirror the nation's political sovereignty: "Our literature, though now dependent, in some measure, on that of the mother country, must soon go alone."

Edgar Allan Poe (PL. 40) agreed with the young Thoreau that American writers had yet to produce a native literature unfettered by British influence. In his manuscript notes for a series of 1846 articles entitled "The Literati of New-York City" (PL. 39), Poe bridled at the "erroneous idea that there is anything very distinctive" about American literature. For Poe, the only way to foster improved American writing was to criticize it honestly.

> We do our literature grosser wrong in overpraising our authors than the British could possibly do in overabusing them. We should drop the gross folly of forcing our readers to relish a stupid book the better because, sure enough, its stupidity was American.

The United States themselves are essentially the greatest poem.

WALT WHITMAN, *Leaves of Grass*

38. [Walt Whitman].
Engraving by Samuel Hollyer, after a daguerreotype by Gabriel Harrison, [1854].

Morgan Library
PML 6068

This informal portrait of the young Whitman in working class attire appeared as a frontispiece to the first edition of *Leaves of Grass* (1855).

Speaking not as a Southerner but as an author "aloof from cliques, swearing by no master," Poe attacked regional literary coteries. He wrote: "The great majority of our books are written and published by Northern men... [resulting in] a depreciation of Southern and Western talent, which upon the whole is greater, more vivid, fresher than that of the North, less conventional, less conservative." One of only a handful of major antebellum writers to emerge from the American South, Poe stood apart from his compatriots in avoiding regional or even national themes. His most famous poem, "The Raven" (PL. 41), was typical in its psychological and otherworldly focus.

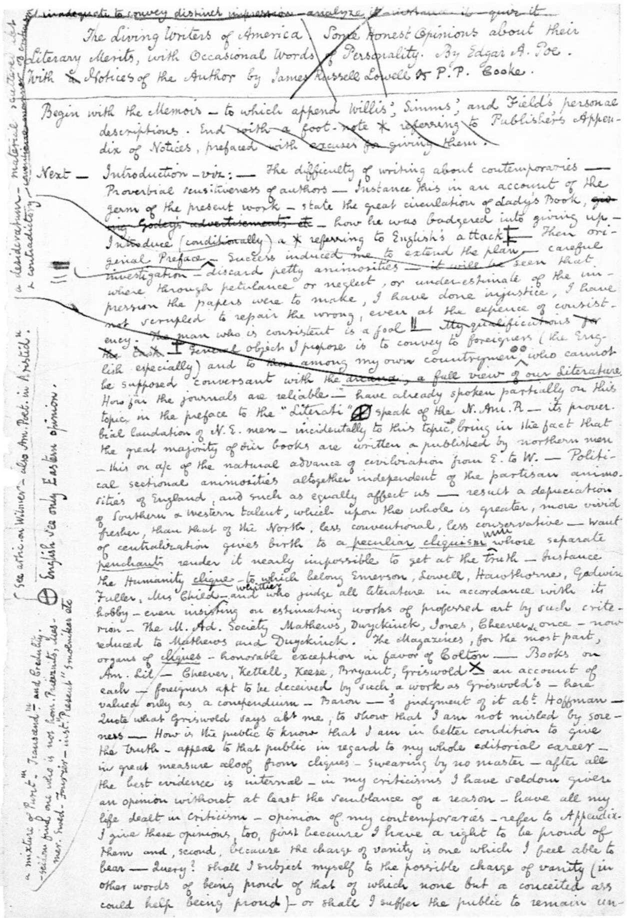
The Living Writers of America. Some Honest Opinions about their
Literary Merits, with Occasional Words of Personality. By Edgar A. Poe.
With Notices of the Author by James Russell Lowell & P. P. Cooke.

Begin with the Memoir – to which append Willis', Simms', and Field's personal
descriptions. End with a foot-note * referring to Publisher's Appendix of Notices, prefaced with excuses for giving them.

Next – Introduction – viz: – The difficulty of writing about contemporaries –
Proverbial sensitiveness of authors – Instance this in an account of the
germ of the present work – state the great circulation of Lady's Book,
Godey's advertisements etc – how he was badgered into giving up –
Introduce (conditionally) a * referring to English's attack – Then original Preface – Success induced me to extend the plan – careful
investigation – discard petty animosities – it will be seen that
where through petulance or neglect, or under-estimate of the im-
pression the papers were to make, I have done injustice, I have
not scrupled to repair the wrong, even at the expence of consist-
ency. The man who is consistent is a fool – My qualifications for
the task – General object I propose is to convey to foreigners (the English especially) and to those among my own countrymen who cannot
be supposed conversant with the arcana, a full view of our Literature
How far the journals are reliable – have already spoken partially on this
topic in the preface to the "Literati" – speak of the N. Am. R. – its proverbial laudation of N. E. men – incidentally to this topic, bring in the fact that
the great majority of our books are written & published by northern men
– this on a/c of the natural advance of civilization from E. to W. – Political sectional animosities altogether independent of the partisan animosities of England, and such as equally affect us – result a depreciation
of Southern & Western talent, which upon the whole is greater, more vivid
fresher, than that of the North, less conventional, less conservative – want
of centralization gives birth to a peculiar cliquism whose separate
penchants render it nearly impossible to get at the truth – Instance
the Humanity clique – to which belong Emerson, Lowell, Hawthorne, Godwin
Fuller, Mrs Child – and Whittier who judge all literature in accordance with its
hobby – even insisting on estimating works of professed art by such crite-
rion – The M. Ad. Society Mathews, Duyckinck, Jones, Cheever, once – now
reduced to Mathews and Duyckinck. The Magazines, for the most part,
organs of cliques – honorable exception in favor of Colton – Books on
Am. Lit – Cheever, Kettell, Keese, Bryant, Griswold – an account of
each – foreigners apt to be deceived by such a work as Griswold's – here
valued only as a compendium – Baron –'s judgment of it abt. Hoffman –
Quote what Griswold says abt me, to show that I am not misled by sore-
ness – How is the public to know that I am in better condition to give
the truth – appeal to that public in regard to my whole editorial career –
in great measure aloof from cliques – swearing by no master – after all
the best evidence is internal – in my criticisms I have seldom given
an opinion without at least the semblance of a reason – have all my
life dealt in criticism – opinion of my contemporaries – refer to Appendix.
I give these opinions, too, first because I have a right to be proud of
them and, second, because the charge of vanity is one which I feel able to
bear – Query? shall I subject myself to the possible charge of vanity (in
other words of being proud of that of which none but a conceited ass
could help being proud) – or shall I suffer the public to remain un-

39. Edgar Allan Poe.
"The Living Writers of America. Some Honest Opinions About Their Literary Merits, with Occasional Words of Personality." Autograph notes, [1846].

Morgan Library
MA 624

In finished form, this work was published in installments as "The Literati of New-York City" in *Godey's Lady's Book* (1846–48) and later in book form as *The Literati* (1850).

40. [Edgar Allan Poe].
Daguerreotype by Masury & Hartshorn, [Providence, Rhode Island, November 1848].

Morgan Library
MA 621

This is one of four extant daguerreotypes of the so-called Ultima Thule image of Poe, taken the year before his death.

Poe was not alone in arguing that American literature could only be stultified by blind praise of American literary mediocrity. In the inaugural issue of their literary and cultural magazine, *The Pioneer* (PL. 42), James Russell Lowell and Robert Carter had made a similar point in 1843.

> We are the farthest from wishing to see what so many ardently pray for—namely, a national literature—for the same mighty lyre of the human heart answers the touch of the master in all ages and in every clime, and any literature, as far as it is national, is diseased.

The Pioneer, though short-lived, was the kind of literary periodical in which much of the most vigorous of American writing of this period

In Europe, the concept of national literature was engendered by each country's linguistic autonomy. But the people of the United States spoke and wrote in English, the language of their cultural and political forebears. As early as 1789, in his "Dissertations on the English Language," Noah Webster called for a vernacular distinct from British English: "Let us then seize the present moment and establish a *national language* as well as a national government." True to his linguistic patriotism, he spent decades preparing *An American Dictionary of the Eng-*

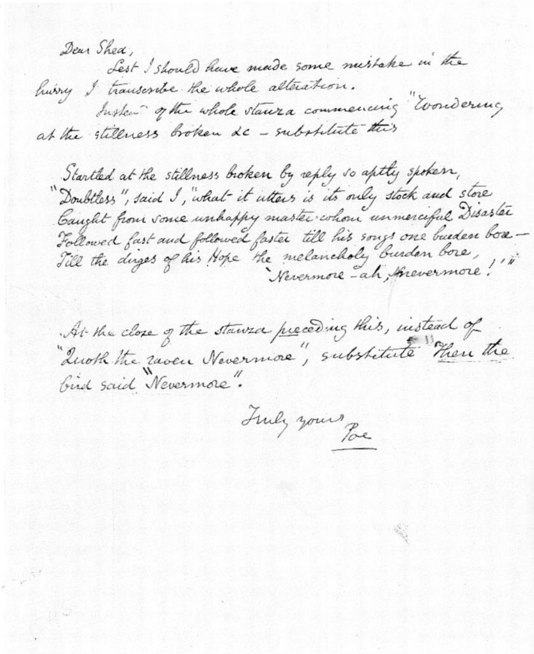
Dear Shea,
Lest I should have made some mistake in the hurry I transcribe the whole alteration.
Instead of the whole stanza commencing "Wondering at the stillness broken &c – substitute this

Startled at the stillness broken by reply so aptly spoken,
"Doubtless", said I, "what it utters is its only stock and store
Caught from some unhappy master whom unmerciful Disaster
Followed fast and followed faster till his songs one burden bore –
Till the dirges of his Hope the melancholy burden bore,
'Nevermore – ah, nevermore!'"

At the close of the stanza preceding this, instead of "Quoth the raven Nevermore", substitute "Then the bird said "Nevermore".

Truly yours
Poe

41. Edgar Allan Poe. Autograph letter signed, dated [New York, November 1845], to John Augustus Shea.

Morgan Library
MA 621

In this letter, Poe sent a revision to "The Raven" for the 4 February 1845 issue of *The New-York Daily Tribune*, Horace Greeley's newspaper. Throughout his life, Poe continued to tinker with the poem, making similar minor revisions.

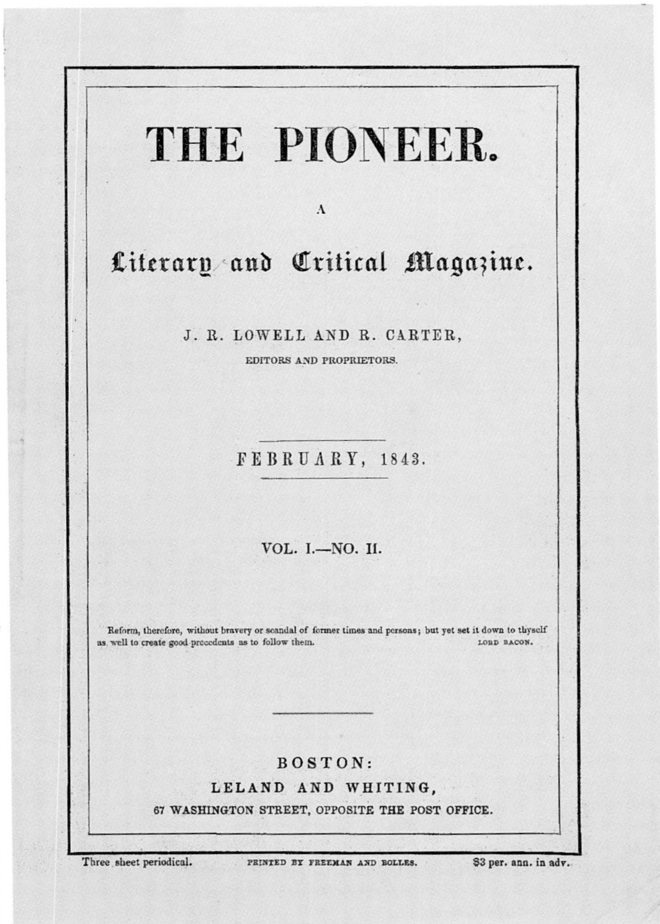
THE PIONEER.

A

Literary and Critical Magazine.

J. R. LOWELL AND R. CARTER,
EDITORS AND PROPRIETORS.

FEBRUARY, 1843.

VOL. I.—NO. II.

Reform, therefore, without bravery or scandal of former times and persons; but yet set it down to thyself as well to create good precedents as to follow them. LORD BACON.

BOSTON:
LELAND AND WHITING,
67 WASHINGTON STREET, OPPOSITE THE POST OFFICE.

Three sheet periodical. PRINTED BY FREEMAN AND BOLLES. $3 per. ann. in adv.

42. James Russell Lowell and Robert Carter, eds. *The Pioneer: A Literary and Critical Magazine*, volume I, no. 2. Boston: Leland and Whiting, 1843.

Morgan Library
PML 125585

This is the second of three issues of Lowell's literary magazine, which featured stories by Poe and Hawthorne along with poetry by Whittier and Very.

appeared. Its three issues featured tales by Nathaniel Hawthorne and Edgar Allan Poe (including "The Tell-Tale Heart"), poetry by John Greenleaf Whittier and Jones Very, and criticism by John Neal and James Russell Lowell. Lowell and Carter saw their magazine as an antidote to "the enormous quantity of thrice-diluted trash, in the shape of namby-pamby love tales and sketches, which is monthly poured out...by many of our popular magazines." Among the innumerable other literary magazines that came and went during these years, *The Dial* was notable as a venue for transcendentalist writing. Under the stewardship of Margaret Fuller and Ralph Waldo Emerson, *The Dial* lasted four years, from 1840 to 1844, fostering the writing of Henry David Thoreau, both the younger and elder William Ellery Channing, Bronson Alcott, and Jones Very.

lish Language (PL. 43), the forerunner of many Webster's dictionaries. His was the first American dictionary and the last to be compiled entirely by a single individual. Ultimately, Webster's dictionary included few Americanisms.

Before the 1850s, writers and critics often decried the sorry state of American literature while anticipating a breakthrough. "Before this generation shall have passed away, the complexion of our literature will be changed," predicted critic John Beauchamp Jones in an 1839 article called "Thoughts on the Literary Prospects of America" for *Burton's Gentleman's Magazine*, one of the most successful literary periodicals of the era. Jones forecast that American literature could not help but attain a glory commensurate with the young country's political eminence.

> What greater work of the intellect can be conceived than the establishment of a novel and perfect system of government, embracing an immense continent and administering to the wants of many millions of people? And if America has excelled in arms, triumphed in legislation, and linked her commerce with every fruitful land, is it to be supposed that she will long remain indifferent to the glories of literature?

Jones's prophecy of a period of American literary ferment was well founded. Within a span of five extraordinary years, 1850 to 1855, writers produced some of the nation's most enduring literature: Hawthorne's *The Scarlet Letter* (1850) and *The House of the Seven Gables* (1851), Emerson's *Representative Men* (1850), Melville's *Moby-Dick* (1851) and *Pierre* (1852), Stowe's *Uncle Tom's Cabin* (1852), Thoreau's *Walden* (1854), Whitman's *Leaves of Grass* (1855), Longfellow's *Song of Hiawatha* (1855), Douglass's *My Bondage and My Freedom* (1855), and Irving's *Life of George Washington* (1855–59). And, though she published virtually nothing, it was during these years that Emily Dickinson began writing in earnest some of the most original poetry in America's history. The fertile 1850s also saw the founding of *The New-York Times* (1851), *Harper's New Monthly Magazine* (1850), and *The Atlantic Monthly* (1857), all of which survive in some form to the present.

If there were ideological reasons that

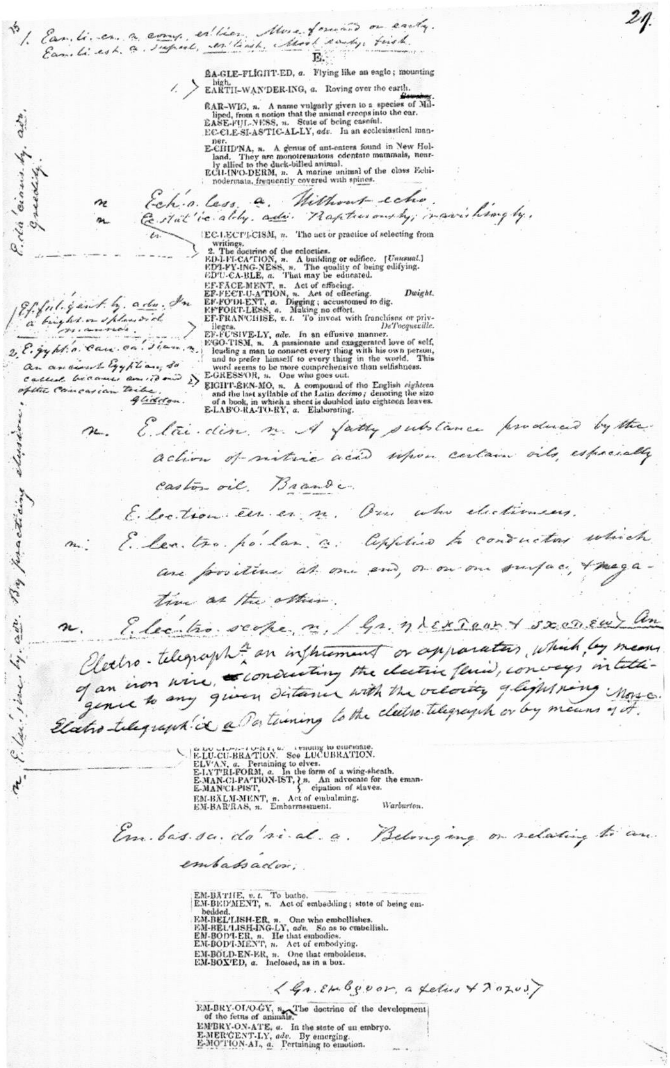

29.

E.

EA-GLE-FLIGHT-ED, *a.* Flying like an eagle; mounting high.
EARTH-WAN'DER-ING, *a.* Roving over the earth.
EAR-WIG, *n.* A name vulgarly given to a species of Milliped, from a notion that the animal creeps into the ear.
EASE-FUL-NESS, *n.* State of being easeful.
EC-CLE-SI-AS'TIC-AL-LY, *adv.* In an ecclesiastical manner.
E-CHID'NA, *n.* A genus of ant-eaters found in New Holland. They are monotrematous edentate mammals, nearly allied to the duck-billed animal.
ECH-IN'O-DERM, *n.* A marine animal of the class Echinodermata, frequently covered with spines.

Ech'o-less, a. Without echo.

EC-LECT'I-CISM, *n.* The act or practice of selecting from writings.
2. The doctrine of the eclectics.
ED-I-FI-CA'TION, *n.* A building or edifice. [*Unusual.*]
ED'I-FY-ING-NESS, *n.* The quality of being edifying.
ED'U-CA-BLE, *a.* That may be educated.
EF-FACE-MENT, *n.* Act of effacing.
EF-FECT-U-A'TION, *n.* Act of effecting. *Dwight.*
EF-FO'DI-ENT, *a.* Digging; accustomed to dig.
EF'FORT-LESS, *a.* Making no effort.
EF-FRAN'CHISE, *v. t.* To invest with franchises or privileges. *DeTocqueville.*
EF-FU'SIVE-LY, *adv.* In an effusive manner.
E'GO-TISM, *n.* A passionate and exaggerated love of self, leading a man to connect every thing with his own person, and to prefer himself to every thing in the world. This word seems to be more comprehensive than selfishness.
E-GRESS'OR, *n.* One who goes out.
EIGHT-EEN-MO, *n.* A compound of the English *eighteen* and the last syllable of the Latin *decimo*; denoting the size of a book, in which a sheet is doubled into eighteen leaves.
E-LAB'O-RA-TO-RY, *a.* Elaborating.

E-lai-din. n. A fatty substance produced by the action of nitric acid upon certain oils, especially castor oil. Brande.

Electro-telegraph. n. an instrument or apparatus, which, by means of an iron wire, conducting the electric fluid, conveys intelligence to any given distance with the velocity of lightning. Morse.
Electro-telegraph'ic a Pertaining to the electro-telegraph or by means of it.

E-LU-CU-BRA'TION. See LUCUBRATION.
ELV'AN, *a.* Pertaining to elves.
E-LYT'RI-FORM, *a.* In the form of a wing-sheath.
E-MAN-CI-PA'TION-IST, } *n.* An advocate for the emancipation of slaves.
E-MAN'CI-PIST,
EM-BALM-MENT, *n.* Act of embalming.
EM-BAR'RAS, *n.* Embarrassment. *Warburton.*

Em-bas-sa-do'ri-al. a. Belonging or relating to an embassador.

EM-BATHE, *v. t.* To bathe.
EM-BED'MENT, *n.* Act of embedding; state of being embedded.
EM-BEL'LISH-ER, *n.* One who embellishes.
EM-BEL'LISH-ING-LY, *adv.* So as to embellish.
EM-BOD'I-ER, *n.* He that embodies.
EM-BOD'I-MENT, *n.* Act of embodying.
EM-BOLD-EN-ER, *n.* One that emboldens.
EM-BOX'ED, *a.* Inclosed, as in a box.

EM-BRY-OL'O-GY, *n.* The doctrine of the development of the fetus of animals.
EM'BRY-ON-ATE, *a.* In the state of an embryo.
E-MER'GENT-LY, *adv.* By emerging.
E-MO'TION-AL, *a.* Pertaining to emotion.

43. Noah Webster.
An American Dictionary of the English Language. Autograph manuscript notes and corrected proofs for a revised edition, [after 1828, before 1843].

Morgan Library
MA 301

On this page of revisions to his American dictionary, Webster added the definition of "electro-telegraph," a device that "conveys intelligence to any given distance with the velocity of lightning." He credits the American inventor Samuel Morse, who developed his design for the telegraph during the 1830s.

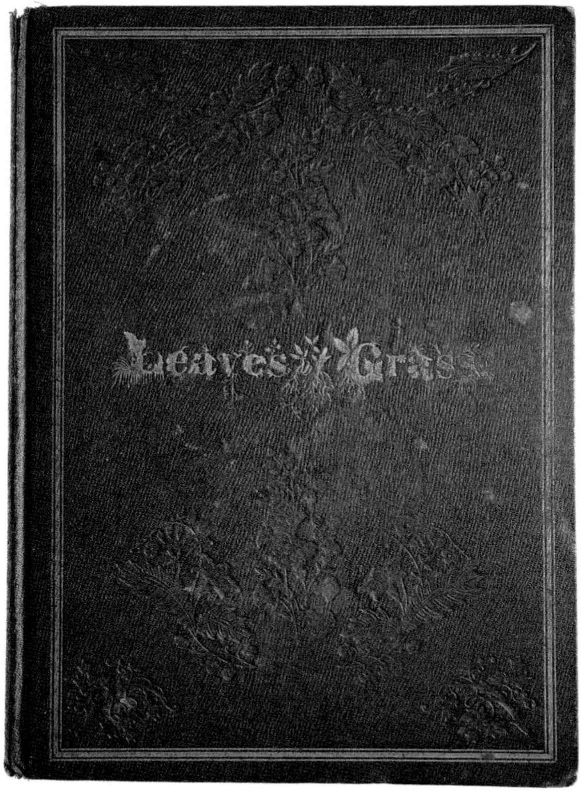

44. Walt Whitman.
Leaves of Grass. Brooklyn: [privately printed], 1855.

Morgan Library
PML 6069

This is the first of many editions and configurations of Whitman's collected poetry.

American authors struggled to find their voice, there were economic factors as well. Writers faced the very practical strictures imposed by the nineteenth-century publishing trade. During the early 1800s, they were forced to assume the financial risk that would later become the publisher's responsibility. To shepherd a book to press, an author required not just a fertile literary imagination but also a keen business sense. To make matters worse, in the absence of an international copyright law, American publishers often found it cheaper to issue reprints of British books than to take a chance on an original American work. In his notes for "The Literati" (see PL. 39), Poe declared unequivocally that "the want of [a] cop[y] r[ight] law...depresses us more than all else." Poe noted that "another source of imitativeness is that our literature (for copyright reasons) is altogether in the hands of a class proverbial for conservatism—the 'gentlemen of elegant leisure.'" It was not until 1891 that guidelines for international copyright were finally implemented.

By mid-century, the American book trade had been overhauled. The roles of author, publisher, printer, wholesaler, distributor, and retailer—convoluted at the start of the century—had settled into the basic arrangement we know today. While many authors benefited in income and reputation from this shift, they sacrificed a degree of artistic autonomy as publishers, in assuming greater financial responsibility, became more concerned with a book's marketability. The publisher's influence was particularly dramatic in the case of Hawthorne (PL. 46). Before the 1850s, Hawthorne's preferred form had been the short story, but collections of his works had not been selling well. For a proposed collection to have been named *Old-Time Legends*, he had written a novella. James T. Fields, of the Boston firm Ticknor, Reed & Fields, convinced Hawthorne to expand the work and issue it separately as his first novel. With the aggressive promotion afforded by its publisher, *The Scarlet Letter* (PL. 48) was a commercial and critical success. Over the next two years, Hawthorne turned out two more novels, *The House of the Seven Gables* (1851) and *The Blithedale Romance* (1852).

The most self-conscious proponent and exponent of a nascent American literary voice was Walt Whitman. The poems first collected as *Leaves of Grass* in 1855 (PL. 44) and revised and augmented over the course of his lifetime constituted what Whitman called "the great psalm of the republic." In the manuscript of his introduction to a proposed British edition of *Leaves of Grass*, Whitman celebrated the vigor and novelty of his own poetry, which he hailed as distinctly American, deliberately democratic.

> Taken as a unity, *Leaves of Grass*, true to its American origin, is a song of "the great pride of man in himself!" It assumes to bring the material and outline the architecture of a more complete, more advanced, idiocratic, masterful, Western personality—the combination and model of a new Man. It does not dwell on the past and cele-

brates in no way the superb old feudal world or its gorgeous reminiscences; it is built forward in the demesnes of the future, and it would seem as if somehow a great coming and regnant democracy—the dream of poets from the time of Plato and before him and since, too—had advanced already and here given genesis to every line.

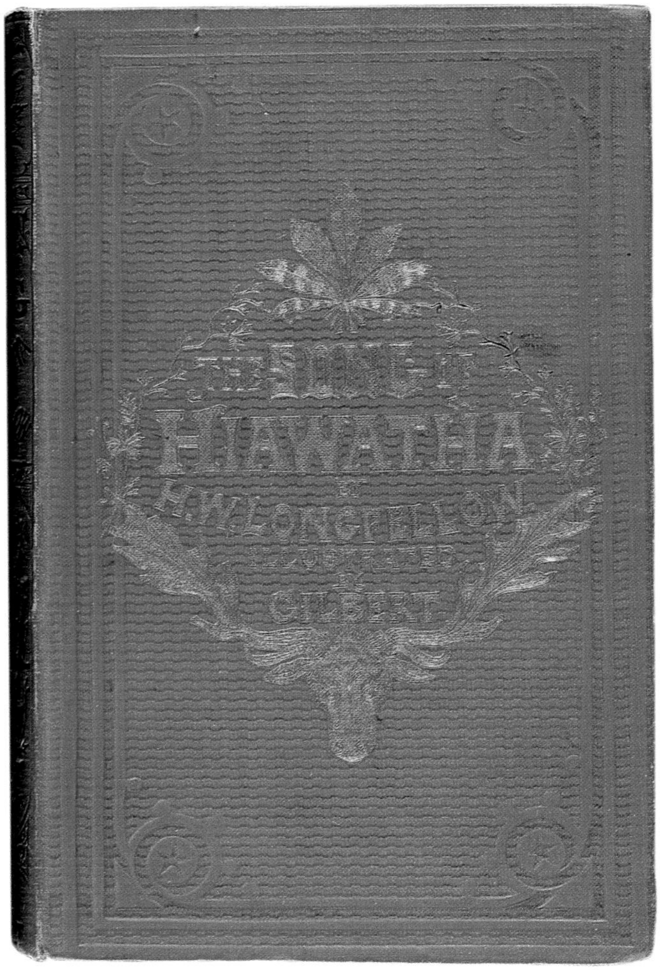

45. Henry Wadsworth Longfellow.
The Song of Hiawatha. London: G. Routledge & Co., 1856 reprint.

Morgan Library
GNR 4510

46. [Nathaniel Hawthorne].
Engraved portrait by Thomas Phillibrowne, after a painting by Cephas Giovanni Thompson. Boston: Ticknor & Fields, 1854.

Morgan Library
MA 611

Whereas some writers and critics considered the nation's relative infancy a hindrance to the production of great literature, Whitman found it liberating. Moreover, he considered his revolutionary abandonment of formal prosody the literary equivalent of American democracy. In his view, political and poetic liberty were inextricable.

In the frontispiece portrait to the first edition of *Leaves of Grass* (PL. 38), Whitman appears in casual working-class attire, bearded and relaxed, hand on hip, looking directly at the viewer. Lest his readers miss this democratic appeal to common people, he added a poetic self-portrait: "Walt Whitman, an American, one of the roughs, a kosmos, / Disorderly fleshy and sensual... eating drinking and breeding, / No sentimentalist... no stander above men and women or apart from them." When Emerson received Whitman's gift of a copy of *Leaves of*

Grass, he was dazzled by this major new talent. Recognizing a distinctive new voice in American letters, he wrote, "I find it the most extraordinary piece of wit and wisdom that America has yet contributed." Whitman, with characteristic self-promoting bravado, not only had the elder writer's letter printed in the next edition of *Leaves of Grass*, but also had his salutation—"I greet you at the beginning of a great career"—embossed on the spine.

While the startlingly novel poetic voices of Walt Whitman and Emily Dickinson emerged during this period, a number of traditional poets were also enjoying popularity. In literary magazines, newspapers, and separate volumes, American verse proliferated. In school and at home, Americans read and memorized verse and often composed amateur rhymes. While an Illinois lawyer, Abraham Lincoln, known later for dramatic oratory but certainly not for poetry, composed "The Bear Hunt." Nathaniel Hawthorne and Henry David Thoreau, who made their reputations as prose authors, began their literary lives as poets. At the age of fourteen, Hawthorne sent some verses to his sister Louisa, saying, "I am full of scraps of poetry, can't keep it out of my brain.... I could vomit up a dozen pages more if I was a mind to." Writing to Thomas Carlyle in 1839, Ralph Waldo Emerson introduced a poetic talent from Concord, Massachusetts: "I have a young poet in this village named Thoreau, who writes the truest verses."

By far the most prominent American poet of the era, spectacularly popular at home and abroad, was Henry Wadsworth Longfellow. His life nearly spanned the nineteenth century, and by his death in 1882 his narrative verses had become crucial to the American mythos. *The Song of Hiawatha* (1855; PL. 45) sold 30,000 copies within six months, becoming the most popular long poem of the century. In his most widely read works—*Evangeline, A Tale of Acadie* (1847), *The Song of Hiawatha*, and *The Courtship of Miles Standish* (1858)—Longfellow drew on American historical themes. At the same time, having been steeped in European traditions of formal prosody, he demonstrated his linguistic agility by employing countless meters. A pioneer in the teaching of modern European languages in America, Longfellow was proficient in Spanish, French, Italian, German, and the Scandinavian languages. Before turning twenty, he was offered the newly created chair of modern languages at his alma mater, Bowdoin College, and went on to serve a distinguished eighteen-year tenure as a professor at Harvard. Immersed as he was in the literature of Europe, Longfellow was among the first American poets to appreciate and practice literary translation from modern sources.

47. [Washington Irving]. Daguerreotype by Mathew Brady, [New York, 1849].

Morgan Library
MA 201

Washington Irving and James Fenimore Cooper were the first American writers to gain international acclaim.

In their efforts to create and advance a native literature, writers naturally turned to America's history, indigenous cultures, and natural landscape. The colonial past was a rich source for talented storytellers Washington Irving (PL. 47) and Nathaniel Hawthorne. Irving's "Rip Van Winkle" and "The Legend of Sleepy Hollow," both published in *The Sketch Book of Geoffrey Crayon, Gent.* (1819–20), have become American folk classics. Irving was the author of factual as well as fictional works based on American history in an era when historical works sold well among the general public. He devoted his final productive years to a multivolume biography of George Washington. Among the many tales set in his native Salem, Massachusetts, Hawthorne's *The Scarlet Letter* stands out as a haunting tale of sin and guilt in colonial society. In the following year, 1851, Hawthorne's friend Herman Melville turned out his own American classic, *Moby-Dick; or, The Whale*. Though deeply indebted to classical literary models, *Moby-Dick* is profoundly American in theme, character, and narrative voice.

With five novels known collectively as *The Leather-Stocking Tales*, James Fenimore Cooper (PL. 49) created a romantic epic of the American frontier. Set in eighteenth-century

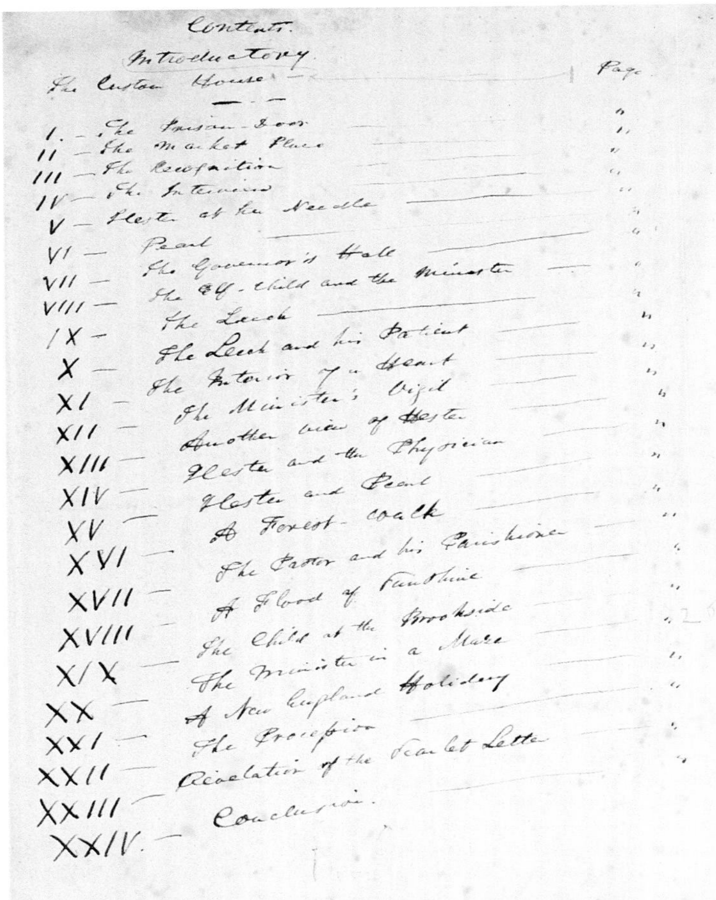
Contents.
Introductory.
The Custom House — Page
I. — The Prison-Door
II — The Market Place
III — The Recognition
IV — The Interview
V — Hester at her Needle
VI — Pearl
VII — The Governor's Hall
VIII — The Elf-Child and the Minister
IX — The Leech
X — The Leech and his Patient
XI — The Interior of a Heart
XII — The Minister's Vigil
XIII — Another View of Hester
XIV — Hester and the Physician
XV — Hester and Pearl
XVI — A Forest-Walk
XVII — The Pastor and his Parishioner
XVIII — A Flood of Sunshine
XIX — The Child at the Brookside
XX — The Minister in a Maze
XXI — A New England Holiday
XXII — The Procession
XXIII — Revelation of the Scarlet Letter
XXIV. — Conclusion.

48. Nathaniel Hawthorne. *The Scarlet Letter.* Autograph manuscript title and contents leaf, [1850].

Morgan Library
MA 571

Only the title page and table of contents from Hawthorne's manuscript of *The Scarlet Letter* survive. According to his friend Annie Adams Fields, with whom he entrusted the manuscript of *The House of the Seven Gables*, Hawthorne burned the *Scarlet Letter* manuscript. "I threw that in the fire," he told her, "put it up the chimney long ago."

49. [James Fenimore Cooper]. Engraved portrait by Henry Bryan Hall, after a daguerreotype by Mathew Brady, [n.d.].

Morgan Library
MA 82

rural New York, Cooper's tales are suffused with the folklore and landscape of the Otsego country, in which native tribes and European Americans coexisted. In his 1850 preface to the novels, Cooper defended his romantic depiction of Native Americans.

> It has been objected to these books that they give a more favorable picture of the red man than he deserves.... To suppose that the red man is to be represented only in the squalid misery or in the degraded moral state that certainly more or less belongs to his condition, is, we apprehend, taking a very narrow view of the author's privileges.

Written during the years in which Native Americans were subject to harsh relocation policies, Cooper's novels were seen by some to be of tremendous documentary value. A reviewer in *The Examiner* wrote, "When nothing but a tradition of the magnificent race of the red Indian shall be left to civilized Americans...thanks to Mr. Cooper, [they] will have lost nothing of their fame; nothing of their native wit, nothing of their hardy truth and rude generosity." There is

50. [Lydia Sigourney]. Engraved portrait, after a painting by Alonzo Chappel. New York: Johnson, Wilson & Co., 1872.

Morgan Library
MA 4500

Lydia Sigourney was a popular poet and Native American rights activist.

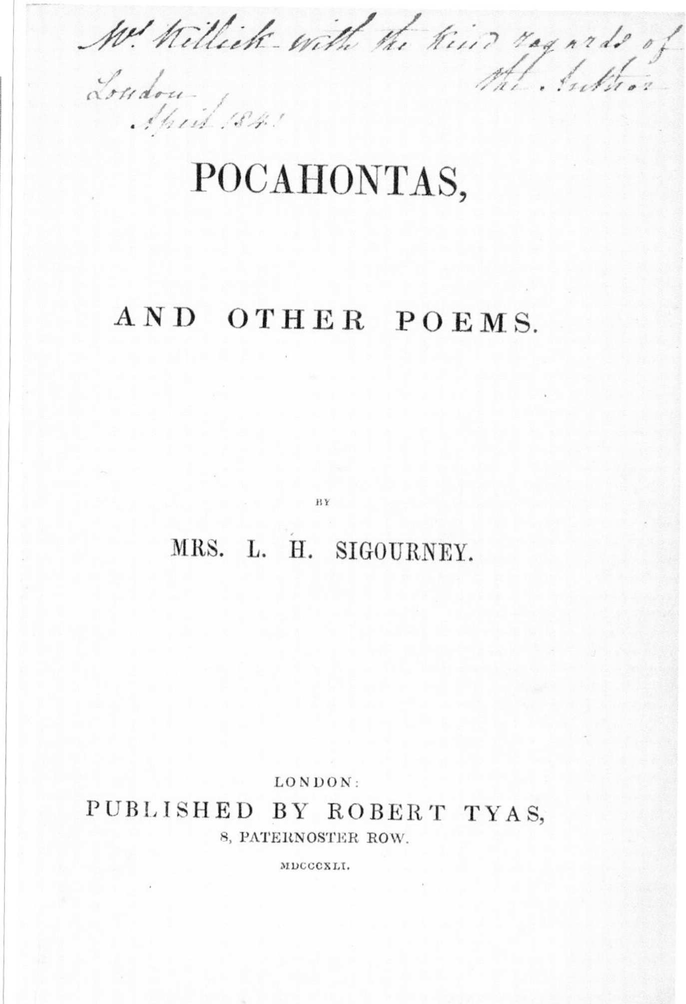

Mr. Willick with the kind regards of the Author
London April 1841

POCAHONTAS,

AND OTHER POEMS.

BY

MRS. L. H. SIGOURNEY.

LONDON:
PUBLISHED BY ROBERT TYAS,
8, PATERNOSTER ROW.
MDCCCXLI.

51. Lydia Sigourney. *Pocahontas, and Other Poems.* London: Robert Tyas, 1841.

Morgan Library
GNR 4616

This copy of the first English edition of *Pocahontas* was inscribed by the author.

no doubt that Cooper's depictions in such novels as *The Last of the Mohicans* (1826) and *The Deerslayer* (1841; PL. 52) contributed to enduring American archetypes—and stereotypes—of Native American cultures.

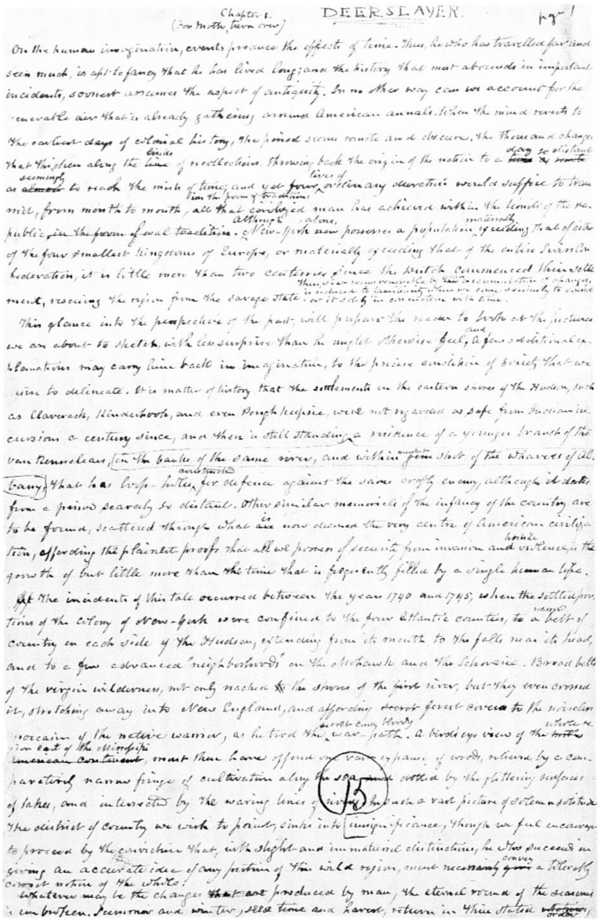

52. James Fenimore Cooper.
The Deerslayer. Autograph manuscript, [1841].

Morgan Library
MA 82

This is the first page of Cooper's manuscript of the novel, which was the earliest in sequence but last written of *The Leather-Stocking Tales.* It chronicles the early years of Natty Bumppo (known variously as Hawkeye, Pathfinder, Deerslayer, Leatherstocking, and the trapper) among the Delaware, around Lake Otsego, New York. The circled number fifteen and bracket are printer's marks, indicating the spot in the text where a compositor began setting up type for page fifteen of the book.

Like Cooper, the popular poet Lydia Sigourney (PL. 50) wrote extensively on Native American themes. Her *Pocahontas* (PL. 51) is a case in point. But while Cooper's aim was to chronicle the vitality, violence, and freedom of frontier America, Sigourney's poetry was a deliberate statement in the service of Native American rights. It would be nearly a century before Native Americans, whose narrative tradition was rich in oral forms, would begin to write extensively in English. This period, however, did see the publication of several Native American autobiographies as well as the first novel by a Native American, *The Life and Adventures of Joaquín Murieta* (1854), by Cherokee author John Rollin Ridge, or Yellow Bird.

While John James Audubon was documenting the birds and quadrupeds of North America in his monumental drawings and folio volumes, Henry David Thoreau was working on his literary rendering of the American landscape. Long before Thoreau, nature writing, as exemplified by William Bartram's popular *Travels Through North and South Carolina, Georgia, East and West Florida* (1791) and the frontier diaries of the Lewis and Clark expedition (1814), was a popular form. Thoreau's work was notable not only for its meticulous descriptions of nature but also for the self-examination and social criticism engendered by his intimate study of the natural world. *Walden; or, Life in the Woods* (1854), based on his solitary two-year stay by Walden Pond in Concord, Massachusetts, represents a fraction of Thoreau's writing about nature and American society. In dozens of journal volumes (PL. 54), Thoreau kept careful track of his reading, observations, thoughts, and revelations. In addition to the forty-odd journals that survive, he left eleven notebooks (PL. 53) filled with translations, excerpts, and notes on his copious reading about Native American cultures.

As he embarked on a life of letters, Thoreau was guided by Ralph Waldo Emerson (PL. 56), an intimate friend and mentor fourteen years his senior. In a letter seeking a British publisher for *Walden*, Emerson touted his protégé: "He is a man of genius, and writes always with force and sometimes with wonderful depth and beauty" (PL. 55). Emerson was the dynamic center of

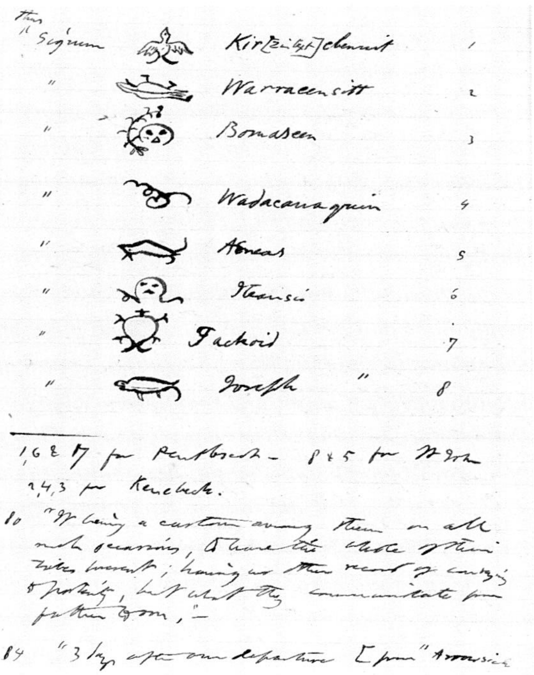

53. Henry David Thoreau. *Extracts Concerning the Indians.* Autograph manuscript journal entry, [1850s].

Morgan Library
MA 606

This entry is recorded in one of eleven journals in which Thoreau made notes on his reading about Native American cultures. On this page he listed the chiefs from various tribes who signed a peace treaty with the English in July 1713. His source was Samuel Penhallow's *The History of the Wars of New-England with the Eastern Indians* (1726).

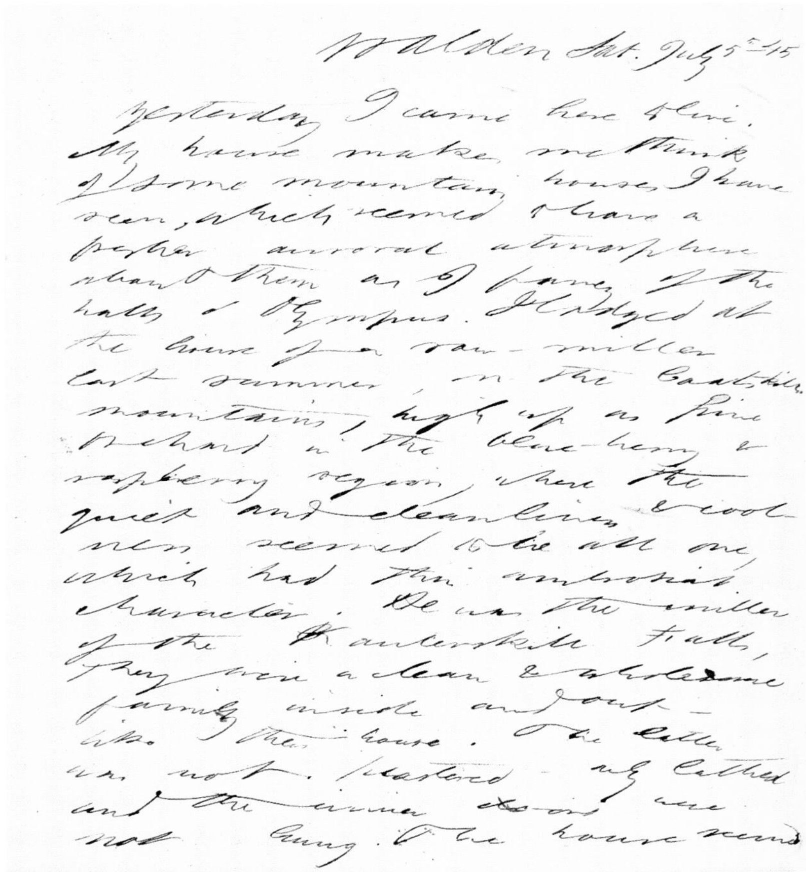

54. Henry David Thoreau. Autograph manuscript journal entry, dated Walden, 5 July 1845.

Morgan Library
MA 1302 (8)

This entry, in which Thoreau documented his move to Walden, is recorded in one of forty of his journal volumes housed in the Morgan Library.

New England transcendentalism, an intellectual movement inspired by German idealism with roots in classical Stoicism. In its American form, transcendentalism sought an ethical model for living derived from nature and intuition. Journal-keeping, as practiced by Thoreau at Emerson's suggestion, was crucial to the introspection and self-development central to American idealism. From his background in the Unitarian church, Emerson had developed a flair for compelling oratory that served him well as the chief American literary sage of the era. His essays, many of which began as lectures, illustrate the way in which the rhetoric of politics and evangelicalism energized much American writing of the period (PL. 57).

For Americans of African descent, the great percentage of whom were enslaved during this period, literacy was not easily attained. Even so, autobiographical accounts proliferated in the form of "slave narratives," some written by black authors, some dictated to whites. By the end of the Civil War, some one hundred slave narratives had been printed in the United States over the course of a century, beginning in 1760 with *A Narrative of the Uncommon Sufferings, and Surprizing* [sic] *Deliverance of Briton Hammon, a Negro Man*. Countless other fugitive slaves and

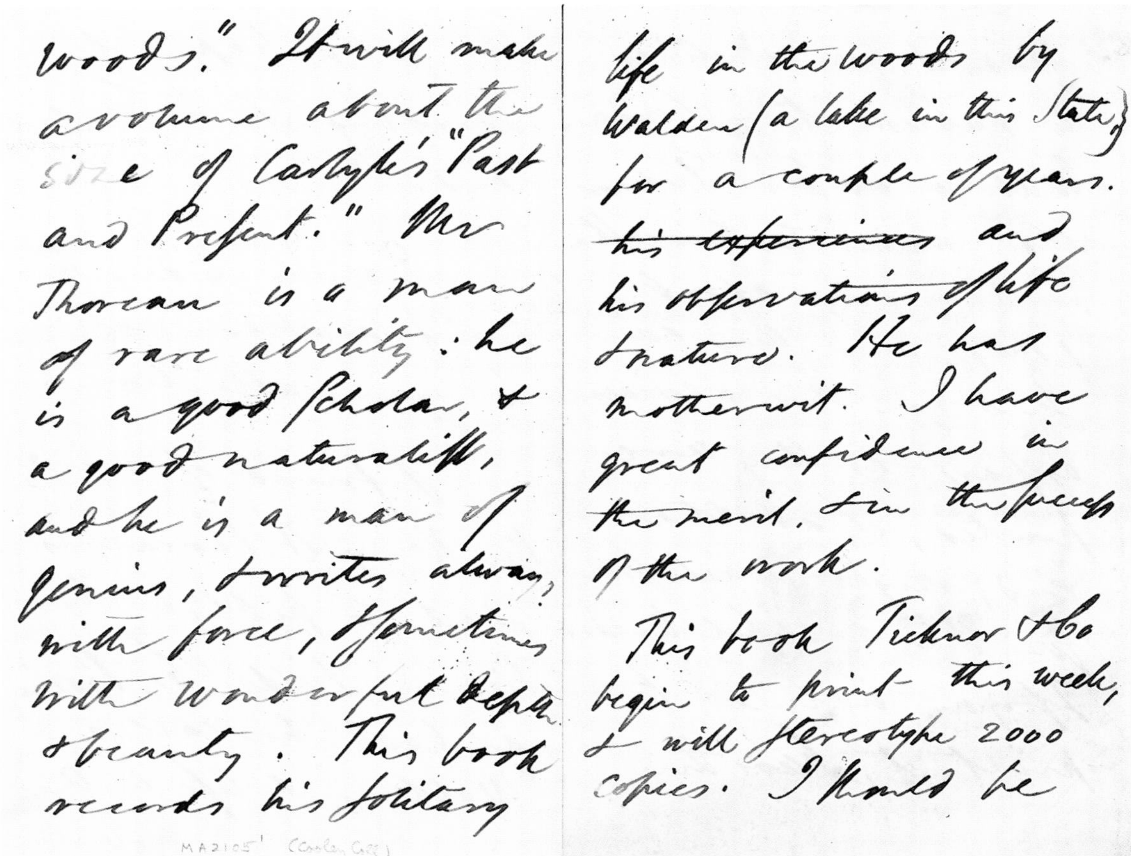

"woods." It will make
a volume about the
size of Carlyle's "Past
and Present." Mr
Thoreau is a man
of rare ability: he
is a good scholar, &
a good naturalist,
and he is a man of
genius, & writes always
with force, & sometimes
with wonderful depth
& beauty. This book
records his solitary

life in the woods by
Walden (a lake in this State)
for a couple of years.
~~his experiences~~ and
his observations of life
& nature. He has
motherwit. I have
great confidence in
the merit, & in the success
of the work.
This book Ticknor & Co
begin to print this week,
& will stereotype 2000
copies. I should be

55. Ralph Waldo Emerson. Autograph letter signed, dated Concord, [Massachusetts], 20 March 1854, to Richard Bentley.

Morgan Library
MA 2105

Emerson wrote this letter to a London publisher, asking him to publish Thoreau's *Walden*: "A friend of mine, Mr. Henry D. Thoreau, is about to publish, by Ticknor, Fields, Co., Boston, a book he calls 'Walden, a Life in the Woods.'"

free blacks told their stories on the antislavery lecture circuit. During the antebellum period, the most extraordinary testimonies of enslavement and freedom were penned by the orator and activist Frederick Douglass, who published three versions of his autobiography: *Narrative of the Life of Frederick Douglass, an American Slave* (1845), *My Bondage and My Freedom* (1855), and *Life and Times of Frederick Douglass* (1881). Douglass's work was subtitled "Written by Himself" to underscore the fact that the tale was fully his own and had not been subject to revision or embellishment by white abolitionists as had many slave narratives of the period. In telling his story, Douglass hoped to "do something toward throwing light on the American slave system and hastening the glad day of deliverance to the millions of my brethren in bonds."

The black experience in America, central as it was to antebellum society, was an inevitable source for white authors as well. Longfellow's slim 1842 volume, *Poems on Slavery*, for example, was acclaimed for its affecting portrayal of the cruel treatment of enslaved blacks. But *The Pioneer*'s reviewer (see PL. 42) did not find Longfellow particularly courageous. "The sentiment of anti-slavery... is spreading so fast and so far over the whole land that its opponents are rapidly dwindling into a minority," he declared, perhaps optimistically, in 1843. "Moreover, such praise, if any there should be, should be given to the early disciples and apostles of this gospel." It was Harriet Beecher Stowe's 1852 novel, *Uncle Tom's Cabin* (PL. 58) that galvanized debate on the antislavery issue. An immediate bestseller, it made Stowe an international literary celebrity. She told the abolitionist journal *National Era* in 1851, "I feel now that the time is come when even a woman or a child who can speak a word for freedom and humanity is bound to speak." By 1860, many New England intellectuals, including Emerson and Thoreau, had become impassioned abolitionists. They organized lectures and memorials in support of archabolitionist John Brown when he was condemned to death for his 1859 raid on Harpers Ferry (see PL. 81).

56. [Ralph Waldo Emerson].
Engraved portrait, [n.d.].

Morgan Library
MA 884

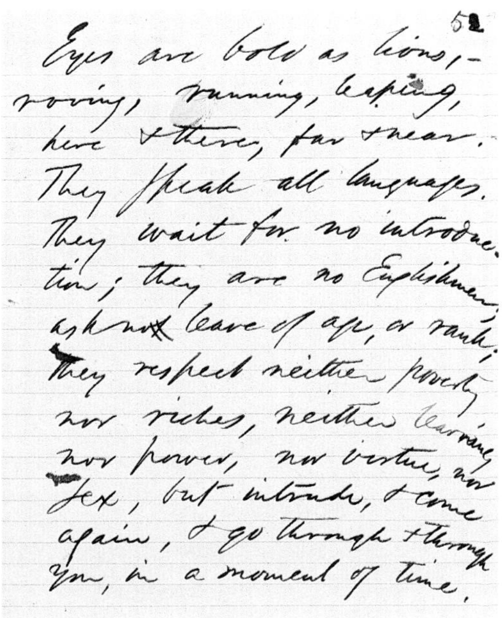

52

Eyes are bold as lions,— roving, running, leaping, here & there, far & near. They speak all languages. They wait for no introduction; they are no Englishmen; ask no leave of age, or rank; they respect neither poverty nor riches, neither learning nor power, nor virtue, nor sex, but intrude, & come again, & go through & through you, in a moment of time.

57. Ralph Waldo Emerson.
"Behavior." Autograph manuscript, [ca. 1851].

Morgan Library
MA 1035

Emerson wrote out this manuscript in a bold hand to facilitate reading from the lectern. First used in a series of lectures he delivered in Pittsburgh in 1851, this essay was later published in *The Conduct of Life* in 1860. In it, Emerson argued that the human body (particularly the eyes) reveals the soul.

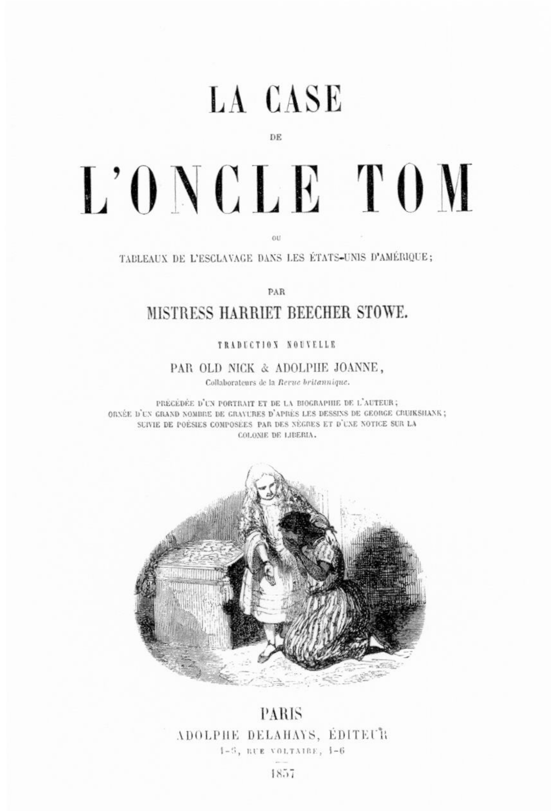

LA CASE
DE
L'ONCLE TOM
OU
TABLEAUX DE L'ESCLAVAGE DANS LES ÉTATS-UNIS D'AMÉRIQUE;
PAR
MISTRESS HARRIET BEECHER STOWE.
TRADUCTION NOUVELLE
PAR OLD NICK & ADOLPHE JOANNE,
Collaborateurs de la *Revue britannique*.
PRÉCÉDÉE D'UN PORTRAIT ET DE LA BIOGRAPHIE DE L'AUTEUR;
ORNÉE D'UN GRAND NOMBRE DE GRAVURES D'APRÈS LES DESSINS DE GEORGE CRUIKSHANK;
SUIVIE DE POÉSIES COMPOSÉES PAR DES NÈGRES ET D'UNE NOTICE SUR LA COLONIE DE LIBERIA.

PARIS
ADOLPHE DELAHAYS, ÉDITEUR
1-3, RUE VOLTAIRE, 1-6
1857

58. Harriet Beecher Stowe.
La Case de l'Oncle Tom, ou Tableaux de l'esclavage dans les Etats-Unis d'Amérique, translated by "Old Nick" (pseudonym of Emile Daurand Forgues) and Adolphe Joanne. Paris: Adolphe Delahays, 1857.

Morgan Library
PML 85460

This is the first French edition of *Uncle Tom's Cabin* (1852), the first American novel to sell over a million copies.

Audubon

and the Artist-Naturalist Tradition in America

THE HIGH ARTISTIC level achieved by John James Audubon in his naturalist drawings was succinctly expressed by the French naturalist Baron Cuvier, who commented in 1828 that Audubon's work "was the most magnificent monument yet raised by art to science." Audubon's reputation as America's preeminent artist-naturalist is in large part derived from his publications *The Birds of America* and *The Viviparous Quadrupeds of North America*. Bold and dynamic in composition, Audubon's drawings communicate his intense passion for and careful observation of nature (PL. 59). To understand the development of the American artist-naturalist tradition and Audubon's position within it, we can look to observations made by early explorers. In October 1492, Columbus's discovery of the island that he called Isabella inspired him to write:

> There are flocks of parrots that obscure the sun and other birds, large and small, of so many kinds, different from ours, that it is wonderful; there are trees of a thousand species, each having its particular fruit and all of marvelous flavor, so that I am in the greatest trouble in the world not to know them, for I am very certain that they are all of great value. I shall take home some of them as specimens and also of the herbs.

Columbus's chagrin points to a desire to catalogue the natural world, an endeavor that would become increasingly refined and sophisticated as the discipline of natural history developed.

The origins and development of the artist-explorer and artist-naturalist working in America were contingent upon the development of a descriptive skill equal to the wildlife and peoples encountered. Textual and painted or drawn accounts became natural companions, frequently leading to the production of important illustrated books on the flora and fauna of America. In 1564, Jacques le Moyne de Morgues, the first artist of quality to work in the United States, accompanied a French expedition led by René Goulaine de Laudonnière to what is now Florida. Le Moyne's impressions of the Timucua people of northeast Florida and their way of life were published in a short history, *Brevis Narratio eorum quae in Florida Americae provincia Gallis acciderunt* (Frankfurt, 1591), with forty-two illustrations and a map of Florida. It was produced by Theodor de Bry as the second part of his publications on the voyages to the New World (Hulton, p. 3). The Library possesses a sketchbook in a limp vellum binding tooled in gold that contains twenty-nine drawings on sixty-eight leaves attributed to Le Moyne (Hulton, p. 177 ff). These range from individual depictions of insects and plants to more elaborate compositions in which insects feed on the leaves and fruit (PL. 60).

> **I drew this hare during one of the days of deepest sorrow I have felt in my life, and my only solace was derived from my labour.**
>
> JOHN JAMES AUDUBON

59. John James Audubon.
Common American Skunk.
Study for plate 42 of *The Quadrupeds.*

Morgan Library
Acc. no. 1976.12:3

60. Attributed to Jacques le Moyne de Morgues.
Apple (folio 51).

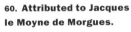

Morgan Library
Acc. no. 1975.18

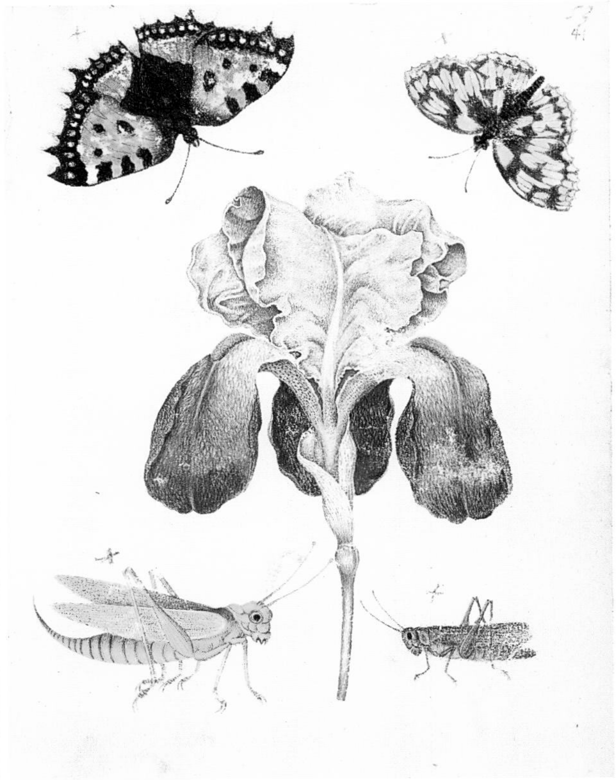

61. Attributed to Jacques le Moyne de Morgues.
Iris (folio 53).

Morgan Library
Acc. no. 1975.18

A delicately colored iris demonstrates the artist's sensitivity and skill (PL. 61). If the attribution is correct, the sketchbook probably predates the Huguenot artist's work in England and Florida but remains an excellent example of an early use of water- and bodycolor, the ideal media for on-site sketching. Le Moyne's technique influenced Virginia colonist John White, an important explorer-artist who was sent to Raleigh as governor of the Roanoke colony in 1587 and was the grandfather of Virginia Dare. White's remarkable watercolors of the flora and fauna and the indigenous peoples of America are now in the British Museum (Hulton and Quinn). De Bry, who greatly admired White's drawings, published his work in *A briefe and true report of the new found land of Virginia... in America* (Frankfurt, 1590).

During the eighteenth century, the tradition of the explorer-naturalist tradition was assiduously maintained by Mark Catesby. Born at Castle Hedingham, Essex, Catesby, whose fascination with wildlife was not limited to that in England, was the first European naturalist to make a systematic study of the flora and fauna of Virginia and the Carolinas. In 1712, he visited his sister and her husband, who had emigrated to Williamsburg, Virginia. He subsequently traveled to the West Indies in 1714 and returned to England in 1719 with botanical specimens and paintings of birds. With funds provided by English naturalists, Catesby returned to America in 1722, at which time he went to South Carolina. In 1725, he visited the Bahamas. *The Natural History of Carolina, Florida and the Bahama Islands* was written and illustrated by Catesby after his return to England in 1726. In his preface, he discusses the origin and development of the work.

> My curiosity was such that, not being content with contemplating the products of our own country, I soon imbibed a passionate desire of viewing as well the animal and vegetable productions in their native countries, which were strangers to England. Virginia was the place (I having relations there) suited most to my convenience to go to, where I arriv'd the 23d of April 1712. I thought then so little of prosecuting a design of the nature of this work, that in the seven years I resided in that country, (I am ashamed to own it) I chiefly gratified my inclination in observing and admiring the various productions of those countries, only sending from thence some dried specimens of plants and some of the most specious of them in tubs of earth, at the request of some curious friends, amongst whom was Mr. Dale of Braintree in Essex, a skilful [sic] apothecary and botanist: to him, besides specimens of plants, I sent some few observations on the country, which he communicated to the late William Sherard, L.L.D., one of the most celebrated botanists of this age, who favoured me with his friendship on my return to England in the year 1719; and by his advice (tho' conscious of my own inability), I first resolved on this undertaking, so agreeable to my inclination.

The first section of Catesby's *Natural History* was completed by 1729, at which time he began to solicit subscriptions to the entire work. The two volumes were published in sections of twenty plates with descriptive texts; he completed the first in 1732 (even though the title page is dated 1731) and the second in 1743. The engravings, colored by hand either by the artist or under his supervision, consist of 100 plates depicting what Catesby considered to be 102 species of American birds. The majority of preparatory drawings for this work are in the Royal Library at Windsor; however, six additional drawings, including the *Frutex Spinosus* (PL. 62) and the *Bead Snake* (PL. 63), with its characteristic bands of yellow, red, and black carefully rendered in watercolor, are preserved in the Morgan Library's copy of the first edition of his book. In his engraved plate for the book (PL. 64), Catesby showed the bead snake wrapped around the potato plant, commenting, "They live mostly underground and are seldom seen above but are frequently found and dug up with potatoes." The artist's association of plants with certain animals demonstrates an awareness of habitat long before ecology became a scientific discipline.

62. Mark Catesby.
Frutex Spinosus.
Study for plate 100 of *The Natural History* (vol. II).

Morgan Library
Acc. no. 1961.6:3

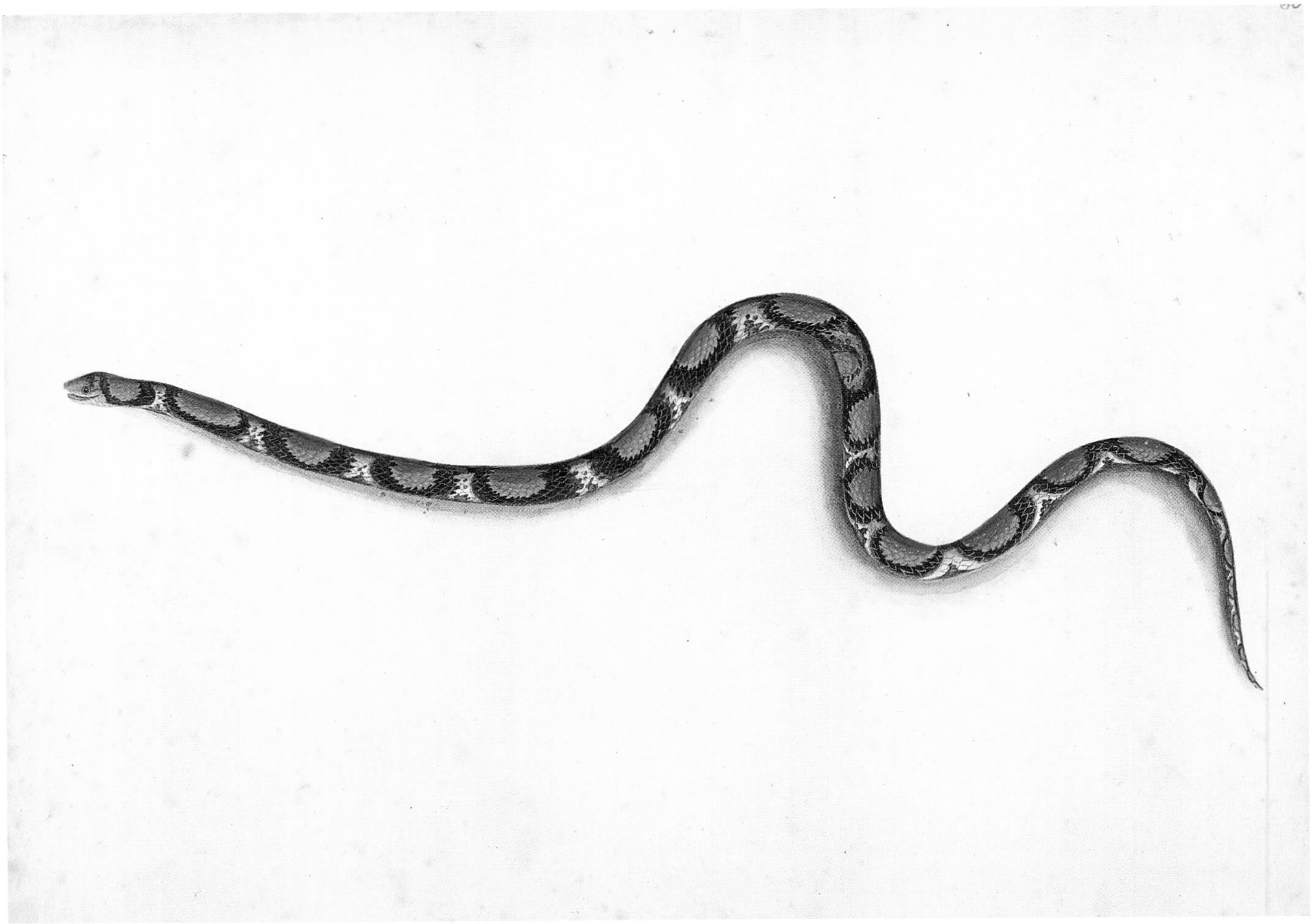

63. Mark Catesby.
Bead Snake.
Study for plate 60 of *The Natural History* (vol. II).

Morgan Library
Acc. no. 1961.6:1

Artist-naturalists such as Catesby were innovators. Combining meticulous examination with an intense curiosity fostered straightforward, realistic depictions of nature. Catesby's "passionate desire of viewing" was somewhat a precursor to the Emersonian ideal of direct contact with the natural environment. This was expressed subsequently in a more sophisticated way by the work of Alexander Wilson and then John James Audubon.

The first native-born American artist-naturalist was William Bartram. The son of the great botanist John Bartram of Philadelphia, his work was influenced by Catesby and Georg Dionysius Ehret. In 1765 Bartram accompanied his father on a collecting trip to the Carolinas, Georgia, and Florida, providing drawings to Dr. John Fothergill, a leading London physician and owner of the largest private botanical garden in England, at Upton, Essex (Ewan, p. 6). In March 1773, Fothergill commissioned Bartram to collect and document plants and shells of the southern colonies. These drawings are presently in the Natural History Division of the British Museum. Having prepared a journal for Fothergill that was never published, Bartram drew upon it for his *Travels through North and South Carolina, Georgia, East and West Florida, the Cherokee Country, the Extensive Territories of the Muscogulges, or Creek Con-*

64. Mark Catesby.
Bead Snake and Potato.
Plate 60 of *The Natural History.*

Morgan Library
PML 45709

federacy, and the Country of the Chactaws. Containing an Account of the Soil and Natural Productions of Those Regions, Together with Observations on the Manners of the Indians. One of the most distinguished and influential books of American natural history, it was published in Philadelphia in 1791 and contains accounts of life in the field as well as descriptions of new species. Bartram's enthusiasm and somewhat quirky observations come across in the illustrations, although some of the immediacy of his early pen-and-ink style seen in the British Museum drawings has been lost. Bartram's artistic appreciation and serious study of nature is evident, and he has been described as "one of the first to achieve [a] combination of scientific knowledge and aesthetic appreciation which he could weld into that rare type of writing—literary prose of true scientific substance" (Ewan, p. 21). The picturesque charm of his descriptions of tropical forests and wilderness life made the work popular with poets such as Coleridge and Southey.

Alexander Wilson, who came to Philadelphia from Scotland in 1794, met William Bartram and members of his circle in 1802. Bartram cultivated Wilson's interest in nature and introduced him to the work of Catesby and Edwards.

Wilson learned to draw from Alexander Lawson, who later was to engrave some of his drawings. By 1805, Wilson was making drawings of birds, a project that would develop into the nine-volume *American Ornithology*, published between 1808 and 1814. His pride in this work was expressed in a letter to his father (25 February 1811) as follows: "The publication of *Ornithology*, though it has swallowed up all the little I have saved, has procured me the honour of many friends, eminent in this country, and the esteem of the public at large" (Hetherington, p. 2). *American Ornithology* was a huge endeavor since Wilson not only did all the research and writing, he singlehandedly made the drawings and engravings of the illustrations and sold subscriptions as well. The decorative patterns developed in his illustrations make his compositions aesthetically appealing. Charles Willson Peale's great picture *Exhumation of the Mastodon* (1806) included, along with those of friends and relatives, portraits of distinguished scientists such as Wilson. Although Wilson was subsequently overshadowed by Audubon, the clarity, freshness of observation, and objectivity of Wilson's illustrations are indicative of American neoclassic taste, and his book is one of its notable manifestations.

Audubon's *Birds of America* established the artist's formidable reputation, which stands today. Until about 1810, Audubon had based his identification of birds on *Natural History* by the French naturalist George-Louis Leclerc, the comte de Buffon (published in nine volumes, 1770–83); but by March that year Audubon met Wilson, who had recently published the first two volumes of *American Ornithology*. Wilson's book served as a guide and a challenge to Audubon, and he even based some of his drawings directly on Wilson's (Davidson, pp. xxvii ff). Audubon spent years painting, collecting birds, and fighting his way through the American wilderness to document them in their natural environment. The outcome was his double-elephant-folio *Birds of America*, the first plates of which were engraved in 1827. The publication included 435 plates, which were hand-colored copies of his paintings, engraved in London by Robert Havell, Jr.; nearly all the original watercolors are at The New-York Historical Society. By 1824, Audubon's technique was to draw birds in watercolor, adding pastel to imitate downy feathers; ink, oil, and egg white to capture the gleaming surface of a bird's eye or beak; and at times scratching the paper to achieve various effects (Davidson, p. xxxi). Audubon's passion for his subject is highly evident in the sharp detail and bold design of the plates.

Following *The Birds of America*, Audubon began to draw mammals for *The Viviparous Quadrupeds of North America*. The Morgan Library has six remarkable Audubon watercolors of mammals that entered the collection in 1900, together with a copy of *Quadrupeds*, all from the collection of Theodore Irwin. These drawings are among seventy-six executed for *Quadrupeds*, the text for which was largely written by Audubon's friend from Charleston, the Reverend John Bachman, who in his youth had collected birds for Wilson. Bachman wrote to the artist: "Employ yourself in drawing every quadruped you can lay your hands on.... Don't flatter yourself that this book is child's play—the birds are a mere trifle compared with this. I have been at it all my life...we all have much to learn in this matter" (Dwight, p. 50). The two (sometimes bound as three) imperial folios of plates for *Quadrupeds* were lithographed and colored by J. T. Bowen of Philadelphia and appeared between 1845 and 1848. When Audubon's health began to fail him in 1846, the project was completed by his son John Woodhouse Audubon, who made his preparatory studies in oil. Another son, Victor Gifford Audubon, supplied a number of the landscape backgrounds of the plates. The publication was originally issued without text to subscribers in thirty parts of five plates each, measuring 28 x 22 inches, at $10 a part or $300 for the lot. Three accompanying octavo volumes of text—mostly Bachman's—were issued in 1846, 1851, and 1854 and included five additional octavo plates.

For mammals, Audubon followed much the same technique that he used for birds, making a life-size drawing from a live or dead specimen. The Library's watercolors attest to his virtuosity in depicting the texture and sheen of a particu-

65. **John James Audubon.**
Brown, or Norway, Rat.
Study for plate 54 of *The Quadrupeds.*

Morgan Library
Acc. no. 1976.12:1

lar animal's fur, subtly describing variations from soft and velvety, as in *Gray Rabbit* (PL. 68), to more bristly, as in *Brown, or Norway, Rat* (PL. 65). According to inscriptions, the latter drawing and *Common American Skunk* (PL. 59) were executed at Minnie's Land, the family home built in 1842 on the Hudson River, in what is now the Fort Washington section of upper Manhattan. Although Audubon's journal records his travels throughout the Northeast in connection with this project, many specimens used for his drawings were from the area of his home.

Audubon's remarkably deft touch is illustrated in his depiction of skunks. The combination of brush and watercolor, heightened with white and enlivened by quick strokes of graphite, particularly impressive in his rendering of the adult skunk's tail, is extraordinary. The drawing of the young was combined with that of the adult and published as plate 42 of *Quadrupeds*. Audubon's instructions that the adult was "to be placed on the rock and the young beneath it" were followed in the lithograph. The practice of cutting out and pasting

66. John James Audubon.
Cat Squirrel. Study for plate 17 of *The Quadrupeds.*

Morgan Library
Acc. no. 1976.12:2

drawings onto a separate sheet was a working method Audubon used in preparing his watercolors for the engraver. On the verso, Audubon carefully noted the weight and measurements of the male skunk.

The subtle variations of watercolor—from dark and golden brown tones to a vivid reddish brown—is especially compelling in Audubon's depiction of the woodchuck (PL. 67). Audubon, apparently feeling very strongly about the animal's disposition, wrote on the back of the sheet: "When these animals aprehend [*sic*] danger or come in contact with it, they issue a loud and shrill whistle capable of being heard more than one hundred yards, and at the following moment they open their mouth laterally and produce a sort of maniacal laugh, which is continued for several minutes and meantime issue a sound as if in a severe fit of aigue [*sic*]. They are extremely savage." Viciousness is conveyed by Audubon's rendering of the center animal that bares its teeth in a snarl.

Audubon's outstanding reputation as a documentarian of natural history rests on his artistic skills. Perhaps the most powerful testimony of his devotion to his art and the comfort he derived from it is that appearing in a poignant inscription on the verso of *Gray Rabbit*, which he finished on 29 August 1841 (PL. 69). Audubon wrote: "I drew this hare during one of the days of deepest sorrow I have felt in my life, and my only solace was derived from my labour. This morning our beloved daughter Eliza died at 2 o'clock. She is now in Heaven, and may our God for ever bless her soul!" Eliza, the daughter of the Reverend John Bachman, was the wife of Audubon's son Victor. She was only twenty-two when she died on 25 May 1841.

67. John James Audubon.
Woodchuck. Study for plate 2 of *The Quadrupeds.*

Morgan Library
Acc. no. 1976.12:6

68. John James Audubon.
Gray Rabbit. Study for plate 22 of *The Quadrupeds*.

Morgan Library
Acc. no. 1976.12:4

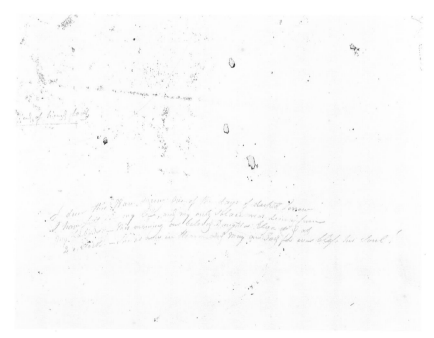

69. Inscription on verso of *Gray Rabbit*.

Morgan Library
Acc. no. 1976.12:4

An Age of

Exploration and Innovation

IN 1800, the vast regions of land west of the Appalachian Mountains were uncharted wilderness. President Thomas Jefferson set the precedent for federal sponsorship of exploration of these areas in 1803, when he obtained appropriation from Congress for Meriwether Lewis and William Clark's expedition into the Louisiana Territory. Setting out from St. Louis in May 1804, the Lewis and Clark expedition traveled through what is now North Dakota and along the Missouri River, eventually crossing the Rocky Mountains to land within sight of the Pacific Ocean before returning to St. Louis in 1806. Lewis and Clark's published observations captivated the public imagination and stimulated further exploration.

The model established by Lewis and Clark was followed in varying degrees by others, among them Zebulon Pike, through present-day Colorado and New Mexico in 1806–7, and Henry Schoolcraft, through what is now southern Missouri and Arkansas in 1817–18. These expeditions mapped previously unknown terrain; recorded geological, botanical, and zoological data; and documented Native American tribes and their languages. They also established transcontinental routes that settlers would later follow.

After Lewis and Clark, expeditions were increasingly mandated to strengthen trade. John Jacob Astor's bold scheme to establish a series of fur-trading posts in Oregon was halted by the War of 1812. After the war, the lucrative fur trade compelled other entrepreneurs to organize treks to the West. Thus motivated, fur trader and explorer Jedediah Smith, in 1829–30, led the first U.S. expedition to enter California from the east and established a route from California to the Pacific Northwest.

Impelled by a deepening sense of expansionism, the government also sponsored expeditions to evaluate terrain for future settlement. When Secretary of War John C. Calhoun authorized an expedition from the Missouri to the Yellowstone River in 1818, its justification was "the mighty growth of our republic... ready to push its civilization and laws to the western confines of the continent."

Advocacy of homesteading compelled Missouri senator Thomas Hart Benton to support the expeditions of his son-in-law, John C. Frémont, through the Rockies and into the Oregon country in 1842–44. Frémont's two published reports provided maps of much of the territory from the Mississippi Valley to the Pacific Ocean, optimistically assessed the fertility of the Northwest, and confirmed the most favorable passages through the Rockies.

> **The Americans arrived but as yesterday on the territory which they inhabit, and they have already changed the whole order of nature for their own advantage.**
>
> ALEXIS DE TOCQUEVILLE, *Democracy in America*

Wednesday. August 2d. 1843. Left Philadelphia for New York. at 10½. A.M. Crossing the Delaware in a Steam Ferry-boat we found ourselves at the Railway Station, at Camden-town, in a few minutes. the whole of the passengers and baggage being stowed away in the cars with some little difficulty - the bell sounded and off we started - an American Railway train is, to a Novice in Transatlantic Locomotion, a very strange looking affair — but a slight sketch will give a better idea of its appearance than the most labored description

70. Septimus Harry Palairet and M. A. Palairet.
Illustrated autograph manuscript journal of their travels in America, 1843.

Morgan Library
MA 2244

This illustration of early American railroading is from a journal kept by the Palairets, an English couple who traveled the Northeast in the summer of 1843. Part of their journey was on New Jersey's first railroad, from Camden to South Amboy.

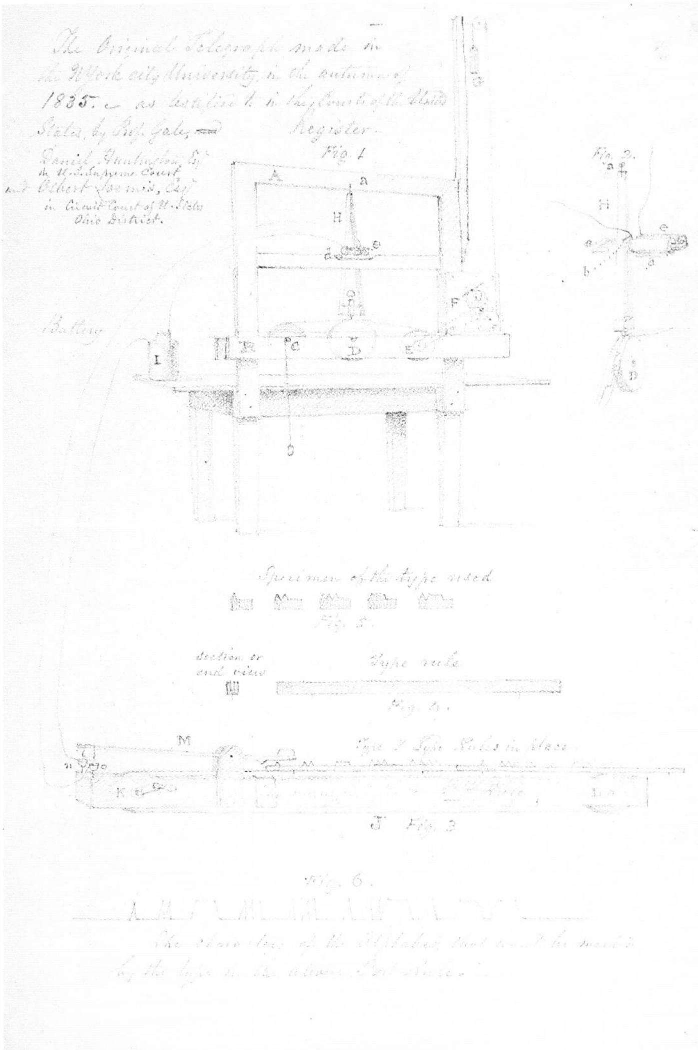

71. Samuel F. B. Morse. Autograph description and drawing of telegraph, [n.d.].

Morgan Library
MA 901

Morse forsook his career as an artist to invent a workable telegraph.

The routes that formed the Oregon Trail from Independence, Missouri, to the Willamette Valley in Oregon had been blazed by explorers and traders preceding Frémont. His detailed maps, broadly disseminated in his popular publications, made the trail accessible to settlers. During the 1840s, almost 12,000 people, beset with "Oregon fever," emigrated to the Northwest. By 1860, some 250,000 had traveled by covered wagon to Oregon and California.

Expeditions did not always render positive assessments of potential sites for settlement. A notable example is Edwin James's *Account of an Expedition from Pittsburgh to the Rocky Mountains Performed in the Years 1819 and '20* (Philadelphia, 1822–23), which declared the Great Plains to be "almost wholly unfit for cultivation and, of course, uninhabitable by a people depending upon agriculture for their subsistence.... [T]he scarcity of wood and water, almost uniformly prevalent, will prove an insuperable obstacle in the way of settling the country." The area between present-day central Nebraska and the Rockies was generally viewed as the "Great American Desert" until the 1847 influx of Mormons into Utah proved that the area was habitable.

As exploration and settlement of the West proceeded, improvements in transportation and a host of inventions transformed American life east of the Mississippi. Land and water shipping and travel were greatly facilitated. The commercial viability of steamboats had been established by Robert Fulton in 1807, when his *Clermont* journeyed from New York City to Albany in thirty-two hours. By the 1820s, more efficient engines reduced the trip to less than eight hours; steamboat companies were operating regularly on the Ohio and Mississippi rivers and Lakes Ontario and Erie. As the speed of steamboat travel increased, fares grew cheaper: a Pittsburgh–Cincinnati trip that cost $12 in 1825 was $6 in 1835, and the New Orleans–Louisville fare likewise halved, from $50 to $25.

Water transport was also boosted by the 1817–25 construction of the Erie Canal. Financed by the New York state legislature, the canal was an immense success. Its cost of $7,000,000 was recouped fairly quickly by tolls, which totaled nearly $500,000 at the end of the first year of operation. The canal reduced the cost of shipping goods between New York City and Lake Erie from approximately $100 to $9 per ton. The resultant boom in canal construction, from 1825 to 1850, linked the Great Lakes to the Mississippi and other major rivers.

Markets that could not be reached by water were served and vastly expanded by railroads (PL. 70). The first passenger railroad in the

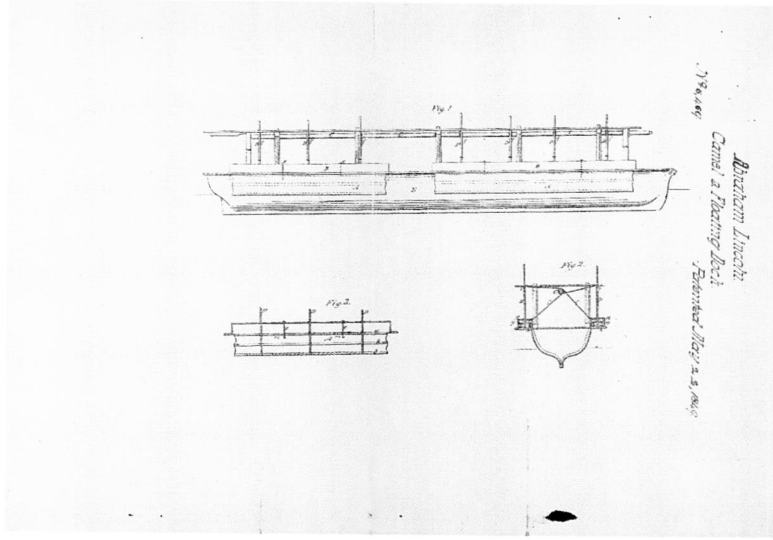

72. [Abraham Lincoln]. U.S. Patent Office. *Abraham Lincoln, of Springfield, Illinois. Buoying Vessels Over Shoals.* Patent No. 6,469, dated 22 May 1849.

Gilder Lehrman Collection GLC 1304

Among American tinkerers was Abraham Lincoln, who was granted a patent for a device to improve water transportation.

United States, the Baltimore & Ohio, began construction in 1828. By 1840, passengers and freight traveled on some 3,000 miles of rail, almost twice the distance of rail in Europe. Between 1840 and 1860, a total of 28,000 miles was added to the American rail system. As the steamboat and the canal system had been, the railroad was an enormous boon to shipping. In 1852, goods traveling by rail took about a week to reach New York City from Cincinnati, a journey that had taken almost two months by boat and wagon in 1817.

As improved transportation spurred economic growth, it also enabled more individuals to move into cities. In New England, the proportion of residents living in urban areas increased from 7 to 36 percent between 1810 and 1860. Between 1820 and 1840, the population of Philadelphia and its suburbs doubled, from 100,000 to 200,000, while Pittsburgh's tripled, from 7,000 to 21,000. Because the land area of the United States remained 1,753,588 square miles, population density increased from 5.5 to 9.7 per square mile during this period.

Accompanying the transportation revolution was the radical change in communication that occurred in 1844 when Samuel F. B. Morse's telegraph successfully transmitted a message over an experimental line from Washington, D.C., to Baltimore (PL. 71). By 1846, 5,000 miles of telegraph wire linked various areas of the country. Morse was one among many of his compatriots who had a scientific aptitude but were much less interested in theory than in application. One of the most influential inventors was Cyrus McCormick, whose reaper allowed farmers to harvest several times more acres of grain than they could by hand. McCormick had patented the reaper in 1834, and by 1850, his factory in Chicago was mass-producing the machine for farmers throughout the expanding nation. Likewise ingenious, but less financially successful than McCormick, Charles Goodyear revolutionized the rubber industry with his 1839 discovery of the vulcanization process, which produced a stronger, more resilient product. The urge to invent was widespread (PL. 72). Between 1836 and 1860, patent applications increased more than tenfold, from 400 to 4,357. With inventors showing a strong inclination for labor-saving devices, the nation's agriculture and manufacturing productivity soared.

By 1850, the United States had developed a complex market economy. Raw materials and finished goods were conveyed over the new networks of canals and railroads more swiftly and in greater variety than ever before. Inventions spurred new manufacturing enterprises that drew growing numbers of the populace from farms to wage-paying jobs in cities. Agriculture began commercializing, with greater numbers of farmers shifting from growing only what was necessary to feed themselves and their families to producing cash crops for market. Prosperity under these market conditions was enjoyed mainly by those who adjusted to a system that encouraged competition and rewarded individual initiative. Even as the gap between rich and poor widened, an American ethos based on individualism and self-advancement took firm hold.

The Annexation of Texas and
The Mexican War

IN 1822, Stephen F. Austin established a colony of Americans near the gulf coast of Texas on land granted by Mexico. Additional land grants by Mexico attracted over 20,000 Americans to Texas during the 1820s. By 1832, Austin's settlement alone had grown from several hundred families to a population of 8,000. Friction arose between American immigrants and Mexican authorities soon after the initial influx. Although the United States had officially renounced claims to Texas in 1819, when it signed the Adams-Onis Treaty with Spain, many Americans still considered the area to fall within the undefined western boundaries of the Louisiana Purchase of 1803. Hoping for eventual annexation by the United States, they withstood assimilation with the resident Mexican population and resisted Mexican government regulations. A particular source of contention was Mexico's ban on importing additional slaves into Texas. Armed conflict erupted in 1835. In 1836, the colonists declared the republic of Texas and won their independence from Mexico (PL. 73).

The new Texas government's application for annexation was a controversial political issue for the United States. As with Missouri, Southern interest in expanding slaveholding territory was met with opposition from antislavery forces that forestalled annexation until 1844, when Texas became an issue in the presidential campaign. By then, the question was no longer only a domestic one regarding the expansion of slavery. Because Britain supported an independent Texas as a bulwark against complete North American dominance by the United States, the issue was also a matter of foreign policy. Initially, both front-runners for their party's presidential nomination, Whig Henry Clay and Democrat Martin Van Buren, opposed annexation for fear of war with Mexico, which had never recognized Texas's independence. Clay won the Whig nomination, but Van Buren's position was rejected by the Democrats. They ultimately nominated James Polk of Tennessee, who favored annexation.

Polk secured the nomination with the enthusiastic support of ex-president Andrew Jackson, who feared British interference with American policies on slavery and Native Americans were Texas not annexed. Before the election, during the summer of 1844, Jackson asserted in a private letter:

> The enticing question between the Democrats and federal Whigs and abolitionists is the annexation of Texas, the Democrats viewing it as absolutely necessary [for the United] States to shut out all British and foreign influence from tampering with the Indians on our western frontiers and with our slaves in the South and West.... Texas is all important to our national defense and safety. How humiliating to every true American, the idea of America, a great and independent nation as we are, to be overawed by the dictates of England. But Texas must and will be ours.

But Texas must and will be ours.

ANDREW JACKSON

UNANIMOUS

DECLARATION OF INDEPENDENCE,

BY THE

DELEGATES OF THE PEOPLE OF TEXAS,

IN GENERAL CONVENTION,

AT THE TOWN OF WASHINGTON,

ON THE SECOND DAY OF MARCH, 1836.

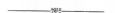

WHEN a government has ceased to protect the lives, liberty, and property of the people, from whom its legitimate powers are derived, and for the advancement of whose happiness it was instituted; and so far from being a guarantee for their inestimable and inalienable rights, becomes an instrument in the hands of evil rulers for their oppression. When the Federal Republican Constitution of their country, which they have sworn to support, no longer has a substantial existence, and the whole nature of their government has been forcibly changed, without their consent, from a restricted Federative Republic, composed of Sovereign States, to a consolidated Central Military despotism, in which every interest is disregarded but that of the army and the priesthood, both the eternal enemies of civil liberty, the ever ready minions of power, and the usual instruments of tyrants. When, long after the spirit of the constitution has departed, moderation is at length so far lost by those in power, that even the semblance of freedom is removed, and the forms themselves of the constitution discontinued, and so far from their petitions and remonstrances being regarded, the agents who bear them are thrown into dungeons, and mercenary armies sent forth to force a new government upon them at the point of the bayonet.

When, in consequence of such acts of malfeasance and abduction on the part of the government, anarchy prevails and civil society is dissolved into its original elements, in such a crisis, the first law of nature, the right of self preservation, the inherent and inalienable right of the people to appeal to first principles, and take their political affairs into their own hands in extreme cases, enjoins it as a right towards themselves and a sacred obligation to their posterity to abolish such government, and create another in its stead, calculated to rescue them from impending dangers, and to secure their welfare and happiness.

Nations, as well as individuals, are amenable for their acts to the public opinion of mankind. A statement of a part of our grievances is therefore submitted to an impartial world, in justification of the hazardous but unavoidable step now taken, of severing our political connection with the Mexican people, and assuming an independent attitude among the nations of the earth.

The Mexican Government, by its colonization laws, invited and induced the Anglo American population of Texas to colonize its wilderness under the pledged faith of a written constitution, that they should continue to enjoy that constitutional liberty and republican government to which they had been habituated in the land of their birth, the United States of America.

In this expectation they have been cruelly disappointed, inasmuch as the Mexican nation has acquiesced in the late changes made in the government by General Antonio Lopez Santa Ana, who having overturned the constitution of his country, now offers, as the cruel alternative, either to abandon our homes acquired by so many privations, or submit to the most intolerable of all tyranny, the combined despotism of the sword and the priesthood.

It hath sacrificed our welfare to the state of Coahuila, by which our interests have been continually depressed through a jealous and partial course of legislation, carried on at a far distant seat of government, by a hostile majority in an unknown tongue, and this too, notwithstanding we have petitioned in the humblest terms for the establishment of a separate state government, and have, in accordance with the provisions of the national constitution, presented to the general congress a republican constitution, which was, without a just cause, contemptuously rejected.

It incarcerated in a dungeon, for a long time, one of our citizens, for no other cause but a zealous endeavour to procure the acceptance of our constitution and the establishment of a state government.

It has failed and refused to secure, on a firm basis, the right of trial by jury, that palladium of civil liberty and only safe guarantee for the life, liberty, and property of the citizen.

It has failed to establish any public system of education, although possessed of almost boundless resources, (the public domain;) and although it is an axiom in political science, that unless a people are educated and enlightened, it is idle to expect the continuance of civil liberty, or the capacity for self government.

It has suffered the military commandants, stationed among us, to exercise arbitrary acts of oppression and tyranny, thus trampling upon the most sacred rights of the citizen, and rendering the military superior to the civil power.

It has dissolved, by force of arms, the state congress of Coahuila and Texas, and obliged our representatives to fly for their lives from the seat of government, thus depriving us of the fundamental political right of representation.

It has demanded the surrender of a number of our citizens, and ordered military detachments to seize and carry them into the interior for trial, in contempt of the civil authorities, and in defiance of the laws and the constitution.

It has made piratical attacks upon our commerce by commissioning foreign desperadoes, and authorizing them to seize our vessels and convey the property of our citizens to far distant parts for confiscation.

It denies us the right of worshipping the Almighty according to the dictates of our own conscience, by the support of a National Religion, calculated to promote the temporal interest of its human functionaries, rather than the glory of the true and living God.

It has demanded us to deliver up our arms, which are essential to our defence—the rightful property of freemen—and formidable only to tyrannical governments.

It has invaded our country both by sea and by land, with the intent to lay waste our territory, and drive us from our homes; and has now a large mercenary army advancing, to carry on against us a war of extermination.

It has, through its emmissaries, incited the merciless savage, with the tomahawk and scalping knife, to massacre the inhabitants of our defenceless frontiers.

It has been, during the whole time of our connection with it, the contemptible sport and victim of successive military revolutions, and hath continually exhibited every characteristic of a weak, corrupt, and tyrannical government.

These, and other grievances, were patiently borne by the people of Texas, until they reached that point at which forbearance ceases to be a virtue. We then took up arms in defence of the National Constitution. We appealed to our Mexican brethren for assistance: our appeal has been made in vain; though months have elapsed, no sympathetic response has yet been heard from the interior. We are therefore forced to the melancholy conclusion, that the Mexican people have acquiesced in the destruction of their liberty, and the substitution therefor of a military government; that they are unfit to be free, and incapable of self government.

The necessity of self preservation, therefore, now decrees our eternal political separation.

We, therefore, the deligates, with plenary powers, of the people of Texas, in solemn convention assembled, appealing to a candid world for the necessities of our condition, do hereby resolve and DECLARE, *that our political connection with the Mexican nation has forever ended, and that the people of Texas, do now constitute a* FREE, SOVEREIGN, *and* INDEPENDENT REPUBLIC, *and are fully invested with all the rights and attributes which properly belong to independent nations; and, conscious of the rectitude of our intentions, we fearlessly and confidently commit the issue to the decision of the supreme Arbiter of the destinies of nations.*

RICHARD ELLIS, *President.*

C. B. STEWART, THOMAS BARNETT. — *Austin.*
JAS. COLLINSWORTH, EDWIN WALLER, ASA BRIGHAM, J. S. D. BYROM. — *Brazoria.*
FRANCISCO RUIS, ANTONIO NAVARO, JESSE B. BADGETT. — *Bexar.*
WILLIAM D. LACY, WILLIAM MENIFEE. — *Colorado.*
JAMES GAINES, W. CLARK, JR., — *Sabine.*
JOHN FISHER, MATT. CALDWELL, — *Gonzales.*
WILLIAM MOTLEY, — *Goliad.*
L. DE ZAVALA, — *Harrisburgh.*
STEPH. H. EVERITT, GEORGE W. SMITH, — *Jasper.*
ELIJAH STAPP, — *Jackson.*
CLAIBORNE WEST, WILLIAM B. SCATES, — *Jefferson.*
M. B. MENARD, A. B. HARDIN, — *Liberty.*
BAILEY HARDIMAN, — *Matagorda.*
J. W. BUNTON, THOS. J. GAZELEY, R. M. COLEMAN, — *Mina.*
ROBERT POTTER, THOMAS J. RUSK, CH. S. TAYLOR, JOHN S. ROBERTS, — *Nacogdoches.*
ROBERT HAMILTON, COLLIN McKINNEE, ALB. H. LATTIMER, — *Red River.*
MARTIN PARMER, E. O. LEGRAND, STEPH. W. BLOUNT, — *San Augustin.*
SYD. O. PENNINGTON, W. CAR'L CRAWFORD, — *Shelby.*
JAMES POWER, SAM. HOUSTON, DAVID THOMAS, EDWARD CONRAD, — *Refugio.*
JOHN TURNER, — *San Patricio.*
B. BRIGGS GOODRICH, G. W. BARNETT, JAMES G. SWISHER, JESSE GRIMES, — *Washington.*

Printed by Baker and Bordens, San Felipe de Austin.

73. *Unanimous Declaration of Independence.*
San Felipe de Austin: Baker and Bordens, [1836].

Gilder Lehrman Collection
GLC 2559

Of the twelve extant copies of Texas's Declaration of Independence, this is one of two surviving from the second printing.

Jackson assisted Polk's campaign by writing similar letters for newspaper publication. Polk won the election. After his inauguration, Congress avoided repeating what had occurred in April 1844, when a treaty of annexation had failed to win the required two-thirds majority in the Senate. In March 1845, Texas was annexed by joint resolution, which required only a simple majority. Admitted as a slave state, Texas became the twenty-eighth state in the Union in December 1845.

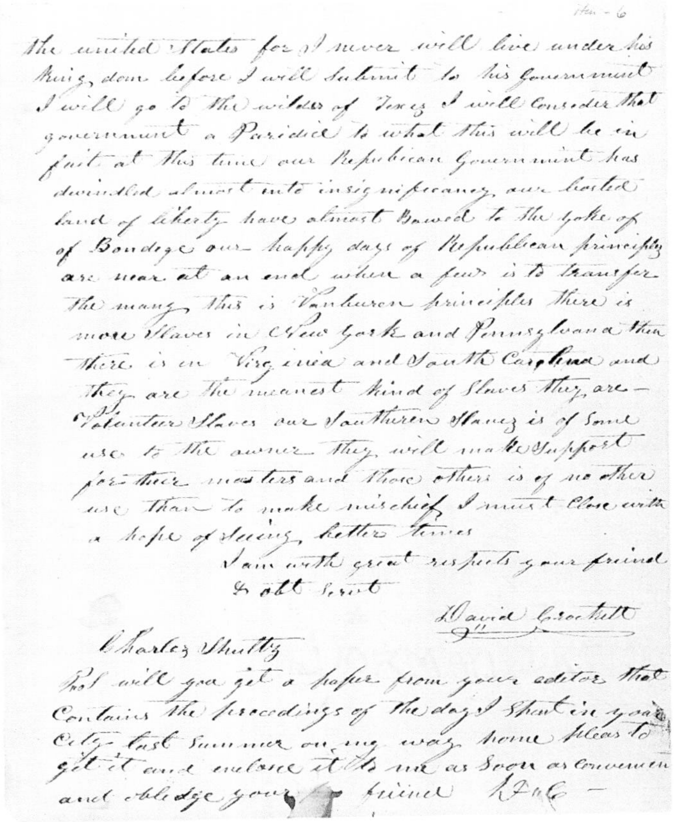
the united States for I never will live under his
Kingdom before I will Submit to his Government
I will go to the wilds of Texes I will Consider that
government a Paridice to what this will be in
fact at this time our Republican Government has
dwindled almost into insignificancy our boasted
land of liberty have almost Bowed to the yoke of
of Bondage our happy days of Republican principles
are near at an end when a few is to transfer
the many this is Vanburen principles there is
more Slaves in New York and Pennsylvania than
there is in Virginia and South Carolina and
they are the meanest kind of Slaves they are
Volunteer Slaves our Southeren Slavez is of Some
use to the owner they will make Support
for their masters and those others is of no other
use than to make mischief I must Close with
a hope of Seeing better times

I am with great respects your friend
& obt Servt

David Crockett

Charles Shultz
Pos will you get a paper from your editor that
Contains the proceedings of the day I Spent in your
City last Summer on my way home pleas to
get it and enclose it to me as Soon as convenien
and obledge your friend DC —

74. David Crockett. Autograph letter signed, dated Washington, [D.C.], 25 December 1834, to Charles Schultz.

Gilder Lehrman Collection
GLC 1162

Politician and frontiersman David Crockett, disgusted by events in Washington, was one of many Americans attracted to "the wild[s] of Texas" in the 1830s.

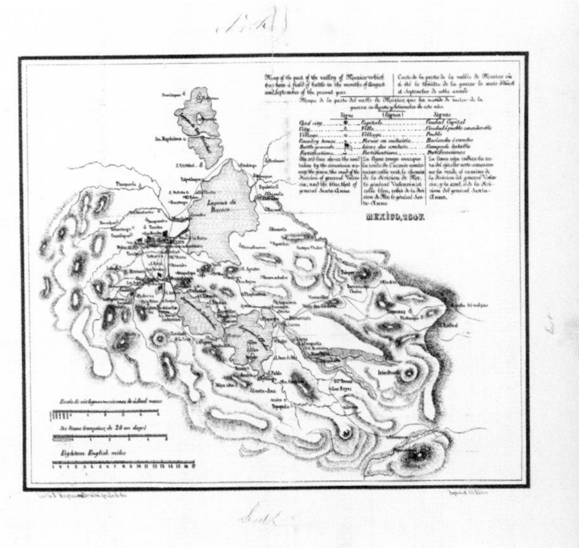

75. ***Map of the Part of the Valley of Mexico Which Has Been a Field of Battle in the Months of August and September of the Present Year.*** Aguila del Oro: M. Murguia, [1847?].

Gilder Lehrman Collection
GLC 155

This map of the interior of Mexico defines the area of battle during August and September 1847 as General Winfield Scott marched his troops toward Mexico City. Contreras and Churubusco, marked by American flags, were the sites of two of Scott's victories.

War with Mexico

Mexico, which still regarded Texas as its own, severed diplomatic relations with the United States when Congress voted for annexation. As President Polk ordered American troops to Texas under General Zachary Taylor, Mexico sent its own forces to the banks of the Rio Grande. Amid the rising tension that summer, an unsigned article about Texas annexation appeared in *The United States Magazine and Democratic Review*. It marked the debut of the term "manifest destiny." The author, later identified as the magazine's editor, John L. O'Sullivan, viewed the annexation of Texas as one step toward "the fulfillment of our manifest destiny to overspread the continent allotted by Providence for the free development of our yearly multiplying millions." For many Americans, the patriotic mission as defined by O'Sullivan justified war with Mexico.

On 13 May 1846, after American lives were lost in skirmishes with Mexican troops, the United States declared war. In a letter transmitting President Polk's war message to American consulates, Secretary of State James Buchanan stated, "Whilst we intend to prosecute the war with vigor, both by land and by sea, we shall bear the olive branch in one hand, and the sword in the other." To combat a Mexican army of 32,000, Congress authorized the enlistment of 50,000 volunteers to supplement the standing army of about 7,500. American troops were deployed in three principal operations: under Zachary Taylor in present-day northern Mexico, under Colonel Stephen Kearney in the west through what is now New Mexico and California, and under General Winfield Scott in the interior of Mexico (PL. 75).

The merits and conduct of the war were questioned by a number of Americans. Artillery officer Abner Doubleday, a member of Zachary Taylor's forces that had captured Monterrey, wrote a despondent, angry letter from there in early 1847.

> What can be more gloomy than the silent streets of a deserted city? The volunteers have committed outrage after outrage until only a few of the lowest class are left, with a few also whose poverty compels them to remain. If these things are not checked, they will bring a stain upon the American name which we can never efface.

The war was attacked by Whigs as expansionist. Some Whigs and other opponents of the war argued that its real purpose was to extend slavery into Mexico, where it was illegal. In the congressional elections of 1846, Whigs won a slim majority in the House. Among the new congressmen was Abraham Lincoln of Illinois. In a speech before the House on 12 January 1848, Lincoln argued the Whig view that the war was unconstitutional because Mexico had not attacked Americans on actual American soil. He assailed Polk for misleading the American public.

> [T]rusting to escape scrutiny by fixing the public gaze upon the exceeding brightness of military glory—that attractive rainbow that rises in showers of blood—that serpent's eye that charms to destroy—he plunged into [the war] and has swept on and on till, disappointed in his calculation of the ease with which Mexico might be subdued, he now finds himself he knows not where.

76. *General Scott's Victorious Entry into the City of Mexico.*
Hand-colored lithograph.
New York: N. Currier, 1849.

Gilder Lehrman Collection
GLC 2918.01

Winfield Scott's capture of Mexico City on 14 September 1847 led to the resumption of peace negotiations and an end to the Mexican war.

Lincoln's speech was delivered as the negotiations for peace were proceeding. By the Treaty of Guadalupe Hidalgo in 1848, Mexico ceded to the United States area that became the New Mexico, California, and Utah territories and agreed to the Rio Grande as the border of Texas. The treaty added 1,193,061 square miles of territory to the United States. Only 1,700 of the almost 13,000 American fatalities were the result of battle. The rest were killed by disease. Despite the dissent and terrible loss of life, many Americans considered the Mexican war glorious. For them, General Winfield Scott's victorious entry into Mexico City was the inevitable realization of the nation's "manifest destiny" (PL. 76). The resolution of the war, while establishing the coast-to-coast sweep of the United States with territorial gains, exacerbated the ongoing debate over the extension of slavery.

Intensification of Sectionalism

THE MISSOURI COMPROMISE of 1820, whereby Missouri was admitted as a slave state and Maine as a free state, only temporarily alleviated the nation's sectional conflict. During the next four decades, several circumstances made the issue of slavery increasingly pervasive. Rapid growth of the slave population further entrenched the system in the South. From just over 1.5 million slaves in 1820, the number more than doubled to 3.2 million by 1850. Also, the practice of slavery became more widespread with westward territorial expansion, particularly with the admission of Arkansas (1836) and Texas (1845). Such firsthand accounts of the horrors of slavery as *Narrative of the Life of Frederick Douglass* (1845), the Fugitive Slave Law of 1850, and other factors accelerated abolitionist militancy.

Northerners were divided on abolition. Some, regarding abolitionists as dangerous extremists, disrupted their rallies throughout the North. Southerners, terrified by Denmark Vesey's planned attack on Charleston in 1822, Nat Turner's rebellion in 1831, and other acts of slave resistance, felt threatened by the efforts of Northern abolitionists to distribute antislavery propaganda in their states. Many Southerners hardened their views. Writing to an abolitionist friend in the North in 1837, E. W. Taylor, a former Northerner, declared readiness for civil war.

> If these matters are going to be carried so far as to the separation of the Union and blood must be spilt, I fight for the South. I could plunge the dagger to the heart almost of a brother in such a glorious cause. It would be for Liberty, Liberty.

As the rift between the two regions deepened, many Northern and Southern politicians maintained a moderate course. They followed Henry Clay, deemed "the Great Compromiser" for his role in forging the Missouri Compromise, as he led in negotiating the Tariff Compromise of 1833, when South Carolina had threatened secession, and the Compromise of 1850, which was another attempt to resolve the question of slavery in the territories. Clay, a Kentuckian and slave owner, had a position on slavery similar to that of Thomas Jefferson and other founders. In 1831, he wrote:

> Slavery is undoubtedly a manifest violation of the rights of man. It can only be justified in America, if at all, by necessity.... That it entails innumerable mischiefs upon our country I think is quite clear.

I could plunge the dagger to the heart almost of a brother in such a glorious cause. It would be for Liberty, Liberty.

E. W. TAYLOR

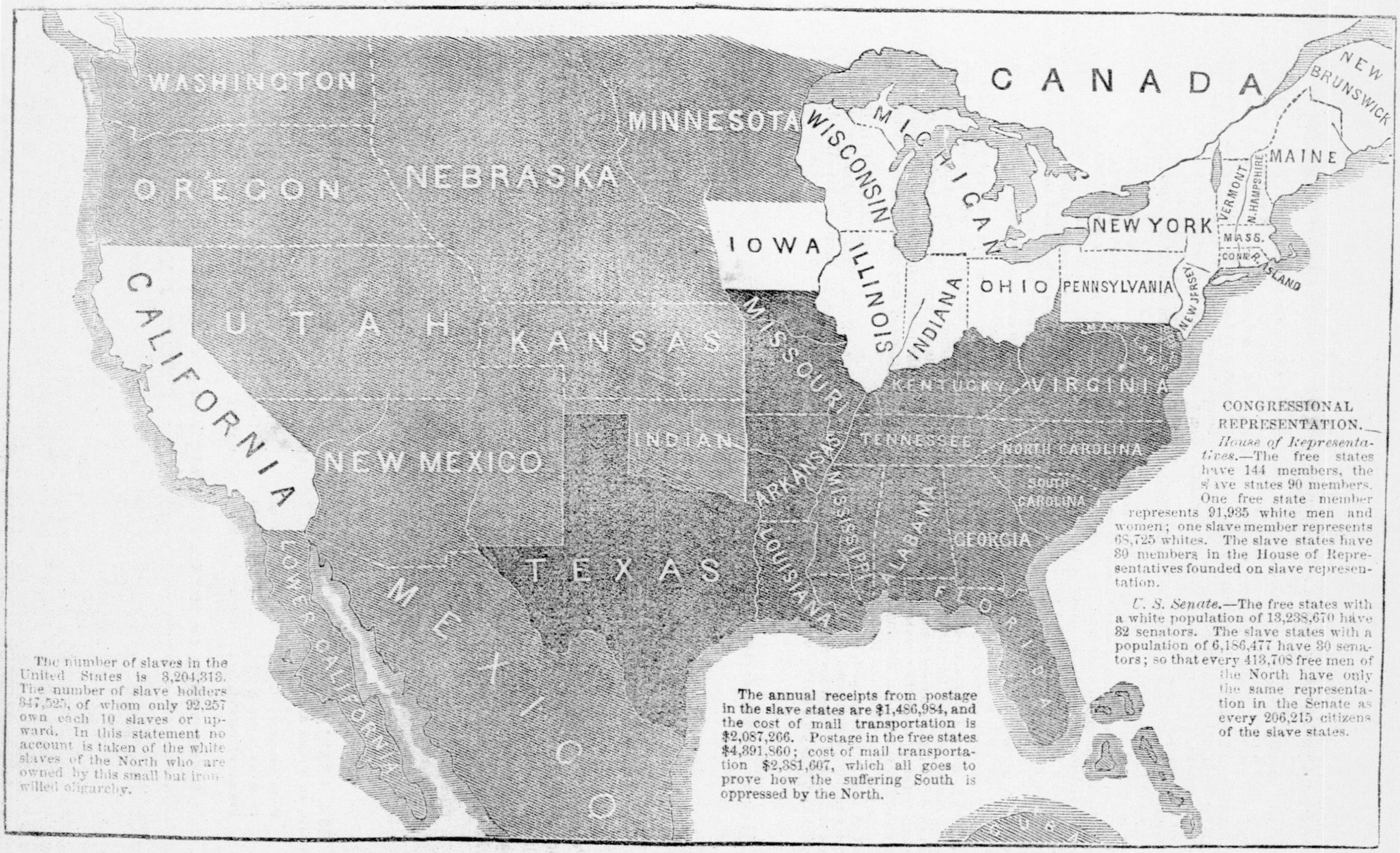
WASHINGTON
OREGON
NEBRASKA
MINNESOTA
CANADA
NEW BRUNSWICK
MAINE
WISCONSIN
MICHIGAN
IOWA
NEW YORK
VERMONT
N. HAMPSHIRE
MASS.
CONN.
R. ISLAND
CALIFORNIA
UTAH
KANSAS
ILLINOIS
INDIANA
OHIO
PENNSYLVANIA
NEW JERSEY
MISSOURI
KENTUCKY
VIRGINIA
INDIAN
NEW MEXICO
TENNESSEE
NORTH CAROLINA
SOUTH CAROLINA
ARKANSAS
MISSISSIPPI
ALABAMA
GEORGIA
LOUISIANA
TEXAS
FLORIDA
LOWER CALIFORNIA
MEXICO
CONGRESSIONAL REPRESENTATION.
House of Representatives.—The free states have 144 members, the slave states 90 members. One free state member represents 91,935 white men and women; one slave member represents 68,725 whites. The slave states have 30 members in the House of Representatives founded on slave representation.
U. S. Senate.—The free states with a white population of 13,238,670 have 32 senators. The slave states with a population of 6,186,477 have 30 senators; so that every 413,708 free men of the North have only the same representation in the Senate as every 206,215 citizens of the slave states.
The number of slaves in the United States is 3,204,313. The number of slave holders 347,525, of whom only 92,257 own each 10 slaves or upward. In this statement no account is taken of the white slaves of the North who are owned by this small but iron-willed oligarchy.
The annual receipts from postage in the slave states are $1,486,984, and the cost of mail transportation is $2,087,266. Postage in the free states $4,891,860; cost of mail transportation $2,381,607, which all goes to prove how the suffering South is oppressed by the North.

FREEDOM AND SLAVERY, AND THE COVETED TERRITORIES

77. *The Border Ruffian Code in Kansas.*
[New York: *Tribune* office, 1856].

Gilder Lehrman Collection
GLB 135

A pamphlet printed by Horace Greeley's *New-York Tribune* office supporting the 1856 Republican campaign included this map outlining the division between the North, South, and Western territories.

78. Louis-Adolphe Gautier, after George Caleb Bingham.
Stump Speaking. Hand-colored engraving. New York: Goupil and Co., 1856.

Gilder Lehrman Collection
GLC 4075

These engravings celebrating the nation's electoral procedures were made after paintings by George Caleb Bingham, an artist and politician from Missouri. They depict calm and order at a time of sectional discord.

Admitting the evil of slavery, Clay argued that the national government was not empowered to free slaves.

> Congress has no power, as I think, to establish any system of emancipation, gradual or immediate, in behalf of the present or any future generation. The several states alone, according to our existing institutions, are competent to make provision on that subject.

Further, Clay held, freed blacks could never be integrated into American society. As president of the American Colonization Society, he advocated that slaves emancipated by states be sent to live in Liberia.

Clay's fellow Whig William Henry Harrison endorsed the position that the federal government had no authority to interfere with slavery in the existing states. In 1838, two years before his election to the presidency, Harrison outlined his position for John Dillon, the author of a pamphlet on slavery.

> [O]ur Union is a union of sovereign independent states.... [I]n every particular where power is not expressly surrendered by that instrument to the general government, it is retained by the states.... The citizens of the free states have the right as individuals to give their opinions to their brethren in the slave states upon the subject of slavery as they can upon the subjects of internal improvements [and] extension of the right of voting, but they have no power whatever to control them upon any of these subjects.

Whereas there was consensus among many leading politicians that federal intervention to emancipate slaves would be unconstitutional,

79. John Sartain, after George Caleb Bingham. *The County Election.* Hand-colored engraving. New York: Goupil and Co., 1854.

Gilder Lehrman Collection
GLC 4074

debate over the extension of slavery became more fierce as the United States expanded westward.

The Compromise of 1850

The Compromise of 1850 evolved from disputes over slavery in the territories won by the United States at the end of the Mexican War in 1848. To resolve the crisis, Henry Clay, in early 1850, put forth several propositions that the Senate deliberated heatedly over the next several months. Precipitating one of the most famous debates in the Senate's history, the resolutions brought about the final confrontation of three of the nineteenth century's senatorial giants: Clay, Daniel Webster of Massachusetts, and John C. Calhoun of South Carolina. Calhoun died in March, while the debate was still in progress, and Webster left the Senate to become secretary of state before the compromise was voted.

Webster did, however, make a decisive mark on the final legislation. In March, while eloquently defending the sanctity of the Union, he condemned abolitionist extremism and urged Northerners to comply with a strengthened fugitive slave law. The speech, published soon after delivery, was intended to conciliate; however, it brought forth an enormous barrage of criticism in New England, particularly from noted abolitionists Ralph Waldo Emerson, Theodore Parker, and John Greenleaf Whittier. Though stung, Webster adhered to his position, and in July, delivered his final speech as a senator. He reiterated his intent to prevent sectional antagonism from escalating into civil war.

[L]ocal divisions are apt to warp the understandings of men and to excite a belligerent feeling between section and section.... Then comes belligerent legislation, and then an appeal to arms. The question is whether we have the true patriotism, the Americanism, necessary to carry through such a trial. For myself, sir, I propose to abide by the principles and purposes which I have avowed. I shall stand by the Union.

Legislation passed in September provided for the admission of California as a free state; the creation of the Utah and New Mexico territories, with the question of slavery left to their state constitutions at the time of admission to the Union; the abolishment of the slave trade in Washington, D.C.; and, most controversial in the North, a fugitive slave act with severe penalties for obstructing the return of escaped slaves to their owners.

The efforts of Webster and Clay to appease both sides did not, finally, work. The fugitive slave law was resented and, in many instances, disobeyed by Northerners. In 1851, James Buchanan, a Pennsylvania Democrat who would be elected president in 1856, urged residents of his home state to respect the law. "What madness it is in the people of the North," he wrote to a friend, "to insist upon the repeal or modification of the only measure of the compromise calculated to benefit the South." He further stipulated, "If we desire to perpetuate the Union, we must let the slaveholding states alone and suffer them to manage their domestic institutions according to their own discretion."

80. Thomas Hovenden. *The Last Moments of John Brown.* Etching on vellum. Philadelphia: George Gebble, 1885.

Gilder Lehrman Collection
GLC 737

John Brown's martyrdom remained a popular icon in the North after the Civil War. This etching by Thomas Hovenden is from a limited series based on his 1884 painting.

The Kansas-Nebraska Act

The next crisis over slavery in the territories occurred in 1854, when Congress passed the Kansas-Nebraska Act. Introduced by Illinois senator Stephen Douglas, the act made law his principle of "popular sovereignty," whereby residents of a territory determined whether it would apply for admission as a slave or free state. The act was a severe defeat to antislavery forces, for it established that the federal government could not intervene in the spread of slavery and subverted the Missouri Compromise provision that slavery would not extend above 36°30' north latitude. Turmoil ensued in Kansas, the southernmost and therefore more likely territory to seek admission as a slave state, as pro- and antislavery settlers battled for control (PL. 77).

John Brown

In 1855, crusading abolitionist John Brown traveled from Ohio to Kansas to aid opponents of slavery. The following year, with four of his sons and two other men, he executed five proslavery settlers at Pottawatomie Creek. This action made him a hero to many abolitionists and a fugitive from the federal government. He eluded capture and continued to engage in agitation. In 1859, with the financial assistance of abolitionists who had determined that slavery could not be ended peacefully, Brown led a raid on the federal arsenal at Harpers Ferry, Virginia. Convicted of treason, he was hanged on 2 December 1859 (PL. 80). In the North, he was commemorated by Ralph Waldo Emerson, Henry David Thoreau, and other abolitionists as a martyr to their cause (PL. 81). For Southerners, Brown's raid confirmed fears of Northerners' willingness to foment insurrection in their midst.

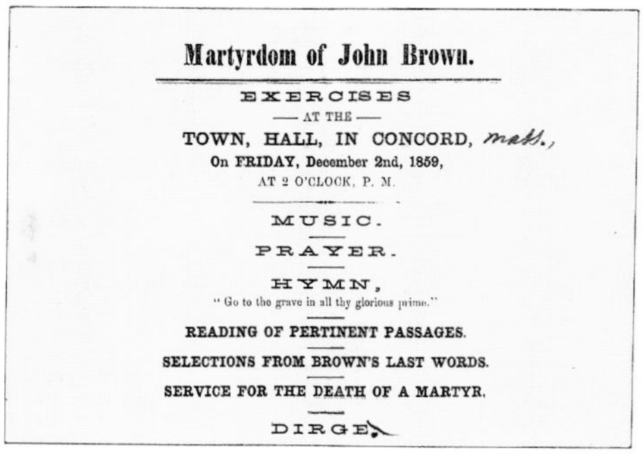
Martyrdom of John Brown.

EXERCISES

— AT THE —

TOWN, HALL, IN CONCORD, mass.,

On FRIDAY, December 2nd, 1859,

AT 2 O'CLOCK, P. M.

MUSIC.

PRAYER.

HYMN,

"Go to the grave in all thy glorious prime."

READING OF PERTINENT PASSAGES.

SELECTIONS FROM BROWN'S LAST WORDS.

SERVICE FOR THE DEATH OF A MARTYR.

DIRGE.

81. *Martyrdom of John Brown.*
Program for exercises held at the Town Hall, Concord, [Massachusetts], dated 2 December 1859.

Morgan Library
MA 884

After John Brown was arrested for his raid in Virginia, Northern supporters organized rallies on his behalf. This program was held in Boston on the day that he was hanged.

The Dred Scott Decision

In 1857, the United States Supreme Court issued one of its most influential and controversial decisions. The Dred Scott decision had immense political as well as legal impact (PL. 82). The case had arisen in 1846, when Dred Scott, the slave of a Missouri family, sued for freedom on the basis of having resided for a time in two free areas, the state of Illinois and the territory of Wisconsin. The Missouri State

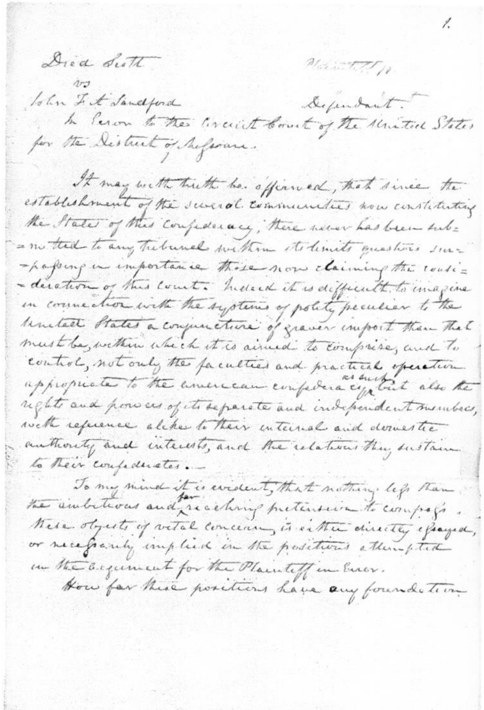
1.

Dred Scott
vs
John F. A. Sandford Defendant.
In Error to the Circuit Court of the United States for the District of Missouri.

It may with truth be affirmed, that since the establishment of the several communities now constituting the States of this Confederacy, there never has been submitted to any tribunal within its limits questions surpassing in importance those now claiming the consideration of this court. Indeed it is difficult to imagine in connection with the systems of polity peculiar to the United States a conjuncture of graver import than that must be, within which it is aimed to comprise, and to control, not only the faculties and practical operation appropriate to the American confederacy as such, but also the rights and powers of its separate and independent members, with reference alike to their internal and domestic authority and interests, and the relations they sustain to their confederates.—

To my mind it is evident, that nothing less than the ambitious and far reaching pretension to compass these objects of vital concern, is either directly essayed, or necessarily implied in the positions attempted in the argument for the Plaintiff in Error.

How far these positions have any foundation

82. Peter V. Daniel.
[Scott vs. Sandford: Opinion of Mr. Justice Daniel]. Autograph manuscript, Washington, D.C., 7 March 1857.

Gilder Lehrman Collection
GLC 2546

The Dred Scott case added to the growing divisiveness between North and South. Justice Peter V. Daniel agreed with the majority decision, adding, "The African was not deemed politically a person."

Supreme Court overturned a lower court's decision in favor of Scott, and the case was appealed to the United States Supreme Court. Determining that Scott must remain a slave, the court majority also declared unconstitutional the Missouri Compromise restriction of slavery to below 36°30' north latitude. In his concurring opinion, Justice Peter V. Daniel concluded that "the African race is not and never was recognized [as citizens] either by language or purposes of the [Constitution]." Such language indicated to antislavery forces that it was highly unlikely that slavery would ever wane or disappear in America. Slavery in the territories had been endorsed by the nation's highest court. The decision exacerbated the national crisis and became a focal point of the debates between Stephen Douglas and Abraham Lincoln.

"A House Divided" and
The Election of 1860

ABRAHAM LINCOLN ENTERED politics as a Whig, serving in the Illinois legislature from 1834 until 1842. After being elected to Congress in 1846 and serving one term, he returned to private law practice in Illinois (PL. 85). An enthusiastic supporter of Henry Clay's "American system" of economic development, Lincoln remained a Whig until the party ceased to be a major force in the presidential election of 1852. As the issue of slavery in the territories gradually overshadowed economic issues, the party disintegrated. When their 1852 platform endorsed the Compromise of 1850 and the Fugitive Slave Act, anti-slavery Whigs refused to support the party's candidate, General Winfield Scott. The election was won by Democrat Franklin Pierce.

In 1856, Lincoln joined the newly formed Republican party and actively supported its first presidential nominee, John C. Frémont. The Republicans espoused free labor as being more economically efficient than the slave system, recognized Congressional authority to control slavery in the territories, and advocated the admission of Kansas as a free state. The election was won by Democrat James Buchanan, who ran on a platform that supported the Kansas-Nebraska Act and Stephen Douglas's principle of popular sovereignty.

In June 1858, at the party's state convention in Springfield, Lincoln was nominated as the Republican candidate for the United States Senate. There, for the first time publicly, he applied the biblical passage "A house divided against itself shall not stand" to his own position on slavery in the territories. His handwritten notes from 1857 and early 1858 reveal that he had been developing the doctrine for some months before the convention. The leaf on which is recorded his earliest known use of the "house divided" phrase also confirms that he regarded the issue of slavery in the territories as more of a moral than a political question (PL. 84). "Why Kansas is neither the whole nor a tithe of the real question," he wrote. The fundamental question was how to halt the spread of slavery to "put it in the course of ultimate extinction." He was equally aware of the issue's divisive ramifications: "I believe the government cannot endure permanently half slave and half free."

> **In your hands, my dissatisfied fellow countrymen, and not in mine, is the momentous issue of civil war. . . .**
>
> **You have no oath registered in Heaven to destroy the government, while I shall have the most solemn one to "preserve, protect, and defend" it.**
>
> ABRAHAM LINCOLN, first inaugural address

83. [Abraham Lincoln]. Photograph by Alexander Hesler, Springfield, 3 June 1860.

Gilder Lehrman Collection
GLC 4347

In June 1860, soon after winning the Republican nomination for president, Abraham Lincoln was photographed in Springfield by Alexander Hesler of Chicago.

Additional pages of notes contain the germs of arguments that he used in campaign debates with his Democratic opponent, Stephen A. Douglas (PL. 86). On one, he denounced the doctrine of popular sovereignty as evasive and morally bankrupt: "Welcome or unwelcome, agreeable or disagreeable, whether this nation shall be an entire slave nation, is the issue before us.... The deceitful cloak of 'self-government' wherewith the 'sum of all villainies'

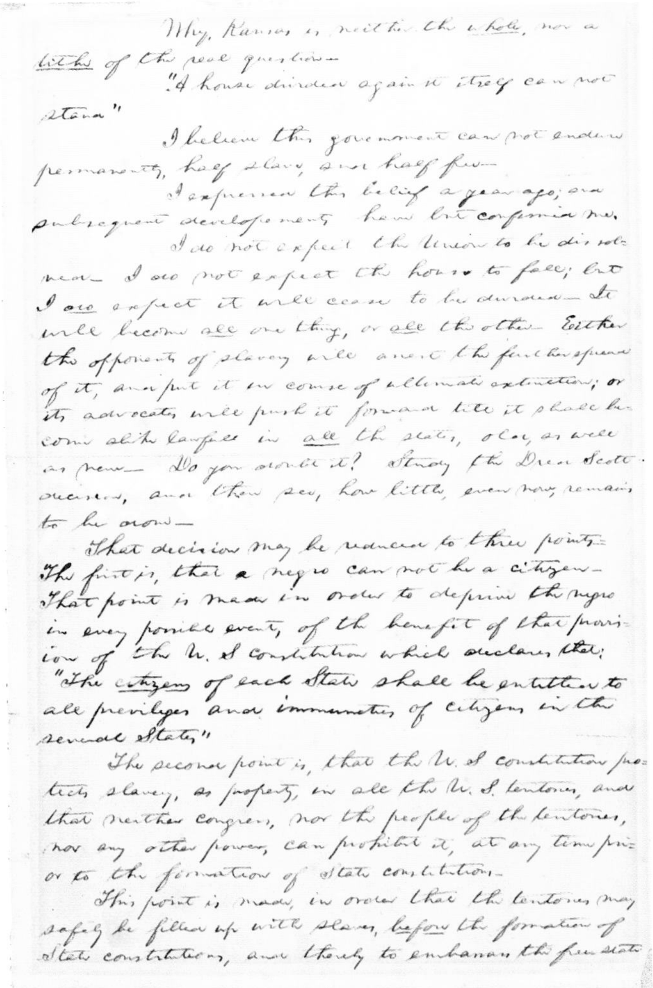

Why, Kansas is neither the whole, nor a tithe of the real question—

"A house divided against itself can not stand"

I believe this government can not endure permanently, half slave, and half free—

I expressed this belief a year ago; and subsequent developments have but confirmed me.

I do not expect the Union to be dissolved— I do not expect the house to fall; but I do expect it will cease to be divided— It will become all one thing, or all the other. Either the opponents of slavery will arrest the further spread of it, and put it in course of ultimate extinction; or its advocates will push it forward till it shall become alike lawful in all the states, old, as well as new— Do you doubt it? Study the Dred Scott decision, and then see, how little, even now, remains to be done—

That decision may be reduced to three points— The first is, that a negro can not be a citizen— That point is made in order to deprive the negro in every possible event, of the benefit of that provision of the U. S. constitution which declares that: "The citizens of each State shall be entitled to all previleges and immunities of citizens in the several States"

The second point is, that the U. S. constitution protects slavery, as property, in all the U. S. territories, and that neither congress, nor the people of the territories, nor any other power, can prohibit it, at any time prior to the formation of State constitutions—

This point is made, in order that the territories may safely be filled up with slaves, before the formation of State constitutions, and thereby to embarrass the free state

84. Abraham Lincoln.
Autograph fragment of a speech, [ca. 1858].

Gilder Lehrman Collection
GLC 2533

This leaf, containing notes for Lincoln's famous "house divided" speech, was preserved by Mary Todd Lincoln's first cousin Elizabeth Todd Grimsley, who kept a number of Lincoln's pre-presidential papers in a trunk at her home in Springfield.

85. [Abraham Lincoln].
Photograph attributed to Nicholas H. Shepherd, Springfield, 1846.

Morgan Library
MA 810

The earliest known photograph of Abraham Lincoln was taken in 1846, the year the thirty-seven-year-old lawyer was elected to Congress.

seeks to express and adorn itself must be torn from its hateful carcass." In another notation, he warned of the consequences of relinquishing the question of slavery to the ballot box, as Douglas advocated.

> If... he shall succeed in... bringing all to declare with him... that if any people want slaves they have a right to them—that Negroes are not men—[that they] have no part in the Declaration of Independence—that there is no moral question about slavery—that slavery and liberty are perfectly consistent... what barrier will be left against slavery being made lawful everywhere?

One fragment reveals Lincoln's conviction that a politician should exemplify moral leadership. "In this age and this country, public sentiment is everything. *With* it, nothing can fail;

against it, nothing can succeed. Whoever molds public sentiment goes deeper than he who enacts statutes or pronounces judicial decisions." Another indicates that the Declaration of Independence was central to his reasoning. "Most governments have been based, practically, on the denial of equal rights.... Ours began by affirming those rights." In public speeches of this time, Lincoln increasingly cited Jefferson's principles, as expressed in the Declaration, as the rationale for keeping slavery out of the territories.

At that time, senators were elected by their state's legislature, and Douglas won the seat by a small majority, even though Republicans had carried the popular vote. Still, Lincoln had refined his thinking on an issue of paramount importance to the nation and positioned himself as a viable Republican candidate.

In February 1860, Lincoln was invited to New York to speak at the Cooper Institute. Employing more historical detail than in any previous speech, he argued forcefully that the founders firmly established the precedent that the federal government had the right to forbid slavery in the territories. He also reasserted that the government should not interfere with slavery as it existed in the South. "Wrong as we think slavery is," he said, "we can yet afford to let it alone where it is." The goal was to confine it. He concluded with the rousing "Let us have faith that right makes might, and in that faith, let us, to the end, dare to do our duty, as we understand it." Confident that he had delivered an important address, he sought absolute accuracy in its publication. He wrote to its publisher, Charles Nott, "So far as [your changes are] intended merely to improve in grammar and elegance of composition, I am quite agreed; but I do not wish the sense changed, or modified, to a hair's breadth."

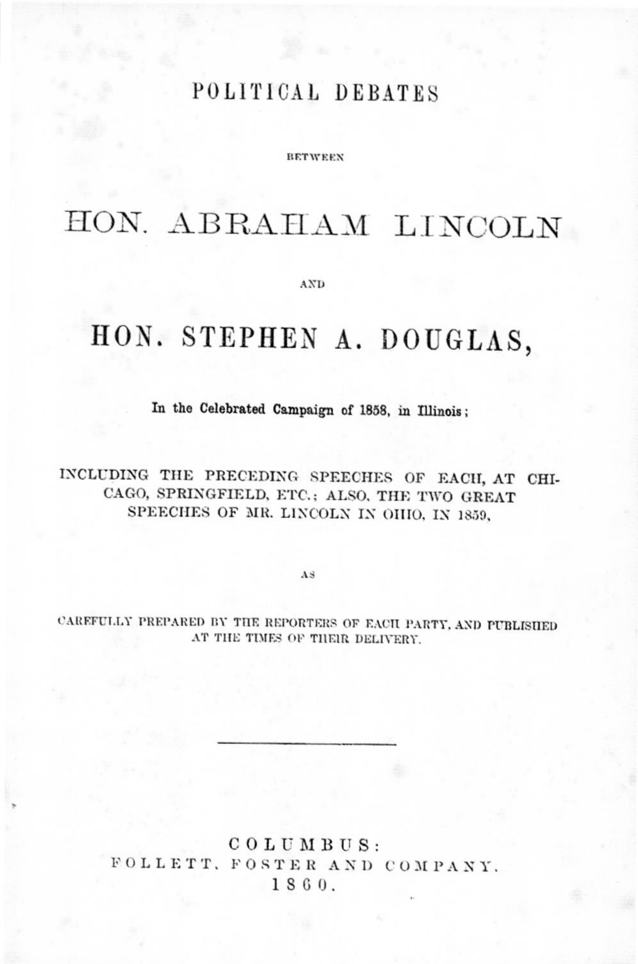
POLITICAL DEBATES

BETWEEN

HON. ABRAHAM LINCOLN

AND

HON. STEPHEN A. DOUGLAS,

In the Celebrated Campaign of 1858, in Illinois;

INCLUDING THE PRECEDING SPEECHES OF EACH, AT CHICAGO, SPRINGFIELD, ETC.; ALSO, THE TWO GREAT SPEECHES OF MR. LINCOLN IN OHIO, IN 1859,

AS

CAREFULLY PREPARED BY THE REPORTERS OF EACH PARTY, AND PUBLISHED AT THE TIMES OF THEIR DELIVERY.

COLUMBUS:
FOLLETT, FOSTER AND COMPANY.
1860.

86. ***Political Debates Between Hon. Abraham Lincoln and Hon. Stephen A. Douglas, in the Celebrated Campaign of 1858, in Illinois.*** Columbus: Follet, Foster & Co., 1860.

Gilder Lehrman Collection
GLC 2957

The debates between Abraham Lincoln and Stephen A. Douglas during their contest for the Senate catapulted Lincoln into the national political scene.

The Election of 1860

In May 1860, Republicans nominated Lincoln for president and Hannibal Hamlin for vice president. The Democratic party split, with Stephen A. Douglas heading the ticket of the Northern wing and John C. Breckinridge of Kentucky being the nominee of Southern Democrats. John Bell of Tennessee was the candidate of the Constitutional Union party. As was customary for presidential candidates at the time, Lincoln did not make campaign appearances. He remained at home in Springfield, while state party organizations conducted a spirited campaign of rallies, barbecues, and other mass gatherings. Throughout the North,

87. *Uncle Sam Making New Arrangements.*
Lithograph. New York: Currier and Ives, 1860.

Gilder Lehrman Collection
GLC 3488

In this cartoon, Uncle Sam awards Abraham Lincoln the White House, while James Buchanan packs his "dirty linen." Political cartoons were abundant during the 1860 campaign. To meet the demand, Currier and Ives published cartoons supporting not only Lincoln but the other three candidates as well.

88. *Wide-Awake Vocalist.* New York: E. A. Daggett, 1860.

Gilder Lehrman Collection
GLC 3430

This campaign songbook was printed for the Republican "Wide-Awakes."

Republican "Wide-Awake" clubs roused voters with parades and music (PL. 88). Lincoln received about 39 percent of the popular vote and, with his sweep of the Northern states, a majority of electoral votes (PLS. 87 and 89).

The euphoria of victory was short-lived. Six weeks after the election, on 20 December 1860, South Carolina seceded. In a letter of 31 December, Mary Todd Lincoln reflected the anxiety of many Americans, expressing hope "that the gloomy cloud, which now hangs over our beloved country, may soon be dispelled and that peace and harmony may be restored." But by the time she and her husband left for Washington, on 11 February 1861, six more states—Mississippi, Florida, Alabama, Georgia, Louisiana, and Texas—had seceded. Lincoln's parting remarks to Springfield friends and supporters were brief and grave. The words were written down later on the train, partially by him and partially by his friend and secretary, John G. Nicolay. "I now leave not knowing when, or whether ever, I may return, with a task before me greater than that which rested upon Washington."

Lincoln's carefully crafted inaugural address was delivered on 4 March 1861. He began in a conciliatory manner, emphasizing that he had "no purpose, directly or indirectly, to interfere with the institution of slavery in the states where it exists." He then stated his belief that "in contemplation of universal law and of the Constitution the Union of the states is perpetual." As his predecessor, Andrew Jackson, had proclaimed when South Carolina threatened secession in 1832, Lincoln affirmed the duty of the president to see "that the laws of the Union be faithfully executed in all the states." Also, as resolutely as had Jackson, Lincoln declared to Southerners that they would be responsible for the consequences of their actions.

> In your hands, my dissatisfied fellow countrymen, and not in mine, is the momentous issue of civil war. The government will not assail you. You can have no conflict without being yourselves the aggressors. You have no oath registered in Heaven to destroy the government, while I shall have the most solemn one to "preserve, protect, and defend" it.... Though passion may have strained,

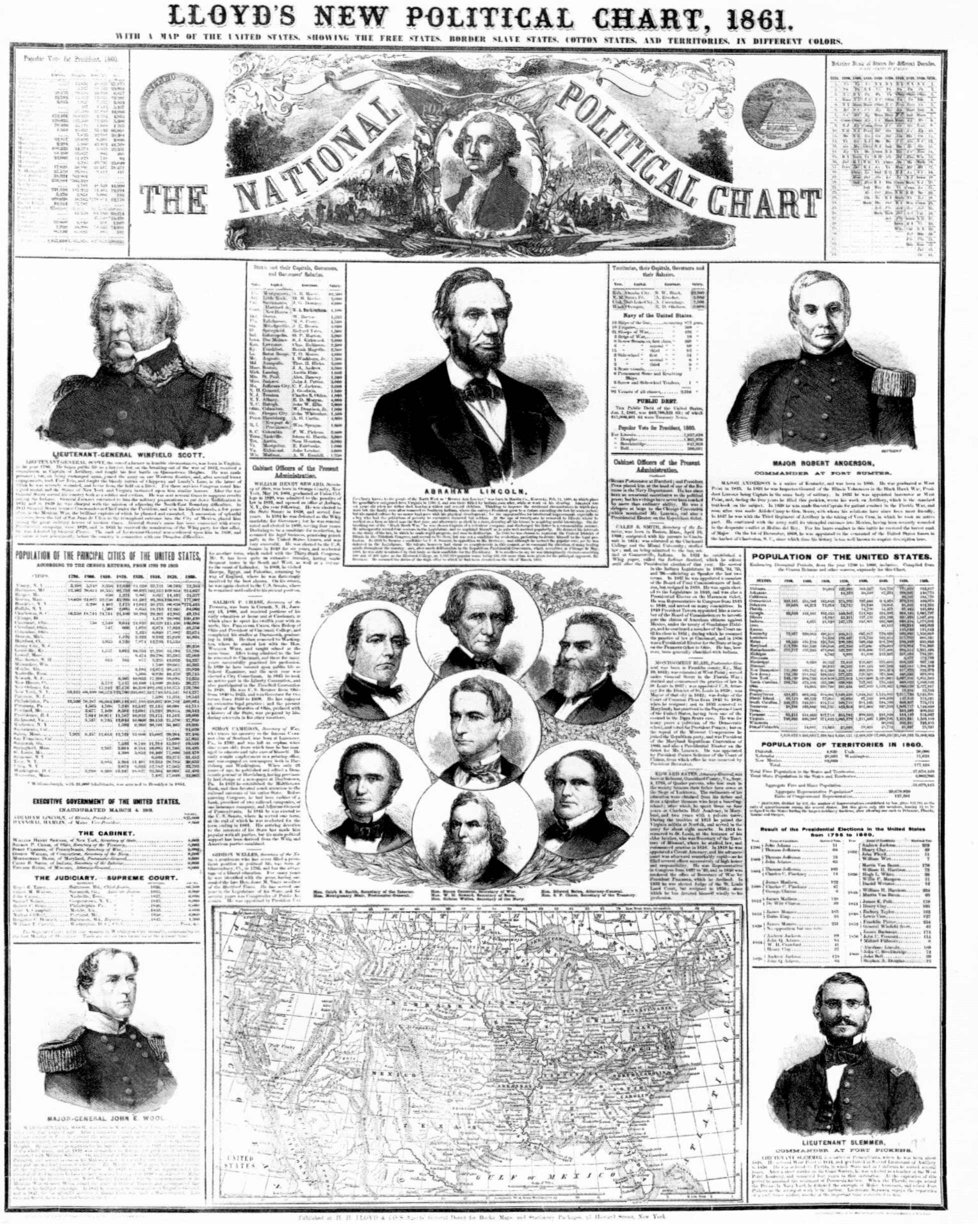

89. ***Lloyd's New Political Chart, 1861.*** *With a Map of the United States, Showing the Free States, Border Slave States, Cotton States and Territories in Different Colors.* New York: H. H. Lloyd, 1861.

Gilder Lehrman Collection
GLC 4243

This broadside, printed after the 1860 election, includes a map of the United States and provides various national statistics, the results of the vote by state, and information on officers in Lincoln's cabinet.

it must not break our bonds of affection. The mystic chords of memory, stretching from every battlefield and patriot grave to every living heart and hearthstone all over this broad land will yet swell the chorus of the Union, when again touched, as surely they will be, by the better angels in our nature.

The South was not mollified. On 12 April, South Carolina forces, under the command of General Pierre G. T. Beauregard, opened fire on Fort Sumter, and the Civil War began.

90. Abraham Lincoln.
Tintype portrait, [n.d.].

Morgan Library

CHECKLIST OF THE EXHIBITION

All items designated "The Gilder Lehrman Collection" are on deposit at the Morgan Library. With the exception of *Narrative of the Life of Frederick Douglass,* which was lent by The New-York Historical Society, all other items in the exhibition are from the permanent collection of the Morgan Library.

John Adams. Autograph letter signed, dated Quincy, [Massachusetts], 1 May 1807, to Benjamin Rush.

Heineman MS 118b. The Dannie and Hettie Heineman Collection. The gift of the Heineman Foundation, 1977.

John Adams. Autograph letter signed, dated Quincy, [Massachusetts], 3 October 1815, to the marquis de Lafayette.

MA 54. Purchased by Pierpont Morgan, 1912.

John Quincy Adams. Autograph letter signed, dated Washington, [D.C.], 3 March 1837, to the inhabitants of the 12th Congressional District of Massachusetts.

GLC 639.05. The Gilder Lehrman Collection.

Louisa May Alcott. Autograph letter signed, dated Concord, [Massachusetts], 11 May [1862], to Sophia Fo[o]rd.

MA 2099. The gift of John L. Cooley, 1961.

Aaron Arrowsmith. *A Map of the United States of North America Drawn from a Number of Critical Researches.* London: A. Arrowsmith, 1 January 1796, revised 1802.

GLC 4318. The Gilder Lehrman Collection.

John James Audubon. Autograph letter signed, dated London, 16 March 1828, to Walter Horton Bentley.

MA 1951. The gift of Henry S. Morgan, 1958.

John James Audubon. Autograph letter signed, dated London, 7 January 1835, to Luman Reed.

MA 1462. The gift of Henry S. Morgan, 1952.

John James Audubon. Autograph letter signed, dated Charleston, 10 January 1837, to Benjamin Phillips.

MA 3864. Purchased on the Fellows Fund, 1970.

John James Audubon. Autograph letter signed, dated New York, 27 September 1841, to William J. Weeks.

MA 1971. The gift of Henry S. Morgan, 1959.

John James Audubon. *The Birds of America; from Original Drawings by John James Audubon.* London: published by the author, 1827–38. Four volumes.

PML 44059–44062. The gift of Henry S. Morgan, 1952.

John James Audubon. *The Birds of America, from Drawings Made in the United States and Their Territories.* New York: J. J. Audubon; Philadelphia: J. B. Chevalier, 1840–44. Seven volumes.

PML 125612–125618. Purchased by Pierpont Morgan with the Irwin collection, 1900.

John James Audubon. "Niagara." Autograph manuscript unsigned of Episode XV in his *Ornithological Biography,* vol. I (1831), pp. 362–63.

MA 3212. Purchased on the Fellows Fund, 1977.

John James Audubon. *Ornithological Biography, or an Account of the Habits of the Birds of the United States of America; Accompanied by Descriptions of the Objects Represented in the Work Entitled The Birds of America, and Interspersed with Delineations of American Scenery and Manners.* Edinburgh: A. Black, 1831–49. Five volumes.

PML 44063–44067. The gift of Henry S. Morgan, 1952.

John James Audubon. Six drawings for *The Viviparous Quadrupeds of North America* (1845–48).

Provenance: Theodore Irwin.

Brown, or Norway, Rat. Preparatory study for plate 54. Watercolor and pencil. 24 1/2 x 32 5/8 inches (622 x 828 mm). Signed and dated at lower right, *Minnie's Land. Jany 18th 1843. / J. J. Audubon.*

Acc. no. 1976.12:1. Purchased by Pierpont Morgan with the Irwin collection, 1900.
PL. 65

Cat Squirrel. Preparatory study for plate 17. Watercolor and pencil. 36 3/4 x 24 1/4 inches (934 x 615 mm). Signed and dated, *New York Decr 9th 1841 / J. J. A.*

Acc. no. 1976.12:2. Purchased by Pierpont Morgan with the Irwin collection, 1900.
PL. 66

Common American Skunk. Preparatory study for plate 42. Watercolor and pencil. 33 x 24 1/2 inches (840 x 622 mm). Signed and dated at lower margin, *The Young drawn at Minnie's Land June 9th 1842. / The Adult drawn at Minnie's Land Jany 22^{d} 1843. From Nature by / John J. Audubon.*

Acc. no. 1976.12:3. Purchased by Pierpont Morgan with the Irwin collection, 1900.
PL. 59

Gray Rabbit. Preparatory study for plate 22. Watercolor and pencil. 23 7/8 x 34 5/16 inches (604 x 870 mm). Signed and dated, *May 21^{t} 1841* (opposite the female) *29th Augt 1841* (below young) *Winter Decr 16 1841* (opposite the male on recto and also on verso near note about the female) *New York J. J. A.* Inscription on verso in Audubon's hand, *I drew this Hare during one of the days of deepest sorrow / I have felt in my life, and my only solace was derived from my Labour.—This morning our beloved Daughter Eliza died at / 2 o'clock.—She is now in Heaven, and May our God for ever bless her Soul!*

Acc. no. 1976.12:4. Purchased by Pierpont Morgan with the Irwin collection, 1900.
PLS. 68–69

Migratory Squirrel. Preparatory study for plate 35. Watercolor and pencil. 34 1/4 x 23 7/8 inches (871 x 606 mm). Inscribed and dated, *New York, Octr 16th, 1841–.*

Acc. no. 1976.12:5. Purchased by Pierpont Morgan with the Irwin collection, 1900.

Woodchuck. Preparatory study for plate 2. Watercolor and pencil. 23 x 33 11/16 inches (584 x 855 mm). Signed and dated, *New York July 11th 1841. / J. J. A.*; variously inscribed throughout.

Acc. no. 1976.12:6. Purchased by Pierpont Morgan with the Irwin collection, 1900.
PL. 67

William Bartram. *Travels through North and South Carolina, Georgia, East and West Florida, the Cherokee Country, the Extensive Territories of the Muscogulges or Creek Confederacy, and the Country of the Chactaws. Containing an Account of the Soil and Natural Productions of Those Regions; Together with Observations on the Manners of the Indians.* Philadelphia: printed by James and Johnson, 1791; London: reprinted for J. Johnson, in St. Paul's Churchyard, 1794.

PML 3484. Purchased by Pierpont Morgan with the Irwin collection, 1900.

Nicholas Biddle. Letter signed, dated Bank of the United States, 25 January 1834, to William Rochester.

GLC 976. The Gilder Lehrman Collection.

Benjamin L. E. Bonneville. Autograph letter signed, dated [n.p., 1839?], to an unidentified general.

GLC 1233.6. The Gilder Lehrman Collection.

The Border Ruffian Code in Kansas. [New York: *Tribune* office, 1856].

GLB 135. The Gilder Lehrman Collection.
PL. 77

John Brown. Autograph letter signed, dated Springfield, Mass[achusetts], 16 April 1857, to Mary Brown.

GLC 2519. The Gilder Lehrman Collection.

[John Brown]. *The Last Moments of John Brown.* Etching on vellum by Thomas Hovenden. Philadelphia: George Gebble, 1885.

GLC 737. The Gilder Lehrman Collection.
PL. 80

[John Brown]. *Martyrdom of John Brown.* Program for exercises held at the Town Hall, Concord, [Massachusetts], 2 December 1859. Bound with autograph speeches of Emerson, Thoreau, et al., listed separately.

MA 884. Purchased by Pierpont Morgan with the Wakeman collection, 1909.
PL. 81

William Cullen Bryant. "The Death of the Flowers." Autograph manuscript signed, New York, 30 June 1830.

MA 34. Purchased by Pierpont Morgan, 1908.

James Buchanan. Autograph letter signed, dated Wheatland, near Lancaster, [Pennsylvania], 6 August 1851, to L. Harper.

GLC 4508. The Gilder Lehrman Collection.

James Buchanan. Printed letter signed, in the form of a "confidential circular," dated Washington, D.C., 14 May 1846, to Seth Sweetser.

GLC 1860.18. The Gilder Lehrman Collection.

John C. Calhoun. *Correspondence Between Gen. Andrew Jackson and John C. Calhoun, President and Vice President of the U. States, on the Subject of the Course of the Latter, in the Deliberations of the Cabinet of Mr. Monroe, on the Occurrences in the Seminole War.* Washington, [D.C.]: Duff Green, 1831.

GLC 3776. The Gilder Lehrman Collection.

The Camp Meeting at Sing Sing, New York, August, 1859. Engraving from *Harper's Weekly*, 10 September 1859.

GLC 1733. The Gilder Lehrman Collection.
PL. 24

Mark Catesby. Three of fourteen drawings for *The Natural History of Carolina, Florida and the Bahama Islands,* (London, 1731–43).

Provenance: Jekyll Catesby; Thomas Pennant; David Pennant; Henry S. Morgan.

Bead Snake. Study for vol. II, pl. 60, of *The Natural History.* Gouache. 10 7/16 x 14 3/4 inches (265 x 375 mm). Inscribed at upper right in pen and brown ink, *Bead S.*; numbered in a different hand, *60*; in left margin, *15*; in pencil at upper left, *Bead.* On verso in pen and brown ink, *Bead S / Bead Snake Potato.*

Acc. no. 1961.6:1. The gift of Henry S. Morgan, 1961.
PL. 63

Frutex Spinosus. Study for vol. II, pl. 100, of *The Natural History.* Gouache and pencil. 14 1/2 x 10 5/8 inches (371 x 268 mm). Inscribed in pen and brown ink at lower center, *Frutex Spinosus Buxi-folijs plurimis Simul Nascentibus, flore / tetrapeta-loide pendulo sordide flavo tubo longissimo, fructu—/ vali croceo, Semina parva continente—.*

Acc. no. 1961.6:3. The gift of Henry S. Morgan, 1961.
PL. 62

Plumeria flore rosea. Study for vol. II, pl. 92, of *The Natural History.* Gouache and pencil on vellum. 14 x 9 inches (355 x 228 mm).

Acc. no. 1961.6:2. The gift of Henry S. Morgan, 1961.

Mark Catesby. *The Natural History of Carolina, Florida and the Bahama Islands.* Autograph manuscript unsigned, [n.d.], of eleven pages of the appendix to vol. II (London, 1743).

MA 6038. The gift of Henry S. Morgan, 1954.

Mark Catesby. *The Natural History of Carolina, Florida and the Bahama Islands.* London: printed at the expense of the author, 1731–43. Two volumes.

PML 45708–45709. The gift of Henry S. Morgan, 1954.
PL. 64

Catherine Cauty. Printed abstinence pledge signed, dated [n.p.], 23 September 1842.

GLC 2542.27. The Gilder Lehrman Collection.

William Ellery Channing. "Concord Walks." Autograph manuscript, [n.d.], portions of which were published in *Thoreau, the Poet-Naturalist* (1873).

MA 1350. Purchased in 1950.

William Ellery Channing. *Mr. Channing's Lectures on Society* [broadside]. [N.p., n.d.].

MA 1350. Purchased in 1950.

Lydia Maria Child. Autograph letter signed, dated New York, 19 November 1844, to the Reverend John Pierpont.

MA 1756. The gift of Mrs. Edward W. McGlenen, Jr., 1955.
PL. 36

Henry Clay. Autograph letter signed, dated Washington, [D.C.], 6 March 1824, to J. D. Godman.

GLC 1028. The Gilder Lehrman Collection.
PL. 9

Henry Clay. Autograph letter signed, dated Washington, [D.C.], 10 August 1827, to the marquis de Lafayette.

MA 54. Purchased by Pierpont Morgan, 1912.

Henry Clay. Autograph letter signed, dated Ashland, [Kentucky], 17 May 1830, to George C. Washington.

MA 2141. The gift of Mrs. Benno Elkan, 1961.

Henry Clay. Autograph letter signed, dated Ashland, [Kentucky], 19 May 1831, to John Switzer.

GLC 3725. The Gilder Lehrman Collection.

James Fenimore Cooper. *The Deerslayer.* Autograph manuscript, [1841].

MA 82. Purchased by Pierpont Morgan, 1895.
PL. 52

James Fenimore Cooper. *The Last of the Mohicans; a Narrative of 1757.* London: John Miller, 1826. Three volumes.

GNR 4237. The bequest of Gordon N. Ray, 1987.

[James Fenimore Cooper]. *Notions of the Americans: Picked up by a Travelling Bachelor.* London: Henry Colburn, 1828. Two volumes.

PML 125589–125590.
Purchased by Pierpont Morgan before 1913.

James Fenimore Cooper. *Satanstoe.* Autograph manuscript, [1845].

MA 83. Purchased by Pierpont Morgan, [1895?].

David Crockett. Autograph letter signed, dated Washington, [D.C.], 4 April 1834, to John Drury.

GLC 931. The Gilder Lehrman Collection.

David Crockett. Autograph letter signed, dated Washington, [D.C.], 25 December 1834, to Charles Schultz.

GLC 1162. The Gilder Lehrman Collection.
PL. 74

Peter V. Daniel. [*Scott vs. Sandford: Opinion of Mr. Justice Daniel*]. Autograph manuscript, Washington, D.C., 7 March 1857.

GLC 2546. The Gilder Lehrman Collection.
PL. 82

Henry Dearborn. Autograph letter signed, dated War Department, 8 July 1803, to Callender Irvine.

MA 6016. Purchased before 1922.

Theodor de Bry. *Brevis Narratio eorum quae in Florida Americae provincia Gallis acciderunt.* Frankfort on the Main, 1590–1634. Seven volumes.

PML 3794–3800. Purchased by Pierpont Morgan with the Irwin collection, 1900.

Declaration of Independence. *In Congress, 4 July 1776, A Declaration* [broadside]. Washington, D.C.: W. J. Stone, [1823].

GLC 154.02. The Gilder Lehrman Collection.
PL. 2

Charles Dickens. Autograph letter signed, dated "on board the steamboat from Pittsburgh to Cincinnati," 1 April 1842, to William Charles Macready.

MA 106. Purchased before 1922.

Emily Dickinson. ["Two—were immortal—twice"]. Autograph manuscript, [ca. 1864].

MA 1641. The gift of W. H. McCarthy, Jr., 1955.

Abner Doubleday. Autograph letter signed, dated Monterrey, Mex[ico], 5 February 1847, to W. S. Rosecrans.

MA 4679. Purchased as the gift of Walter S. Rosenberry III, 1991.

Stephen A. Douglas. Autograph letter signed, dated Washington, D.C., 29 June 1860, to N. Prescott.

GLC 4625. The Gilder Lehrman Collection.

[Frederick Douglass]. *Expulsion of Negroes and Abolitionists from Tremont Temple, Boston, Massachusetts, on December 3, 1860.* Engraving from *Harper's Weekly*, 15 December 1860.

GLC 1733. The Gilder Lehrman Collection.
PL. 34

Frederick Douglass. *Narrative of the Life of Frederick Douglass, an American Slave. Written by Himself.* Boston: Anti-Slavery office, 1845.

Lent by The New-York Historical Society.

Ralph Waldo Emerson. *An Address Delivered Before the Senior Class in Divinity College, Cambridge, Sunday Evening, 15 July, 1838.* Boston: James Munroe and Company, 1838.

PML 38017. Purchased in 1944.

Ralph Waldo Emerson. Autograph letter signed, dated Concord, [Massachusetts], 8 August 1839, to Thomas Carlyle.

MA 2104. The gift of the Fellows, 1961.

Ralph Waldo Emerson. Autograph letter signed, dated Concord, [Massachusetts], 20 March 1854, to Richard Bentley.

MA 2105. The gift of the Fellows, 1961.
PL. 55

Ralph Waldo Emerson. Autograph letter, dated Concord, [Massachusetts], 3 August 1859, to Elizabeth Hoar.

MA 2106. The gift of the Fellows, 1961.

Ralph Waldo Emerson. "Behavior." Autograph manuscript, [ca. 1851], published in *The Conduct of Life* (1860).

MA 1035. Purchased in 1925.
PL. 57

[Ralph Waldo Emerson]. Carte-de-visite, signed.

MA 1939. The gift of George S. Hellman, 1958.

Ralph Waldo Emerson. "Considerations by the Way." Autograph manuscript, [ca. 1851], published in *The Conduct of Life* (1860).

MA 575. Purchased by Pierpont Morgan with the Wakeman collection, 1909.

Ralph Waldo Emerson. *Essays.* Boston: James Munroe and Company, 1841.

GNR 4264. The bequest of Gordon N. Ray, 1987.

[Ralph Waldo Emerson]. *Order of Services at the Ordination of Mr. Ralph Waldo Emerson as Junior Pastor of the*

Second Church and Society in Boston, on Wednesday, March 11, 1829. Boston: Isaac R. Butts, 1829.

MA 1756. The gift of Mrs. Edward W. McGlenen, Jr., 1955.

Ralph Waldo Emerson. *Representative Men. Seven Lectures.* London: John Chapman, 1850.

GNR 4269. The bequest of Gordon N. Ray, 1987.

Ralph Waldo Emerson, Henry David Thoreau, et al. Autograph speeches delivered at John Brown Relief and Memorial Meetings held at Salem and Concord, Massachusetts, 1859–60.

MA 884. Purchased by Pierpont Morgan with the Wakeman collection, 1909.

Abigail Kelley Foster. Autograph letter signed, dated Worcester, [Massachusetts], 9 March 1881, to Harriet Robinson.

GLC 2076. The Gilder Lehrman Collection.

Margaret Fuller. Autograph letter signed, dated Florence, 10 May 1850, to William Wetmore Story.

MA 1975. The gift of John L. Cooley, 1959.

[Margaret Fuller, J. F. Clarke, and Ralph Waldo Emerson]. *Memoirs of Margaret Fuller Ossoli.* Boston: Phillips, Sampson and Company, 1852.

PML 59490–59491. Purchased in 1968.

Robert Fulton. Autograph letter signed, dated Philadelphia, 25 January 1807, to [Robert R. Livingston].

GLC 3107, The Livingston Papers. The Gilder Lehrman Collection.

Albert Gallatin. *A Table of Indian Tribes of the United States, East of the Stony Mountains, Arranged According to Languages and Dialects* [broadside]. [N.p.], 1826.

PML 127693. The gift of Mrs. Margaret Gallatin Cobb, 1995.

William Lloyd Garrison. Autograph letter signed, dated Baltimore, [Maryland], 14 July 1830, to Ebenezer Dole.

GLC 4516. The Gilder Lehrman Collection.

William Lloyd Garrison. "The Free Mind." Autograph manuscript signed, Salem, [Massachusetts], 16 October 1858.

MA 6036. Probably purchased by Pierpont Morgan before 1913.
PL. 32

Louis-Adolphe Gautier, after George Caleb Bingham. *Stump Speaking* [hand-colored engraving]. New York: Goupil & Co., 1856.

GLC 4075. The Gilder Lehrman Collection.
PL. 78

Charles Goodyear. Autograph letter signed, dated New York, 20 August 1842, to Benjamin Stillman.

GLC 2480.9. The Gilder Lehrman Collection.

Horace Greeley. Autograph letter signed, dated New York, 1 March 1851, to E[lizabeth] O[akes] Smith.

GLC 496.26. The Gilder Lehrman Collection.

Horace Greeley. *The Crystal Palace and Its Lessons.* Autograph manuscript, [ca. 1852].

MA 6037. Purchased by Pierpont Morgan with the Ford collection.

Horace Greeley. *The Crystal Palace and Its Lessons.* New York: DeWitt and Davenport, 1852.

PML 125594. Purchased by Pierpont Morgan with the Ford collection.

Angelina Emily Grimké. *Appeal to the Christian Women of the South.* [New York: American Anti-Slavery Society, 1836].

GLB 243. The Gilder Lehrman Collection.
PL. 35

Alexander Hamilton, James Madison, and John Jay. *The Federalist: A Collection of Essays.* New York: J. and A. McLean, 1788.

GLC 1551. The Gilder Lehrman Collection.

William Henry Harrison. Autograph letter signed, dated Bogotá, [Colombia], 3 August 1829, to J. Cleves Short.

GLC 632. The Gilder Lehrman Collection.

William Henry Harrison. Autograph letter signed, dated North Bend, [Ohio], 12 December 1838, to John B. Dillon.

GLC 2946. The Gilder Lehrman Collection.

Nathaniel Hawthorne. [American notebooks]. Autograph manuscript journal in six volumes, dated 1835–53.

MA 569, 577–580. Purchased by Pierpont Morgan with the Wakeman collection, 1909.

MA 3100. The gift of Mrs. Charles W. Engelhard, 1977.

Nathaniel Hawthorne. Autograph letter signed, dated Salem, 28 September 1819, to Maria Louisa Hathorne.

MA 611 (1). Purchased by Pierpont Morgan with the Wakeman collection, 1909.

Nathaniel Hawthorne. *The Blithedale Romance.* Autograph manuscript signed, [1852].

MA 573. Purchased by Pierpont Morgan with the Wakeman collection, 1909.
PL. 26

Nathaniel Hawthorne. [English notebooks; French and Italian notebooks]. Autograph manuscript journal of his travels, in eleven volumes, dated 1853–62.

MA 581–591. Purchased by Pierpont Morgan with the Wakeman collection, 1909.

Nathaniel Hawthorne. *The Scarlet Letter.* Autograph manuscript title and contents leaf, [1850].

MA 571. Purchased by Pierpont Morgan with the Wakeman collection, 1909.
PL. 48

Hinton Rowan Helper. *Compendium of the Impending Crisis of the South.* New York: A. B. Burdick, 1857.

GLC 267.74. The Gilder Lehrman Collection.

Harm Jan Huidekoper. Autograph letter signed, dated Meadville, Pennsylvania, 28 May 1829, to the Reverend John Pierpont.

MA 1756. The gift of Mrs. Edward W. McGlenen, Jr., 1955.

Washington Irving. *Astoria, or, Anecdotes of an Enterprise Beyond the Rocky Mountains.* Portion of the autograph manuscript, [ca. 1836], in an album with the autograph manuscript of Irving's *Abbotsford,* [1835].

MA 4718.The gift of Irving Kingsford, 1991.

Washington Irving. *A Chronicle of the Conquest of Granada.* Autograph manuscript, [1826–28].

MA 681 (Title page and introduction).

Purchased in 1911.

MA 1214 (Chapters 1–19). Purchased in 1945.

MA 201 (Chapters 20–end). Purchased by Pierpont Morgan before 1913.

Washington Irving. *A Chronicle of the Conquest of Granada. From the Mss. of Fray Antonio Agapida.* Paris: Baudry, at the Foreign Library, 1829. Printed by Jules Didot, Sr. Three volumes.

GNR 4354. The bequest of Gordon N. Ray, 1987.

[Washington Irving]. Daguerreotype by Mathew Brady, [New York, 1849].

MA 201. Purchased by Pierpont Morgan before 1913.
PL. 47

Washington Irving. *Life of George Washington.* Approximately thirty-nine pages of the autograph manuscript, [1859].

MA 1300. Purchased by Pierpont Morgan before 1913.

PML 58492. The gift of Mrs. John J. Ide, 1968.

Washington Irving. *Sketch Book of Geoffrey Crayon Gent.* New York: G. P. Putnam, 1864.

PML 125587. Purchased by Pierpont Morgan before 1913.

Andrew Jackson. Autograph letter signed, dated Camp near Fort Williams, 25 April 1814, to Rachel Jackson.

GLC 522. The Gilder Lehrman Collection.
PL. 20

Andrew Jackson. Autograph letter signed, dated Headquarters, Division of the South, Nashville, [Tennessee], 23 October 1816, to James Monroe.

GLC 151. The Gilder Lehrman Collection.

Andrew Jackson. Autograph letter signed, dated Knoxville, 26 March 1819, to Major William B. Lewis.

MA 811. Purchased by Pierpont Morgan with the Ford collection.
PL. 8

Andrew Jackson. Autograph letter signed, dated Washington, [D.C.], 11 January 1825, to Major William B. Lewis.

MA 811. Purchased by Pierpont Morgan with the Ford collection.

Andrew Jackson. Autograph letter signed, dated Washington [D.C.], 27 February 1825, to Major William B. Lewis.

MA 811. Purchased by Pierpont Morgan with the Ford collection.

Andrew Jackson. Autograph letter signed, dated Washington, D.C., 18 July 1831, to R. G. Dunlap.

GLC 1690. The Gilder Lehrman Collection.

Andrew Jackson. Autograph letter signed, dated Washington, [D.C.], 4 March 1834, to Moses Dawson.

GLC 1736. The Gilder Lehrman Collection.

Andrew Jackson. Autograph letter signed, dated Hermitage, Tennessee, 8 July 1844, to William Russell.

GLC 4365. The Gilder Lehrman Collection.

Andrew Jackson. Check signed, dated Washington, D.C., 8 January 1835, to Andrew Jackson, Jr.

GLC 1994.01. The Gilder Lehrman Collection.
PL. 16

[Andrew Jackson]. Engraving by James B. Longacre, after a painting by Thomas Sully. From an extra-illustrated copy of John Trumbull's *Autobiography and Reminiscences.* New York: [Wiley & Putnam], 1841–73.

PML 18081–18085. Purchased by Pierpont Morgan, 1908.
PL. 7

Andrew Jackson. *Farewell Address of Andrew Jackson* [broadside]. [New York]: Israel Sackett, [1837].

GLC 3680. The Gilder Lehrman Collection.
PL. 18

[Andrew Jackson]. Funeral ribbon. [New York], 1845.

MA 6035.
PL. 17

[Andrew Jackson]. *Monumental Inscriptions* [broadside]. [N.p., 1828].

GLC 1825. The Gilder Lehrman Collection.
PL. 10

Andrew Jackson. *President's Message* [broadside]. Published as a *Hartford Times* Extra, 9 December 1829.

GLC 2009. The Gilder Lehrman Collection.

Andrew Jackson. *Proclamation, by Andrew Jackson, President of the United States* [broadside, on silk]. New York: G. F. Hopkins, 10 December 1832.

GLC 1895. The Gilder Lehrman Collection.
PL. 13

[Rachel Jackson]. Miniature attributed to Mary Catherine Strobel. Watercolor on ivory.

GLC 2793.19. The Gilder Lehrman Collection.
PL. 11

Edwin James, comp. *Account of an Expedition from Pittsburgh to the Rocky Mountains, Performed in the Years 1819 and '20, by Order of the Hon. J. C. Calhoun, Sec'y of War: Under the Command of Major Stephen H. Long. From the Notes of Major Long, Mr. T. Say, and Other Gentlemen of the Exploring Party.* Philadelphia: H. C. Carey and I. Lea, 1823.

GLC 4143. The Gilder Lehrman Collection.

Thomas Jefferson. Autograph letter signed, dated [Monticello], 6 December 1813, to Baron Alexander von Humboldt.

Heineman MS 118. The Dannie and Hettie Heineman Collection. The gift of the Heineman Foundation, 1977.

Thomas Jefferson. Autograph letter signed, dated Monticello, 7 February 1820, to James Ronaldson.

GLC 496.41. The Gilder Lehrman Collection.

Thomas Jefferson. Autograph letter signed, dated Monticello, 26 December 1820, to the marquis de Lafayette.

MA 54. Purchased by Pierpont Morgan, 1912.
PL. 5

Thomas Jefferson. Autograph letter signed, dated Monticello, 5 September 1822, to Samuel McKay.

GLC 639.14. The Gilder Lehrman Collection.

Thomas Jefferson. Autograph letter signed, dated Monticello, 28 October 1822, to the marquis de Lafayette.

MA 54. Purchased by Pierpont Morgan, 1912.

Thomas Jefferson. *Notes on the State of Virginia.* Paris: privately printed by Phillipe Denis Pierres, 1785.

PML 3734. Purchased by Pierpont Morgan with the Irwin collection, 1900.
PL. 19

Thomas Jesup. Letter signed, dated Fort Mitchell, [Florida Territory], 18 June 1836, to Winfield Scott.

GLC 2640. The Gilder Lehrman Collection.

Andrew Johnson. Autograph letter signed, dated Washington, D.C., 23 January 1858, to David T. Patterson.

GLC 324. The Gilder Lehrman Collection.

John Beauchamp Jones. "Thoughts on the Literary Prospects of America," in *Burton's Gentleman's Magazine and American Monthly Review.* Philadelphia: William E. Burton, November 1839.

PML 16850. Purchased by Pierpont Morgan, 1910.

Rufus King. *Substance of Two Speeches, Delivered in the Senate of the United States on the Missouri Bill.* New York: Kirk and Mercein, 1819.

GLC 2384. The Gilder Lehrman Collection.

Henry Lee. *A Vindication of the Character and Public Services of Andrew Jackson; in Reply to the Richmond Address, Signed by Chapman Johnson, and to Other Electioneering Calumnies.* Boston: True and Greene, 1828.

GLB 100. The Gilder Lehrman Collection.
PL. 12

The Legion of Liberty! And Force of Truth, Containing the Thoughts, Words, and Deeds, of Some Prominent Apostles, Champions, and Martyrs. 10th edition. New York: American Anti-Slavery Society, 1847.

Archives of the Morgan Library.
PL. 30

Jacques le Moyne de Morgues, attributed to. *Sketchbook.* Twenty-nine drawings on sixty-eight leaves, many of which serve as cover sheets for the drawings. Tempera with some silver and gold wash, over faint indications in black chalk; bound in limp vellum tooled in gold. Leaf: 7 1/8 x 5 1/2 inches (183 x 142 mm). Binding: 7 1/3 x 6 inches (185 x 150 mm).

Acc. no. 1975.18. Purchased as the gift of Henry S. Morgan, Mr. and Mrs. William S. Paley, Mr. and Mrs. Richard Salomon, and Mrs. Carl Stern, 1975.
PLS. 60–61

Abraham Lincoln. *The Address of the Hon. Abraham Lincoln, in Indication of the Policy of the Framers of the Constitution and the Principles of the Republican Party, Delivered at Cooper Institute, February 27th, 1860.* Charles C. Nott and Cephas Brainerd, eds. New York: George P. Nesbitt & Co., 1860.

GLC 533. The Gilder Lehrman Collection.

Abraham Lincoln. Autograph fragment of a speech beginning "In this age, and this country, public sentiment is every thing." [Ca. 1858].

MA 230. Purchased by Pierpont Morgan before 1913.

Abraham Lincoln. Autograph fragment of a speech beginning "Made so plain by our good Father in Heaven, that all feel and understand it, even down to brutes and creeping insects." [Ca. 1858].

GLC 3251. The Gilder Lehrman Collection.

Abraham Lincoln. Autograph fragment of a speech beginning "Welcome, or unwelcome, agreeable, or disagreeable, whether this nation shall be an entire slave nation, is the issue before us." [Ca. 1858].

MA 230. Purchased by Pierpont Morgan before 1913.

Abraham Lincoln. Autograph fragment of a speech beginning "Why, Kansas is neither the whole, nor a tithe of the real question." [Ca. 1858].

GLC 2533. The Gilder Lehrman Collection.
PL. 84

Abraham Lincoln. Autograph letter signed, dated Springfield, Illinois, 31 May 1860, to Charles C. Nott.

GLC 4436. The Gilder Lehrman Collection.

Abraham Lincoln. Autograph list of election results in Sangamon County, Illinois, dated Sangamon County, Illinois, 9 September 1842, to [Mary Todd].

GLC 1978. The Gilder Lehrman Collection.

Abraham Lincoln. "The Bear Hunt." Autograph manuscript, [Springfield, ca. 6 September 1846].

MA 229. Purchased by Pierpont Morgan, 1905.

[Abraham Lincoln]. Campaign tokens, [1860].

GLB 99. The Gilder Lehrman Collection.

Abraham Lincoln. *Inaugural Message of Abraham Lincoln* [broadside]. Published as a *Chicago Tribune* Extra, 4 March 1861.

GLC 2316. The Gilder Lehrman Collection.

[Abraham Lincoln]. Photograph by Alexander Hesler, Springfield, 3 June 1860.

GLC 4347. The Gilder Lehrman Collection.
PL. 83

[Abraham Lincoln]. Photograph attributed to Nicholas H. Shepherd, Springfield, 1846.

MA 810. Purchased by Pierpont Morgan, 1906 or 1910.
PL. 85

Abraham Lincoln. *Speech of Mr. Lincoln of Illinois on the Reference of the President's Message in the House of Representatives, Wednesday, Jan. 14, 1848.* Washington: J. & G. S. Gideon, 1848.

GLC 1638. The Gilder Lehrman Collection.

[Abraham Lincoln]. Tintype portrait, ca. 1858.

GLC 3950. The Gilder Lehrman Collection.

[Abraham Lincoln]. Tintype portrait, [n.d.]

Purchased by Pierpont Morgan before 1913.
PL. 90

[Abraham Lincoln]. *Uncle Sam Making New Arrangements* [lithograph]. New York: Currier and Ives, 1860.

GLC 3488. The Gilder Lehrman Collection.
PL. 87

[Abraham Lincoln]. U.S. Patent Office. *Abraham Lincoln, of Springfield, Illinois. Buoying Vessels Over Shoals.* Patent No. 6,469, dated 22 May 1849.

GLC 1304. The Gilder Lehrman Collection.
PL. 72

[Abraham Lincoln]. *Wide-Awake Vocalist* [songbook]. New York: E. A. Daggett, 1860.

GLC 3430. The Gilder Lehrman Collection.
PL. 88

[Abraham Lincoln and Stephen A. Douglas]. *Political Debates Between Hon. Abraham Lincoln and Hon. Stephen A. Douglas, in the Celebrated Campaign of 1858, in Illinois.* Columbus: Follet, Foster & Co., 1860.

GLC 2957. The Gilder Lehrman Collection.
PL. 86

[Abraham Lincoln, Stephen A. Douglas, and John Bell]. Campaign tokens, [1860].

GLC 4102. The Gilder Lehrman Collection.

Mary Todd Lincoln. Autograph letter signed, dated Springfield, 31 December [1860], to Fanny Barrow.

GLC 4030. The Gilder Lehrman Collection.

Lloyd's New Political Chart, 1861. *With a Map of the United States, Showing the Free States, Border Slave States, Cotton States and Territories in Different Colors* [broadside]. New York: H. H. Lloyd, 1861.

GLC 4243. The Gilder Lehrman Collection.
PL. 89

Henry Wadsworth Longfellow. "The Children's Hour." Autograph manuscript signed, [n.d.].

MA 623. Purchased by Pierpont Morgan with the Wakeman collection, 1909.

Henry Wadsworth Longfellow. *The Courtship of Miles Standish, and Other Poems.* London: W. Kent & Co., 1858.

GNR 4512. The bequest of Gordon N. Ray, 1987.

Henry Wadsworth Longfellow. *Outre-Mer; a Pilgrimage Beyond the Sea.* New York: Harper & Brothers, 1835. Provenance: James Russell Lowell. Two volumes.

PML 75348–75349. The bequest of Tessie Jones in memory of her father, Herschel V. Jones, 1968.

Henry Wadsworth Longfellow. *Poems on Slavery.* Cambridge: John Owen, 1842.

PML 125591. Purchased by Pierpont Morgan before 1913.

Henry Wadsworth Longfellow. *The Song of Hiawatha.* London: G. Routledge & Co., 1856.

GNR 4510. The bequest of Gordon N. Ray, 1987.
PL. 45

Henry Wadsworth Longfellow. *Syllabus de la grammaire italienne.* Boston: Gray et Bowen, 1832.

PML 125588. Purchased by Pierpont Morgan before 1913.

James Russell Lowell and Robert Carter, eds. *The Pioneer: A Literary and Critical Magazine.* Boston: Leland and Whiting, 1843. Three issues.

PML 125584–125586. Purchased by Pierpont Morgan before 1913.
PL. 42

James Madison. Autograph letter signed, dated Montpelier, [Virginia], 25 November 1820, to the marquis de Lafayette.

MA 54. Purchased by Pierpont Morgan, 1912.
PL. 6

Map of the Part of the Valley of Mexico Which Has Been a Field of Battle in the Months of August and September of the Present Year. Aguila del Oro: M. Murguia, [1847?].

GLC 155. The Gilder Lehrman Collection.
PL. 75

John Marshall. [*Osborn v. the Bank of the U.S.*]. Autograph manuscript, [Washington], 1824.

GLC 3653. The Gilder Lehrman Collection.
PL. 15

Harriet Martineau. *Society in America.* Autograph manuscript, [ca. 1836–37].

MA 873. Purchased by Pierpont Morgan, 1910.

The May Session of the Woman's Rights Convention. Engraving from *Harper's Weekly*, 11 June 1859.

GLC 1733. The Gilder Lehrman Collection.
PL. 37

Cyrus McCormick. Autograph letter signed, dated National Hotel, Washington, [D.C.], 24 June 1852, to the President of the Agricultural Convention.

GLC 974. The Gilder Lehrman Collection.

Thomas L. McKenney and James Hall. *History of the Indian Tribes of North America, with Biographical Sketches and Anecdotes of the Principal Chiefs. Embellished with One Hundred and Twenty Portraits, from the Indian Gallery in the Department of War, at Washington.* Philadelphia: D. Rice & A. N. Hart, 1855. Three volumes.

PML 125596–125598.

John Melish. *A Map of the United States with the Contiguous British and Spanish Possessions.* Engraved by J. Vallance and H. S. Tanner. Philadelphia: James Fmlayson, 1823, copyright 1820.

GLC 4319. The Gilder Lehrman Collection.
PL. 4

Herman Melville. *Moby-Dick; or, The Whale.* New York: Harper & Brothers, 1851.

PML 75359. The bequest of Tessie Jones in memory of her father, Herschel V. Jones, 1968.

A Mirror for the Intemperate [broadside, on silk]. Boston: N. Boynton, [1831].

GLB 200. The Gilder Lehrman Collection.
PL. 28

Samuel F. B. Morse. Autograph description and drawing of the telegraph, [n.d.].

MA 901. Purchased by Pierpont Morgan, 1905.
PL. 71

An Ordinance to Dissolve the Union Between the State of South Carolina and Other States United with Her Under the Compact Entitled "The Constitution of the United States of America." Published as a *Charleston [South Carolina] Mercury* Extra, 20 December 1860.

GLC 2688. The Gilder Lehrman Collection.

Septimus Harry Palairet and M. A. Palairet. Illustrated autograph manuscript journal of their travels in America, 1843.

MA 2244. The gift of Arnold Whitridge, 1962.
PL. 70

John Pierpont. *The Anti-Slavery Poems of John Pierpont.* Boston: O. Johnson, 1843.

Archives of the Morgan Library.

Edgar Allan Poe. Autograph letter signed, dated [New York, November 1845], to John Augustus Shea.

MA 621. Purchased by Pierpont Morgan, 1909.
PL. 41

[Edgar Allan Poe]. Daguerreotype by Masury & Hartshorn, [Providence, Rhode Island, November 1848].

MA 621. Purchased by Pierpont Morgan, 1909.
PL. 40

Edgar Allan Poe. *Hans Phaall* [later published as *The Unparalleled Adventure of One Hans Pfaall*]. Autograph manuscript signed, [April or May 1835].

MA 950. Purchased by J. P. Morgan, Jr., 1919.

Edgar Allan Poe. "The Living Writers of America. Some Honest Opinions About Their Literary Merits, with Occasional Words of Personality." Autograph notes, [1846], for "The Literati of New-York City," published in *Godey's Lady's Book* (1846–48) and in book form as *The Literati* (1850).

MA 624. Purchased by Pierpont Morgan with the Wakeman collection, 1909.
PL. 39

Edgar Allan Poe. Printed prospectus for *Penn Magazine*, with an autograph letter dated Philadelphia, 22 January 1841, to Judge Robert Taylor Conrad written on the blank page.

MA 1301. Purchased by Pierpont Morgan, 1906.

Edgar Allan Poe. *Tamerlane.* Autograph manuscript, [1827].

MA 570. Purchased by Pierpont Morgan with the Wakeman collection, 1909.

W. Rawle. Pennsylvania Society for Promoting the Abolition of Slavery. Printed circular signed, dated [Philadelphia, Pennsylvania], 13 April 1820.

GLC 777. The Gilder Lehrman Collection.

Read and Ponder the Fugitive Slave Law! [broadside]. [Boston]: printed and for sale at *The Spy* office, [1850].

GLC 1862. The Gilder Lehrman Collection.
PL. 33

John Sartain, after George Caleb Bingham. *The County Election* [hand-colored engraving]. New York: Goupil and Co., 1854.

GLC 4074. The Gilder Lehrman Collection.
PL. 79

[Winfield Scott]. *General Scott's Victorious Entry into the City of Mexico* [hand-colored lithograph]. New York: N. Currier, 1849.

GLC 2918.01. The Gilder Lehrman Collection.
PL. 76

[Lydia Sigourney]. Engraved portrait, after a painting by Alonzo Chappel. New York: Johnson, Wilson & Co., 1872.

MA 4500. The bequest of Gordon N. Ray, 1987.
PL. 50

Lydia Sigourney. *Pocahontas, and Other Poems.* London: Robert Tyas, 1841.

GNR 4616. The bequest of Gordon N. Ray, 1987.
Pl. 51

Slave Market of America [broadside]. New York: American Anti-Slavery Society, 1836.

GLC 4557. The Gilder Lehrman Collection.
PL. 29

Songs for the Anniversary of the Jerry Rescue [broadside]. [N.p., 1852].

Archives of the Morgan Library.

William Wetmore Story. *Two Studies of Robert Browning Reading.* Pencil. 9 5/8 x 14 11/16 inches (245 x 374 mm). Signed and dated, *W. W. Story / Sep. 19th 1869.*

Acc. no. 1954.4. The gift of Mrs. Herbert N. Straus, 1954.

Harriet Beecher Stowe. Autograph letter signed, dated Andover, [Massachusetts], 14 December 1852, to Ralph Wardlaw.

GLC 4631. The Gilder Lehrman Collection.
PL. 31

Harriet Beecher Stowe. *La Case de l'Oncle Tom, ou Tableaux de l'esclavage dans les Etats-Unis d'Amérique*, translated by "Old Nick" (pseudonym of Emile Daurand Forgues) and Adolphe Joanne. Paris: Adolphe Delahays, 1857.

PML 85460. The gift of Miss Elisabeth Ball, 1965.
PL. 58

E. W. Taylor. Autograph letter signed, dated Charleston, 25 January 1837, to J. Wilbur.

GLB 76. The Gilder Lehrman Collection.

[Texas]. *Unanimous Declaration of Independence.* San Felipe de Austin: Baker and Bordens, [1836].

GLC 2559. The Gilder Lehrman Collection.
PL. 73

William Makepeace Thackeray. Autograph letter signed, dated New York, 5 April 1853, to Alice Jane Trulock.

MA 4500. The bequest of Gordon N. Ray, 1987.

Henry David Thoreau. "Advantages and Disadvantages of Foreign Influence on American Literature." Autograph manuscript, [1836].

MA 2392. The gift of the Fellows, 1965.

Henry David Thoreau. Autograph journal in forty volumes, dated 1837–61, with pine box.

MA 1302. Purchased by Pierpont Morgan with the Wakeman collection, 1909.
PL. 54

Henry David Thoreau. *Extracts Concerning the Indians.* Autograph manuscript journal in eleven volumes, [1850s].

MA 596–606. Purchased by Pierpont Morgan with the Wakeman collection, 1909.
PL. 53

Henry David Thoreau. *Nature Notes.* Autograph manuscript, [1850s].

MA 610. Purchased by Pierpont Morgan with the Wakeman collection, 1909.

Henry David Thoreau. *Walden; or, Life in the Woods*. Boston: Ticknor and Fields, 1854.

GNR 4629. The bequest of Gordon N. Ray, 1987.

The Times-Picayune, New Orleans. *Picayune Supplement* [newspaper]. New Orleans, 30 May 1858.

GLC 4201. The Gilder Lehrman Collection.
PL. 22

Alexis de Tocqueville. *De la démocratie en Amérique*. Paris: Librarie de Charles Gosselin, 1835–40. Four volumes.

GNR 5252. The bequest of Gordon N. Ray, 1987.

Frances Trollope. *The Domestic Manners of Americans*. London: Whittaker, Treavler, and Co., 1832. Two volumes.

PML 9317–9318. Purchased by Pierpont Morgan with the Irwin collection, 1900.
PL. 27

John Tyler. Autograph letter signed, dated Sherwood Forest [near Richmond, Virginia], 8 March 1859, to Robert Tyler.

GLC 948. The Gilder Lehrman Collection.

U.S. Congress. House of Representatives, Committee on Indian Affairs. Report no. 474, 23d Congress, 1st session, *Regulating the Indian Department*. To accompany bills H.R. nos. 488, 489, and 490. [Washington]: Gales and Seaton, 1834.

GLC 4132. The Gilder Lehrman Collection.
PL. 21

U.S. Congress. Senate. [Bill of Rights]. *Journal of the First Session of the Senate of the United States of America, Begun and Held at the City of New-York, March 4th, 1789, and in the Thirteenth Year of the Independence of the Said States*. New York: Thomas Greenleaf, 1789.

GLC 172. The Gilder Lehrman Collection.

U.S. Constitution. [Philadelphia]: Dunlap and Claypoole, [18 or 19 September 1787].

GLC 258. The Gilder Lehrman Collection.
PL. 1

U.S. Continental Congress, 1787. *An Ordinance for the Governing of the Territory of the United States, North-west of the River Ohio*. [Cincinnati: printed for William Maxwell, 1796].

GLC 1042. The Gilder Lehrman Collection.

[*U.S. Treaty with Cherokee Nation*]. Manuscript, Washington, D.C., 6 August 1846.

GLC 1233.5. The Gilder Lehrman Collection.
PL. 23

U.S. War Department. *The Causes of the Existing Hostilities Between the United States, and Certain Tribes of Indians North-West of the Ohio, Stated and Explained from Official and Authentic Documents, and Published in Obedience to the Orders of the President of the United States*. Philadelphia: D. C. Claypoole, [1792].

GLC 2437, The Henry Knox Papers. The Gilder Lehrman Collection.

Daniel Webster. Autograph letter signed, dated Boston, 7 May 1833, to Joel Poinsett.

MA 2123. Purchased in 1961.
PL. 14

Daniel Webster. *Discourse in Commemoration of the Lives and Services of John Adams and Thomas Jefferson, Delivered in Faneuil Hall, Boston, August 2, 1826*. Boston: Cummings, Hilliard and Co., 1826.

PML 125583. Purchased by Pierpont Morgan with the Irwin collection, 1900.
PL. 3

Daniel Webster. *Speech of the Honorable Daniel Webster, on the Compromise Bill* [signed pamphlet]. Washington, [D.C.]: Gideon & Co., 1850.

GLC 1946. The Gilder Lehrman Collection.

Noah Webster. *An American Dictionary of the English Language*. Autograph manuscript notes and corrected proofs for a revised edition, [after 1828, before 1843].

MA 301. Purchased by Pierpont Morgan with the Ford collection.
PL. 43

[Walt Whitman]. Engraving by Samuel Hollyer, after a daguerreotype by Gabriel Harrison, [1854]. Frontispiece to *Leaves of Grass*. Brooklyn: [privately printed], 1855.

PML 6068. Purchased by Pierpont Morgan with the Irwin collection, 1900.
PL. 38

Walt Whitman. Introduction for a London edition of *Leaves of Grass*. Autograph manuscript, [1867].

MA 1056. Purchased in 1927.

Walt Whitman. *Leaves of Grass*. Brooklyn: [privately printed], 1855.

PML 6069. Purchased by Pierpont Morgan before 1913.
PL. 44

John Greenleaf Whittier. *Poems Written During the Progress of the Abolition Question in the United States, Between the Years 1830 and 1838*. Boston: Isaac Knapp, 1837.

PML 125592. Purchased by Pierpont Morgan before 1913.

John Greenleaf Whittier. "The Slaves of Martinique." Autograph manuscript signed, [1848].

MA 1304. Purchased by Pierpont Morgan with the Wakeman collection, 1909.

Alexander Wilson. *American Ornithology; or, the Natural History of the Birds of the United States*. London: Whittaker, Treacher, & Arnot, 1832. Three volumes.

PML 56060–56062. The gift of Henry S. Morgan, 1966.

[Brigham Young]. *General Epistle from the Council of the Twelve Apostles, to the Church of Jesus Christ of Latter Day Saints Abroad, Dispersed Throughout the Earth*. [N.p., 1848].

GLC 4149. The Gilder Lehrman Collection.
PL. 25

FOR FURTHER READING

Many sources were consulted in preparing this exhibition and publication. Noted here is a selection of works of interest to the general reader who wishes to explore in greater depth issues and personalities of the period from 1820 to 1860.

One hundred sixty years after its publication, Alexis de Tocqueville's *Democracy in America* (1835) continues to engage readers with first-hand observations of Jacksonian America. David Brion Davis, whose essay introduces this volume, provides modern historical insights in "Expanding the Republic, 1820–1860," which appears in *The Great Republic: A History of the American People* (1992). Broad, single-volume summaries are offered by Daniel J. Boorstin in *The Americans: The National Experience* (1965), James MacGregor Burns in *The Vineyard of Liberty* (1981), and Page Smith in *The Nation Comes of Age* (1981). Arthur Schlesinger, Jr.'s *The Age of Jackson* (1945) is a highly readable study of the Jacksonian era. More recently, Charles G. Sellers, in *The Market Revolution: Jacksonian America, 1815–1848* (1991), examines social and political controversies of the day.

Biographies of the era's most influential personalities are also rich resources. The most comprehensive life of Andrew Jackson is Robert V. Remini's three-volume work, *Andrew Jackson and the Course of American Empire* (1977), *Andrew Jackson and the Course of American Freedom* (1981), and *Andrew Jackson and the Course of American Democracy* (1984). Professor Remini is also the author of a biography of one of Jackson's principal political adversaries, *Henry Clay: Statesman for the Union* (1991). Clay and two other opponents of Jackson are represented in Merrill D. Peterson's *The Great Triumvirate: Webster, Clay, and Calhoun* (1987). Two studies of Abraham Lincoln's political life before his presidency are Don E. Fehrenbacher's *Prelude to Greatness: Lincoln in the 1850s* (1962) and Gabor S. Borrit's *Lincoln and the Economics of the American Dream* (1978). Mark E. Neeley, Jr.'s *The Last Best Hope on Earth: Abraham Lincoln and the Promise of America* (1993) is a concise biography written as the companion volume to a 1993–94 namesake exhibition at the Huntington Library. The exhibition catalogue of the same title (1993), with text by John Rhodehamel and Thomas F. Schwartz, includes color illustrations of many important Lincoln-related documents. The most recent biography is David Herbert Donald's *Lincoln* (1995).

Study of major reform movements and their leaders is crucial to understanding the era's dynamic spirit. Three recent explorations of the abolition and women's rights movements are Carolyn L. Karcher's *The First Woman in the Republic: A Cultural Biography of Lydia Maria Child* (1994), Wendy Hamand Venet's *Neither Ballots nor Bullets: Women Abolitionists and the Civil War* (1991), and William S. McFeely's *Frederick Douglass* (1991).

The literature of the period is treated in many fine critical editions, literary histories, and biographies. William Charvat's classic study of the nineteenth-century American book trade, *Literary Publishing in America, 1790–1850* (1959) is available in a 1993 edition with an afterword by Michael Winship. Broad studies include F. O. Matthiessen's standard work, *American Renaissance: Art and Expression in the Age of Emerson and Whitman* (1941), Larzer Ziff's *Literary Democracy: The Declaration of Cultural Independence in America* (1981), Michael T. Gilmore's *American Romanticism and the Marketplace* (1985), Lawrence Buell's *New England Literary Culture: From Revolution through Renaissance* (1986), Donald E. Pease's *Visionary Compacts: American Renaissance Writings in Cultural Context* (1987), and David S. Reynolds's *Beneath the American Renaissance: The Subversive Imagination in the Age of Emerson and Melville* (1988). Among many highly readable biographies of individual authors are Robert D. Richardson, Jr.'s *Henry Thoreau: A Life of the Mind* (1986) and *Emerson: The Mind on Fire* (1995), David S. Reynolds's *Walt Whitman's America: A Cultural Biography* (1995), Joan D. Hedrick's *Harriet Beecher Stowe: A Life* (1994), Kenneth Silverman's *Edgar A. Poe: Mournful and Never-Ending Remembrance* (1991), and James R. Mellow's *Nathaniel Hawthorne in His Times* (1980). For writing by African Americans of the period, Charles T. Davis and Henry Louis Gates, Jr.'s *The Slave's Narrative* (1985) and John W. Blassingame's *Slave Testimony: Two Centuries of Letters, Speeches, Interviews, and Autobiographies* (1977) contain useful introductions.

In addition to the primary sources discussed, a few selected texts related to John James Audubon and the artist-naturalist tradition in America are Paul Hulton, *The Work of Jacques le Moyne de Morgues* (1977); Paul Hulton and David Beers Quinn, *The American Drawings of John White, 1577–1590* (1964); Joseph Ewan, *William Bartram, Botanical and Zoological Drawings, 1756–1788* (1968); W. M. Hetherington, *Memoir of Alexander Wilson, The American Ornithologist* (1831); George Frederick Frick and Raymond Phineas Stearns, *Mark Catesby, The Colonial Audubon* (1961); Marshall B. Davidson, *The Original Water-Color Paintings by John James Audubon for The Birds of America* (1966); Munson-Williams-Proctor Institute, Utica, and The Pierpont Morgan Library, New York, *Audubon Watercolors and Drawings* (1965), catalogue by Edward H. Dwight.

Published by The Pierpont Morgan Library

Julianne Griffin
Publisher

Patricia Emerson
Editorial Coordinator

Noah Chasin
Publications Administrator

Deborah Winard
Publications Associate

Project Staff

Robert Parks
Robert H. Taylor Curator,
Department of Autograph Manuscripts

Christine Nelson
Associate Curator, Department of Autograph Manuscripts

Stephanie Wiles
Associate Curator,
Department of Drawings and Prints

Lori E. Gilbert
Gilder Lehrman Curatorial Assistant,
Department of Autograph Manuscripts

David A. Loggie
Chief Photographer

Edward J. Sowinski
Assistant, Photography Department

Marilyn Palmeri
Administrator, Photographic Services,
Rights and Reproductions

David Coleman
Associate, Photographic Services,
Rights and Reproductions

Patricia Reyes, *Mellon Conservator*

Mary Cropley
Assistant Conservator

Timothy Herstein
Assistant, Conservation Department

Designed by David Comberg

Printed and bound by Imprimeries Réunies Lausanne S.A.
Lausanne, Switzerland

From Jackson to Lincoln: Democracy and Dissent was composed using four American typefaces: New Caledonia, Franklin Gothic, Willow and Matrix Wide, all digitally redrawn from original metal and wood designs. The wood type used on the cover and fly sheets was set by Bowne & Co., NY.

THIS DAY IT IS
TAKING SHAPE,
NOT TO BE LESS SO,

BUT
TO BE MORE SO,
CAPRICIOUSLY,
STORMILY,
ON NATIVE
PRINCIPLES,

WITH SUCH VAST PROPORTIONS OF PARTS.

WALT WHITMAN "Letter to Ralph Waldo Emerson," in *Leaves of Grass* (1856)